More Lovecraftian People and Places

MORE LOVECRAFTIAN PEOPLE AND PLACES

Ken Faig, Jr.

Hippocampus Press

New York

Copyright © 2025 by Ken Faig, Jr.
Published by Hippocampus Press
P.O. Box 641, New York, NY 10156.
www.hippocampuspress.com

All rights reserved.
No part of this work may be reproduced in any form or by any means without the written permission of the publisher.

Cover artwork from "Map of Lovecraft's Providence"
© 2018 by Jason C. Eckhardt, eck-art.net
Cover design and images pp. 108 and 339 by Dan Sauer, dansauerdesign.com
Hippocampus Press logo designed by Anastasia Damianakos.

First Edition
1 3 5 7 9 8 6 4 2

ISBN 978-1-61498-439-9 trade paperback

Contents

Abbreviations 7
Relatives 9
   Clergymen among Lovecraft's Paternal Ancestors 11
   Franklin C. Clark (1847–1915) 43
   In Memoriam: Ethel Phillips Morrish (1888–1987) 75
Educators 95
   Abbie Ann Hathaway (1852–1917) 97
   Arthur Palmer May (1880–1941) Lovecraft's Tutor 110
Helpers and Neighbors 117
   Delilah Townsend (ca. 1868–1944) 119
   Mariano De Magistris (1862–1939) 127
   The People of 169 Clinton Street 145
   The People of 10 Barnes Street 158
Others 177
   Lovecraft and the Irish 179
   Edwin Baird: The Man Who Discovered Lovecraft 195
   Lovecraft's 1937 Diary 218
Places 247
   Providence's Poe Street 249
   Lovecraft's Travelogues of Foster, Rhode Island 259
   Boy in Summer 319
Early Recognition 327
   The First Public Lecture on H. P. Lovecraft 329
Sources 341

ABBREVIATIONS

AAV   S. T. Joshi and David E. Schultz, ed. *Ave atque Vale: Reminiscences of H. P. Lovecraft*. West Warwick, RI: Necronomicon Press, 2018.

AG   *Letters to Alfred Galpin and Others*. Ed. S. T. Joshi and David E. Schultz. New York: Hippocampus Press, 2020.

AT   *The Ancient Track: Complete Poetical Works*. Ed. S. T. Joshi. New York: Hippocampus Press, 2013.

CE   *Collected Essays*. Ed. S. T. Joshi. New York: Hippocampus Press, 2004–06. 5 vols.

CF   *Collected Fiction: A Variorum Edition*. Ed. S. T. Joshi. New York: Hippocampus Press, 2015–17. 4 vols.

CLM   *Letters to C. L. Moore and Others*. Ed. David E. Schultz and S. T. Joshi. New York: Hippocampus Press, 2017.

DS   *Dawnward Spire, Lonely Hill: The Letters of H. P. Lovecraft and Clark Ashton Smith*. Ed. David E. Schultz and S. T. Joshi. New York: Hippocampus Press, 2017.

DW   *Letters with Donald and Howard Wandrei and to Emil Petaja*. Ed. S. T. Joshi and David E. Schultz. New York: Hippocampus Press, 2019.

EHP   *Letters to E. Hoffmann Price and Richard F. Searight*. Ed. David E. Schultz and S. T. Joshi. New York: Hippocampus Press, 2021.

ES   *Essential Solitude: The Letters of H. P. Lovecraft and August Derleth*. Ed. David E. Schultz and S. T. Joshi. New York: Hippocampus Press, 2013. 2 vols.

ET   *Letters to Elizabeth Toldridge and Anne Tillery Renshaw*. Ed. David E. Schultz and S. T. Joshi. New York: Hippocampus Press, 2014.

FLB   *Letters to F. Lee Baldwin, Duane W. Rimel, and Nils Frome*. Ed. David E. Schultz and S. T. Joshi. New York: Hippocampus Press, 2016.

IAP	S. T. Joshi. *I Am Providence: The Life and Times of H. P. Lovecraft*. Hippocampus Press, 2010. 2 vols.
JFM	*Letters to James F. Morton*. Ed. David E. Schultz and S. T. Joshi. New York: Hippocampus Press, 2014.
JVS	*Letters to J. Vernon Shea, Carl F. Strauch, and Lee McBride White*. Ed. S. T. Joshi and David E. Schultz. New York: Hippocampus Press, 2016.
LL	S. T. Joshi and David E. Schultz. *Lovecraft's Library*. 5th rev. ed. New York: Hippocampus Press, 2024.
LFF	*Letters to Family and Family Friends*. Ed. S. T. Joshi and David E. Schultz. New York: Hippocampus Press, 2020. 2 vols.
MF	*A Means to Freedom: The Letters of H. P. Lovecraft and Robert E. Howard*. Ed. S. T. Joshi, David E. Schultz, and Rusty Burke. New York: Hippocampus Press, 2009. 2 vols.
ML	*Miscellaneous Letters*. Ed. David E. Schultz and S. T. Joshi. New York: Hippocampus Press, 2022.
MWM	*Letters to Maurice W. Moe and Others*. Ed. David E. Schultz and S. T. Joshi. New York: Hippocampus Press, 2018.
OFF	*O Fortunate Floridian: H. P. Lovecraft's Letters to R. H. Barlow*. Ed. S. T. Joshi and David E. Schultz. Tampa, FL: University of Tampa Press, 2007.
RB	*Letters to Robert Bloch and Others*. Ed. David E. Schultz and S. T. Joshi. New York: Hippocampus Press, 2017.
RK	*Letters to Rheinhart and Others*. Ed. S. T. Joshi and David E. Schultz. New York: Hippocampus Press, 2020.
SP	*A Sense of Proportion: The Letters of H. P. Lovecraft and Frank Belknap Long*. Ed. David E. Schultz and S. T. Joshi. New York: Hippocampus Press, 2025.
WBT	*Letters to Wilfred B. Talman and Helen V. and Genevieve Sully*. Ed. David E. Schultz and S. T. Joshi. New York: Hippocampus Press, 2019.
WH	*Letters to Woodburn Harris and Others*. Ed. S. T. Joshi and David E. Schultz. New York: Hippocampus Press, 2022.

Relatives

Clergymen among Lovecraft's Paternal Ancestors

In Memory of My Friends Chris J. Docherty and A. Langley Searles

Rotten with Reverends?

Lovecraft wrote to his friend Frank Belknap Long in November 1927: "The Lovecraft line is fairly rotten with Reverends. It trickles Theology and radiates rural rectors. God help it" (*SP* 455). He expounded further in his letter to Maurice W. Moe dated 5 April 1931:

> The overwhelming majority—virtually totality—of my ancestry on both sides is of the staid and stolid country-gentry class, with an abnormally high percentage of *clergymen* droning their amiably well-meaning matins and liturgies across the well-clipt hedges of a subdu'd and commonplace rural mead. I can scare up a full-fledged cleric—the Rev. Francis Fulford, Vicar of Dunsford—in four generations, that is, he is my great-great grandfather—and by two generations behind him they come thick and fast. (*MWM* 292)

Undoubtedly, Lovecraft harbored mistaken notions regarding the social class and occupations of his paternal ancestors. In *Devonshire Ancestry of Howard Phillips Lovecraft* (2003), my co-authors Chris J. Docherty, A. Langley Searles, and I found these occupations for Lovecraft's ancestors in his direct paternal (Lovecraft) line in England: great-grandfather Joseph Lovecraft (1774–1850), carpenter and worsted-spinner (declared bankrupt in 1831, after his emigration to America); 2×-great-grandfather John Lovecraft (1742–1780), mariner; 3×-great-grandfather Joseph Lovecraft (1703–1781), farmer; 4×-great-grandfather Will Lovecraft (1675?–1736+), weaver (DSF 18–24, 42). In fact, both Will Lovecraft and his bride George[1] Merifeild, who married in Broadhempston parish, Devonshire, on 27 December 1699, were weavers. Will's and George's son Joseph and their grandson John both resided in adjoining Woodland parish, while their great-grandson the emigrant Joseph Lovecraft lived in Pulsford (Woodland parish) (1813 to 1820+) and Bickington parish (1828 to 1831) before his emigration to America in 1831 (DSF 13–17). S. T. Joshi mentioned our research on Lovecraft's paternal ancestry in the latest edition of his biography of Lovecraft (*IAP* 3). We acknowledge that Lovecraft's beliefs concerning his ancestry remain important even when they have been proven erroneous (*QAT* 27).[2]

Rev. Francis Fulford (1734–1772), Vicar of Dunsford, cannot have been Lovecraft's ancestor, since he had in fact been dead for nearly a decade by the time Lovecraft's great-grandmother was born during the summer of 1782. In fact, Lovecraft's great-grandfather, the emigrant Joseph Lovecraft, married Mary Full (1782–1864), the daughter of Richard and Elizabeth (Brusey) Full of Denbury parish, in Woodland parish church on 26 September 1805 (DSF 12). The maiden name of Joseph Lovecraft's 1805 bride Mary was Full, not Fulford.[3] Her

---

1. George was an uncommon, but not unknown, given name for females; some given names were borne both by males and by females. Today the female version of this name would usually be Georges, Georgene, or Georgette.

2. In my essay on HPL's ancestry (2008) I wrote: "My colleagues and I have certainly caught the Lovecraft family genealogist—be it great-aunt Sarah Allgood or some other person—in a number of apparently deliberate falsehoods, but we realize at the same time that what HPL believed is important, whether it is true or not. Nevertheless, we take much greater pride in Will Lovecraft and George Merifeild, weavers, married in Broadhempston Parish (Devon) in December 1699, than we do in highly questionable noble or royal descents" (QAT 27).

3. The fact that Joseph and Mary Lovecraft named their first child, baptized in Woodland parish on 7 September 1806, John Full Lovecraft provides a substantial clue regarding Mary's maiden name (DSF 13).

parents, Richard Full and Elizabeth Brusey of Torbryan parish, had been married in Torbryan parish church on 15 August 1782, with James Brusey and William Hooper as witnesses. Mary's father Richard Full had been baptized at Woodland parish church on 18 June 1758, the son of Richard and Mary (Tapper) Full. Mary's mother, Elizabeth Brusey, had been baptized at Denbury parish church on 24 May 1763, the daughter of John and Joan (Knapman) Brusey. Mary Full herself was baptized privately at Denbury parish church on 10 September 1782, less than a month after her parents' marriage, and was publicly received into the church two weeks later on 24 September 1782 (DSF 12–13). There is not a clergyman in sight among Lovecraft's Full family ancestors for three generations in back of Joseph Lovecraft's 1805 bride Mary Full.

Reaching for Ancestors among the Landed Gentry (With Family Seats and Coats of Arms)

Lovecraft was at best an amateur family historian. The paternal family charts that he borrowed from his great-aunt Sarah Allgood[4] for copying in 1905 (*SP* 452) themselves contained substantial inaccuracies. On the basis of these charts, Lovecraft claimed that his 2×-great-grandfather Thomas Lovecraft (1745–1826) had been forced to sell his property, Minster Hall near Newton Abbot, in 1823 (*SP* 455, *MWM* 294), evidently in order to liquidate debts incurred for "wine, horses, and the fair" (*MWM* 393–94). According to a note in the Allgood chart, one Thomas Lovecroft bore as arms "a chevron[5] or [i.e., gold] between three towers or on a field vert [i.e., green]" as early as

---

4. Sarah Allgood (1830–1908) was a younger sister of Helen Allgood (1820–1881). Helen married HPL's grandfather George Lovecraft (1815–1895) in 1839.
5. In heraldry, a chevron is an upside-down V-shaped band.

1500 (*SP* 454).⁶ According to the same source, Lovecraft's ancestor John Lovecroft of Minster Hall bore as arms in 1560 "a chevron, engrailed,⁷ or, between three foxes' heads, erased,⁸ or, on a field vert" (*MWM* 293).⁹ In fact, the arms "vert a chevron between three towers or" occur only with different tinctures as quarterings in the arms of the Elliott and Boscawen families¹⁰ in the 1620 Visitation of Cornwall (DSF 3). R. P. Graham-Vivian, M.V.C., Norroy & Ulster King of Arms, wrote to Henry L. P. Beckwith, Jr. concerning these arms on 19 June 1969: "The fact that it appears only as an ancient Quartering by the time of the Visitations means that whatever it was, and it was unnamed, was extinct in the male line, and even the name lost sight of" (DSF 3).

In fact, no Devonshire manor or estate bearing the name

---

6. Regarding the older version of the arms, Henry L. P. Beckwith, Jr. opines: "It appears that another branch of the family cadenced the coat by the substitution of towers for the heads, and it may be that the towers in this coat, and in H.P.L.'s crest, derive from the arms of a family with which the Lovecrafts were intermarried, the cadet line deriving from this match" (94).

7. An engrailed pattern in heraldry has boundaries or borders consisting of a series of circular arcs with outward points. It is the chevron (i.e., the upside-down V-shaped band) that is engrailed in the Lovecraft arms.

8. The foxes' (or rather wolves') heads are erased in the Lovecraft arms, which means that only the heads are depicted, with jagged edges as if severed from their bodies at their necks.

9. The later Lovecraft family coat of arms and crest were blazoned by Henry L. P. Beckwith, Jr. and were reproduced first in Beckwith's book (95) and then (hand-colored by Beckwith) as the frontispiece for DSF. Beckwith believes that HPL was in error when he stated that the later version of the arms depicted foxes' rather than wolves' heads (94). He believes that the later Lovecraft family arms represent a "punning" coat, based on the French *louve* (meaning wolf bitch) and *croft* meaning place, farm, field, lair, cave, den (DSF 3). See also Beckwith's article "The Lovecraft Family Arms," which appeared in my own *Moshassuck Review* [Esoteric Order of Dagon Amateur Press Association] for February 1998 (2–3). Beckwith blazons the later arms as "Vert [green], a chevron engrailed and three wolves' heads gold," and the crest "A tower gold" (94).

10. For more on the Boscawen and Elliott families of Cornwall, see DSF 3–7.

"Minster Hall" has been identified.[11] Docherty, Searles, and I were not able to identify any Thomas Lovecraft[12] in Lovecraft's direct paternal line (DSF 26–27). Lovecraft probably used family resources, including his 1905 copy of the Allgood chart, and the Providence Public Library for most of the genealogical research he conducted prior to his 1924–26 residency in New York City. By 1927 his friend Wilfred B. Talman, a much more dedicated genealogist, had taught Lovecraft to use the richer genealogical resources of the Rhode Island Historical Society, then housed in its cabinet on Waterman Street in Providence[13] (QAT 15–16).

Lovecraft's introduction to these resources, which included Burke's *Peerage* and Burke's *Landed Gentry*, proved to be a mixed blessing. Like many amateur family historians of his day, Lovecraft could not resist linking the surnames he found in the Allgood chart to the principal lines included in these references. Lovecraft probably descended from "cadet" branches of families like the Allgoods and the Morrises rather than the principal lines

---

11. A more extended treatment of Minster Hall may be found in DSF 8–11. The term minster (Old English mynster) was originally used for a monastic church or a religious house but later was applied to any large church, such as a collegiate or cathedral church, but especially to churches with secular canons (e.g., York, Beverley, Ripon, Southwell, Lincoln, Lichfield, and Wimborne). Minster Hall has fascinated readers and students of HPL's work over the decades. It is the setting for a major part of S. T. Joshi's novel *The Assaults of Chaos*.

12. A son Thomas Lovecraft of Jonah and Elizabeth (Ludgar) Lovecraft was baptized in Woodland parish on 22 November 1736. Thomas Lovecraft and Martha Hollock (or Hollett) of Torbryan were married in Torbryan parish church on 4 August 1772; it is not certain that the 1772 Torbryan groom Thomas Lovecraft was the son Thomas Lovecraft of Jonah and Elizabeth (Ludgar) Lovecraft baptized in Woodland parish in 1736 (DSF 26–27). Jonah Lovecraft (1705–1780) was a younger brother of HPL's ancestor Joseph Lovecraft (1703–1781) (DSF 43).

13. The Rhode Island Historical Society Library is now located on Hope Street; its former cabinet on Waterman Street is now the copying center for Brown University.

that he claimed for his ancestors in his letters to Long and Moe[14] (QAT 21). Alan Taylor, the leading authority on the Edgecombe family, was unable to identify either of the Edgecombe brides (sisters Letitia and Ellen) whom Lovecraft claimed for Thomas Lovecraft and Rev. Francis Fulford, respectively (DSF 26). In summary, many of the "great" lines claimed by Lovecraft on the authority of the Allgood chart probably do not actually occur among his ancestors: e.g., Fulford, Edgecombe, Chichester, Carew, Musgrave, and Reed (QAT 21).

We must probably reject Lovecraft's claim that his paternal ancestry was dominated by landed gentry and clergymen. In my essay "Quae Amamus Tuemur: Ancestors in Lovecraft's Life and Fiction" (2008) I wrote:

> Where he sought for intellectuals, he generally found sturdy yeomen and their wives, earning a hard living from the soil. His spurious English ancestry may have been ridden with clergymen, but his real English ancestry included carpenters, mariners, farmers, weavers. Lovecraft's ancestors prove that ordinary seed may produce from time to time an extraordinary flowering. (QAT 29)

---

14. I question the credibility of HPL's account of his Allgood and Morris lines beyond his great-grandparents William Allgood and Rachel Morris, who married in Trevethin, Monmouth, on 8 June 1817. I doubt whether Rachel Morris (b. 1790? Pontypool, Monmouth) was the daughter of Thomas Morris (1777–1817), M.A. (Oxon.) and the granddaughter of Sir John Morris, Baronet, of Clasemont, Glamorganshire, Wales, as HPL asserted in his letter to Frank Belknap Long in November 1927 (SP 453). HPL probably lifted these claimed Morris ancestors directly from the Morris entry in Burke's *Landed Gentry*. Similarly, HPL probably lifted the father Lancelot Allgood and the grandfather Sir Lancelot Allgood, whom he claimed for his great-grandfather William Allgood (b. 1786, Trevethin, Monmouth), directly from the Allgood entry in Burke's *Landed Gentry*. I did include a "cadet" line of Allgood ancestors in my article on HPL's ancestry (QAT 21). My Allgood "cadet" line differs from HPL's account of his Allgood ancestry, although both lines originated in Northumberland.

I think I can write with confidence that Chris J. Docherty, A. Langley Searles, and I regarded the weavers, farmers, mariners, carpenters, and spinners whom we discovered among Lovecraft's paternal ancestors with as much pride as we would have felt had we discovered landed gentry or clergy. In many ways the ancestors whom we discovered for Lovecraft reflect more closely the mainstream of social and economic life in Devonshire, particularly Broadhempston and Woodland parishes, than would more illustrious putative predecessors.[15] We concluded our study *Devonshire Ancestry of Howard Phillips Lovecraft* with these remarks: "That the Devon Lovecrafts and Lovecrofts were ancient but hardly illustrious families seems apparent. This fact, however, does not reduce the interest of the family's Devon origins for the many thousands of readers who admire the work of Howard Phillips Lovecraft" (DSF 40–41).

The History of the Lovecraft and Lovecroft Surnames

Lovecraft's account of the Lovecroft and Lovecraft name variants is especially interesting. Richard D. Squires's *Stern Fathers 'neath the Mould: The Lovecraft Family in America* (1995) contains an excellent chart that carefully reflects Lovecraft's account of his paternal line in England (49). Therein George Lovecraft, great-grandson of the 1560 armiger John Lovecroft of Minster

---

15. According to Rev. H. R. Evans, Devonshire was a major exporter of wool by the 15th century. Evans wrote further that Woodland parish in particular lent itself to sheep pasture and that local water sources served admirably for the washing of wool (EVW 168–69, 196; DSF 38). So it is not surprising that Will Lovecraft and his 1699 Broadhempston bride George Merifeild were both weavers. It is possible that the weaver John Lovecraft, who was buried in Broadhempston in 1705/06, was Will Lovecraft's father or grandfather, so that multiple generations of the Lovecraft family may have worked as weavers, a very common occupation in Broadhempston and Woodland parishes and the whole of Devonshire from the 15th century onward.

Hall, married Hester Lovecroft in 1649. In his November 1927 letter to Long, Lovecraft describes Hester Lovecroft as "one of the old line with uncorrupted name and the original arms with the three towers instead of foxes' heads" (*SP* 455).[16] In Lovecraft's account, the surname of the proprietors of Minster Hall changed from Lovecroft to Lovecraft during the interval between John Lovecroft in 1560 and his great-grandson George Lovecraft in 1649. Henry L. P. Beckwith, Jr. joins Lovecraft in believing that Lovecroft was the older form of the surname (DSF 3).

In *A Dictionary of Surnames* (1988), Patrick Hanks and Flavia Hodges assert that the Old English *croft* refers to an arable enclosure, normally adjoining a house. Thus they believe that the "croft" suffix surnames are habitation names deriving from the dwelling places of the bearers of the name. According to the same source, the Old English *croeft* refers to a craft, skill, machine, engine, or mill. Regarding the prefix "Love," Hanks and Hodges state: "English and Scots: nickname from ANF *louve* female wolf (a fem. Form of *lou* cf. Low 3). This nickname was fairly commonly used for men, in an approving sense. It may have been bestowed on a staunch soldier, with reference to the ferocity with which the she-wolf defends her young."

Beckwith, who notes that there were wolves in the Exmoor area as late as 1200,[17] believes that the later surname Lovecraft may have been borne by families whose living (i.e., craft) included wolf-hunting, hence the three wolves' heads, not foxes' heads as Lovecraft incorrectly states, in the later version of the coat of arms (DSF 3). Whether they were soldiers or wolf-hunters or both, the early male bearers of the Lovecraft surname were

---

16. HPL noted that Hester's father was one Richard Lovecroft (d. 1642), but stated that the Allgood chart did not trace her ancestry beyond her father (*SP* 454).

17. Letter from Beckwith to me dated 4 April 1997.

doubtless brave men and skilled fighters. Perhaps the prowess of the Lovecraft men caused the family arms to be added as quarterings in the Boscawen and Elliott family arms when women of the Lovecraft family married into these families centuries before the final flourishing of the Lovecraft family name in Broadhempston and Woodland parishes in the seventeenth and eighteenth centuries—perhaps as early as the twelfth or thirteenth centuries, long before the Lovecroft name first appeared in the Teign Valley in the middle of the fifteenth century according to the Allgood chart (*SP* 454). Beckwith opines that the Lovecraft family arms are ancient: "Though it is impossible to establish the date of first usage of the coat by H.P.L.'s ancestors, internal design evidence suggests that it is of considerable antiquity. I refer here specifically to the use of the tincture vert (green), and to the composition of the coat—a chevron between three items" (94).

The Lovecra(o)ft and the Luc(k)raft surnames probably have common origins in the remote past. Hanks and Hodges state that Lucraft is a habitation name deriving from Luckcroft in Ashwater, Devon, whose name derives from the Old English *loca* (enclosure) and the Old English *croft* (paddock). They state that the Luckraft variant is first found c. 1554 in Stoke Gabriel (335). Luc(k)raft family authority Ian Lucraft, in his presentation "Devon Origins in the South Hams," delivered before the Luc(k)raft Family Conference in Exeter in May 1999, identified one Richard de Loccroft, assessed for eighteen pence in Essewater (Ashwater) parish of Black Torrington, north of Okehampton, in the 1332 lay subsidy. In the 1524 lay subsidy, Lucraft found five occurrences of the Lovecroft and Lovecrofte surnames (four in Loddiswell parish and one in Harberton parish), one occurrence of Lowcrofte in Harberton parish, one occurrence of Lomecrofte in Bridford parish, and one occurrence of Lowcroffthe in Exeter St. Sidwell parish.[18] The Devon muster roll for 1569 includes three occurrences of these related surnames: pikeman Luke Luckrafte in Revelstock parish, Plympton hundred; archer William Lockroste in Littlehempston parish, Haytor hundred; and billman John Lovecroft, South Milton Parish, Stanborough hundred.[19]

The earliest Lovecraft surname parish records found by the Devon Record Office (DRO) for Docherty, Searles, and me, by type, relate to the baptism of Richard Lovecraft, son of Xpofer [Christopher], in Loddiswell on 20 November 1559; the burial of Agnise Lovecraft in Loddiswell on 30 August 1560; and the marriage of Steven Lovecraft and Joane Wakeham in Loddiswell on 3 June 1567 (DSF 29–30, DSF2 90). The earliest Lovecroft surname parish records, by type, were those for the marriage of Margaret Lovecroft and Vincent Cutmore in Stokeinteighhead on 2 July 1576; the burial of Walter Luckroft in Loddiswell on 30 May 1591; and the baptism of Jehan Lovecraft, daughter of William, at Loddiswell in 1605 (DSF 29–30, 2.91–92). By the time of the Devon protestation returns of 1641, there are only four occurrences of the Lovecraft surname: one (Henry) in Cornwood parish, Ermington hundred; and three (John, Samuel, and Thomas) in Broadhempston parish, Haytor hundred. By way of contrast, there are no occurrences of the Lovecroft surname and twenty-one occurrences of the more common Lu(k)raft surnames and variants (DSF 29).[20]

---

18. Ian Lucraft published his findings in *The Luc(k)raft Newsletter* [Sheffield, UK] No. 7 (December 1999). Lucraft maintains a website for his Luc(k)raft One-Name Study at www.lucraft.org.

19. See A. J. Howard and T. L. Stoate, *The Devon Muster Roll for 1569* (Bristol, UK: T. L. Stoate, 1977).

20. See A. J. Howard, *The Devon Protestation Returns 1641* (Privately printed, 1973).

The Lovecroft variant of the surname had become uncommon by the seventeenth century. In Loddiswell parish, even the more common Lovecraft surname was beginning to wane in favor of Luc(k)raft. The last Lovecraft baptism in Loddiswell was 17 December 1628; the last marriage, 1 November 1617; the last burial, 5 May 1624 (DSF 2.94).[21] The Lovecraft surname held out the longest in any number in Broadhempston and Woodland parishes, where the earliest baptisms for the surname were recorded in 1613 and 1692, respectively (DSF 37). Of eighteen seventeenth-century Lovecraft and Lovecroft marriages in Devon found for us by DRO, Docherty, Searles, and I identified six in Broadhempston, five in Torbryan, five in Loddiswell, and one each in Ashburton and Littlehempston (DSF 29). Of the forty-four eighteenth-century Lovecraft marriages contained in the index maintained by the Devon Family History Society (DFHS), more than seventy percent occurred in Broadhempston or Woodland parishes: Broadhempston, sixteen; Woodland, fifteen; Denbury, Torbryan, and Staverton, two each; Chagford, Ashburton, Cornworthy, Widdecombe in the Moor, St. Peter Exeter, Plymouth St. Charles, and Rockbeare, one each (DSF 29).

The last Lovecraft burial in Woodland parish was that of John Lovecraft, age 71—perhaps an older brother of the emigrant Joseph Lovecraft (1774–1850)—on 4 December 1844 (DSF 32). The last Lovecraft burial in Broadhempston parish was that of William Lovecraft (1776–1855) on 20 February 1855. William, the son of innkeeper Joshua Lovecraft (1739–1811) and his wife Sarah (Ashweek) Lovecraft (1740–1808), was baptized in Broadhempston on 6 February 1776 and married Elizabeth Ben-

---

21. That some memory of the Lovecraft surname was retained in Loddiswell parish in the 18th century is indicated by the fact that the 8 December 1735 Loddiswell burial record of John Luccraft has his surname struck out and replaced by Lovecraft (DSF 31).

nett there on 3 December 1799. He and his wife raised a family of twelve children baptized in Broadhempston between 1800 and 1823. William moved to London to conduct his tailoring business after the death of his wife, Elizabeth (Bennett) Lovecraft, in 1835, but retired to Broadhempston in 1850 and built the handsome home "Greenhill" (known today as "Sneydhurst") (DSF 33).

By the late nineteenth century, the Lovecraft name was dying out in England. There were only six Lovecrafts enumerated in the 1881 UK census, two of them being London residents William Lovecraft (1803–1883) and Sarah Lovecraft (1800–1889), both children of the Broadhempston tailor William Lovecraft and his wife, Elizabeth (Bennett) Lovecraft (DSF 34). The last English Lovecraft, excluding non-bloodline Lovecrafts who later assumed the surname in honor of H. P. Lovecraft, was apparently John Lovecraft, who died at St. Thomas, Devonshire, at the stated age of seventy-one during the first quarter of 1911 (DSF 2.66). It seems likely that H. P. Lovecraft was the last surviving male bloodline Lovecraft when he died in 1937, unless he was survived by his elusive second cousin George Elliott Lovecraft (1866/67–1933/34+) (a.k.a. George A. Lovecraft and Eliot George Lovecraft), last noted in the 1933–34 New York City directory.[22]

Willimus Lovecroft(e)

Although Docherty, Searles, and I questioned Lovecraft's assertion that landed gentry and clergymen predominated among his paternal ancestors, the Clergy of the Church of England database does tell us of one Lovecroft (note the use of the early spelling) who attained major orders. Record ID 66335 of the database[23]

---

22. For George Elliott Lovecraft, see my work *George Elliott Lovecraft: Lost Scion of the House of Lovecraft* [LSHL]. R. Alain Everts discovered that George E. Lovecraft died in New York City in December 1932.
23.   db.theclergydatabase.org.uk/jsp/DisplayOrdination.jsp?CDBOrdRedID

indicates that one Willimus Lovecroft, residing in the diocese of Exeter, Devonshire, was ordained to the subdiaconate in the parish church of Hanborough, Oxfordshire, on 19 December 1556 by Bishop John Holyman of Bristol. Holyman was born in Cuddington, Buckinghamshire, and became a fellow of Oxford as early as 1512, attaining a bachelor's degree in canon law in 1514 and a doctorate in canon law in 1526. He became rector of Hanborough in 1534 and retained this holding when he was consecrated as Bishop of Bristol in November 1554. He resigned his rectorship in February 1558, shortly before his death. Hanborough, where Lovecraft was ordained as subdeacon, belonged to the diocese of Oxford under Bishop Robert King. Holyman, the Bishop of Bristol, probably performed the ordination because of his close association with Hanborough, where he still served as rector. Originally a Cistercian monk, Robert King became Bishop of Thane and Oseney in 1541 and the first Bishop of Oxford in 1542. He returned to the Catholic faith under Queen Mary and was one of the judges of Archbishop Thomas Cranmer, burned at the stake on 21 March 1556. Bishop King died in 1558.[24]

The second record relates to Willimus Lovecrofte, doubtless the same man despite the slight difference in the spelling of his surname. Record ID 64454 of the database[25] indicates that Willimus Lovecrofte was ordained to the diaconate in the Capella Sancti Gabrielis (chapel of St. Gabriel) in Cliste (probably Bishop's Clist) in the diocese of Exeter on 13 March 1557 by

---

=66335, viewed 11 May 2014. The source of this record is given as OCRO Oxf. Dioc. Papers d. 105 (Episcopal Register).

24. The information relating to Anglican Bishops Holyman and King derives from Wikipedia, viewed 11 May 2014.

25. db.theclergydatabse.org.uk/jsp/DisplayOrdination.jsp?CDBOrdRedID =64454, viewed 11 May 2014. The source of this record is given as Devon RO. Chanter 18 (Register).

Bishop James Turberville of Exeter. Born in Beare, Dorsetshire, Turberville received his bachelor's degree from Oxford on 17 June 1516 and his master's degree from the same institution on 26 June 1520. He was consecrated as Bishop of Exeter on 8 September 1555. He refused the oath of supremacy instituted under Queen Elizabeth in 1559 and was deprived of his office in 1560. He retired to private life and died about the year 1570.[26]

There end the facts I have so far been able to discover about Willimus Lovecroft(e). He attained major orders (subdeacon, deacon) in the Church of England under Queen Mary and therefore probably recognized the supremacy of the Pope over the English church. I have not been able to determine what became of him after he was ordained as deacon on 13 March 1557. Queen Mary died on 17 November 1558 and was succeeded by her half-sister Elizabeth, who severed ties with the papacy and restored the independence of the Church of England. Like his superior, Bishop Turberville of Exeter, deacon Lovecrof(e) may have refused the oath of supremacy required by Parliament in 1559 and, like Turberville, may have been deprived of his office. On 25 February 1570, with his bull *Regnans in Excelsis,* Pope Pius V excommunicated Elizabeth and released her subjects from obedience to her. In 1588 Catholic Spain sent the Armada against England and persecution of Catholics reached full tilt, to continue with somewhat diminishing severity into the following century under Elizabeth's successors, James I and Charles I. The Act Against Jesuits and Seminarists (27 Elizabeth, cap. 2) adopted by Parliament in 1585[27] declared Catholic priests ordained abroad after 1559 who entered English territory guilty of treason, punishable

---

26. The information relating to Anglican Bishop Turberville derives from Wikipedia, viewed 11 May 2014.
27. The text of this act may be viewed at history.hanover.edu/texts/ENGref/er85.html, viewed 15 May 2014.

by hanging, disemboweling, and quartering, and persons who aided them guilty of a felony, punishable by hanging only. Several hundred Catholic priests and laypersons were executed under this act; some of these have subsequently been beatified or canonized as martyrs by the Catholic Church. Catholics did not attain full civil rights in England until 1829, and a Catholic diocesan structure was not instituted until 1850. The Act of Settlement of 1701 still prohibits Catholics or individuals with Catholic spouses from being head of the Church of England, an office always held by the English monarch.[28]

If Willimus Lovecroft(e) did attain the priesthood, his priestly ordination is not recorded in the Church of England database. During this period subdeacon and deacon were usually temporary offices in preparation for the priesthood, both in the Church of England and the Catholic Church. (Today the office of permanent deacon has been revived in the Catholic Church.) Did Willimus Lovecroft(e) complete his education at one of the continental seminaries established to educate Catholic priests for service in England? There were such institutions, sometimes called English colleges, in Rome, Douai, Valladolid, and Seville. Did he thereafter return clandestinely to England to serve as chaplain for one of the Catholic gentry, hiding in a "priest's hole" when necessary to avoid apprehension? Did he serve as a priest outside England? Did he abandon the clerical state once the oath of supremacy was required of Church of England clerics under Queen Elizabeth? It seems to me unlikely that he remained a deacon permanently, either in the Church of England

---

28. It has been proposed to amend the act to allow the head of the Church of England to marry a Catholic, but it has been objected that church requirements that Catholic parents raise their children as Catholics could pose a problem for the succession if the monarch is allowed to marry a Catholic.

or in the Catholic Church. It is possible that he died early, before he was able to complete the requirements for ordination to the priesthood. I emphasize that I have at present no evidence that Lovecroft(e) ever held any clerical orders other than subdeacon and deacon in the Church of England.

Willimus Lovecroft(e)'s ordinations antedate any Devon parish record for the Lovecraft(e) or Lovecroft(e) surnames found by DRO for Docherty, Searles, and me. Apart from the individuals identified in the 1524 lay subsidy, Willimus Lovecroft(e) is the earliest individual we know to have borne the Lovecraft(e) or Lovecroft(e) surnames, unless one accords that honor to Richard de Loccroft of the 1332 lay subsidy. How Willimus Lovecroft(e) links to H. P. Lovecraft's ancestral lines is unknown, although it seems likely that he is related to some degree, albeit remotely. (If Willimus became a celibate Catholic priest, he was probably not one of Lovecraft's direct ancestors, unless he broke his vows.) Willimus is to my knowledge so far the only Church of England clergyman who bore the Lovecroft(e) family name or any of its close variants (e.g., Lovecraft(e), Lowcroft(e), Lowcraft(e)). If H. P. Lovecraft was troubled that his ancestry as revealed by the Allgood chart was "rotten" with Church of England clergymen, one wonders how he might have felt about Willimus Lovecroft(e), the Church of England subdeacon (1556) and deacon (1557) who may later have become a Catholic priest.

Did Will Lovecraft of Broadhempston Parish Have Father John Lovecraft and Grandfather John Lovecraft (Weaver)?

Docherty, Searles, and I speculated concerning the possible ancestors of Will Lovecraft (1675?–1736+) (DSF 24–25). A John Lovecraft, Jr. was buried in Broadhempston on 28 May 1696, while another John Lovecraft, a weaver, was buried there on 10

January 1705/06. It is possible that these two John Lovecrafts were father and grandfather of Will Lovecraft. Based upon the Allgood chart, Lovecraft gives his direct paternal line of descent as Howard(4) Winfield(3) George(2) Joseph(1) Thomas(A) John(B) Joseph(C) George(D) William(E) Richard(F) John(G) (*SP* 454–55). The emigrant Joseph Lovecraft (1774–1850) is Joseph(1) in this enumeration. Docherty, Searles, and I were in agreement with the Allgood chart for generations 1–4 in America, but we found that Lovecraft's paternal ancestors in England were John(A) Joseph(B) Will(C). Note how the succession of John(B) Joseph(C) in the Allgood chart matches John(A) Joseph(B) in the DSF account of Lovecraft's direct paternal (Lovecraft) descent. The Allgood chart interjects a generation George(D) between Joseph(C) and William(E), while the DSF account goes directly from Joseph(B) to Will(C). If we accept John Lovecraft, Jr. (d. 1696) and John Lovecraft (d. 1705/06) as father and grandfather for Will Lovecraft, the DSF account becomes John(A) Joseph(B) Will(C) John (D–E). Allowing twenty-five years for each generation, we might assign years of birth c. 1650 for John(D) (d. 1696) and c. 1625 for John(E) (d. 1705/06).

The abundance of seventeenth-century parish register entries for the Lovecraft surname in Broadhempston (DSF 2.92–101) makes it difficult to validate a father John and a grandfather John for Will Lovecraft (1675?–1736+). If the John Lovecraft, Jr. who was buried on 28 May 1696 is the same person as the John Lovecraft, son of John, baptized on 15 September 1687, then John, Jr. did not live long enough to form a link in Lovecraft's paternal ancestry. There were three marriages involving a John Lovecraft in Broadhempston parish in the 1680s: 9 November 1682, with Susanna Venning; 5 August 1683, with Jane Predham; 26 February 1684/85, with Dorothy Furnace. The burial record does not disclose the age of John Lovecraft (weaver), buried in Broadhempston on 10 January 1705/06 (DSF 2.63). It is possible that he was young enough (say, born c. 1650) to have been one of the Broadhempston parish grooms of the 1680s; however, another John Lovecraft was buried in Broadhempston on 26 February 1724/25 (DSF 2.63). A John Lovecraft, son of Thomas Junier, was baptized in Broadhempston on 11 November 1638 (DSF 2.61), which is interesting because of the presence of the name Thomas in the Allgood chart. This John Lovecraft could also have been one of the Broadhempston grooms of the 1680s. John, Samuel, and Thomas Lovecraft were all residing in Broadhempston parish (Haytor hundred) in 1641 according to the 1641 protestation returns (DSF 2.95).

The Allgood Chart's Thomas(A) Lovecraft and the Emigration of Joseph(1) Lovecraft

Docherty, Searles, and I (DSF 27–28) discussed the possibility that Thomas(A) of the Allgood chart may have been a family patron rather than an ancestor. For example, White's 1850 Devon directory recorded one Thomas Maye Luscombe as a gentleman residing at Broadhempston Hall (the former Rowe family dower house at Beaston). John Grant Luscombe, yeoman, was still in possession of Oakhill Farm at Beaston in Morris's 1870 Devon directory (DSF 27–28). Is it possible that this Thomas Maye Luscombe assisted Joseph(1) Lovecraft (1774–1850), financially or otherwise, in his emigration to America? The Allgood chart family historian may have chosen to interject an illustrious patron like Thomas Maye Luscombe into the family history.

Another possible reason for interjecting the name of Thomas Lovecraft (1745–1826) as the father of the emigrant Joseph Lovecraft might have been to deflect attention from Joseph himself. Writing to Moe in 1931, Lovecraft blamed the financial ruin of the family on Thomas Lovecraft:

In 1745 we find born a restless egg who probably felt the blind stultification of all this oppressive respectability; for according to common report this Thomas Lovecraft struck out to live while he lived, aided by wine, horses, and the fair. I hope he had a good time, for his legacy to posterity was a general property scattering which shot everything to hell before he croaked—so that he had to sell even his family seat in 1823 . . . historick date, on which the Lovecrafts ceased to be gentlemen according to the original and technical definition. Possibly the shock killed the old reprobate, for he himself bumped off three years after that. Out of the wreckage climbed sundry of his numerous lawful progeny—I can't answer for the doubtless numerous rest—including his sixth child and their son[29] Joseph, already married and with six children of his own. (*MWM* 293–94)

Writing to Rheinhart Kleiner in 1916, Lovecraft stated that his grandfather George Lovecraft (1815–1895) emigrated to America in 1847 "on account of a loss of fortune" (*RK* 61). Even once he acknowledged Joseph Lovecraft as the original emigrant in his 1927 letter to Long and his 1931 letter to Moe, Lovecraft minimized the role of Joseph by stating incorrectly that he died soon after his emigration to America (*MWM* 294).

By 1828 Joseph(1) Lovecraft had left Pulsford, where he resided from 1813 to 1820+, to found his worsted spinning business in Bickington (*DSF* 14–15). The sale of Minster Hall (1823) and the death of Thomas Lovecraft (1826) as narrated by Lovecraft initiate a period of major changes in Joseph(1) Lovecraft's life—i.e., his removal to Bickington (1828) and his removal to America (1831f.). In 1927 and 1931, Lovecraft dated Joseph's emigration to the year 1827 (*SP* 455, *MWM* 294).

---

29. By writing "their" son, HPL apparently intended to refer both to Thomas Lovecraft (1745–1826) and his alleged 1766 bride Letitia Edgecombe. According to HPL's account, Letitia and Ellen Edgecombe were sisters who married, respectively, Thomas Lovecraft and Rev. Francis Fulford (*SP* 455).

In his letter to Maurice W. Moe of 5 April 1931, he stated that Joseph settled first in Ontario before arriving in New York, "in whose northern reaches he settled down on an experimental farm and promptly died" (*MWM* 294). In actuality, Joseph Lovecraft was listed in the first Rochester city directory in 1834 and continued to live there until his death at the age of seventy-five in March 1850 (Squires 11–12).

The Date(s) of Emigration of Various Members of the Lovecraft Family

Citing a family Bible record, Squires states that Joseph's son William (1808–1882) departed from England on 4 May 1831 (21). Squires states further that Joseph's son Joseph, Jr. (1810–1879) arrived in Rochester on 24 May 1831 (24).[30] If these dates are correct, Joseph, Jr. probably traveled in advance of William, because twenty days' passage from England to America would have been very fast for the times. Forty-seven days' passage from Torquay to Quebec (or longer if bad weather was encountered) was still typical in the 1850s (DSF 14n54). Exactly when Joseph (1774–1850) and Mary (Full) Lovecraft (1782–1864) emigrated is not known; Squires opines only that their emigration must have occurred between 1827 and 1831 (10). I do not believe they would have left England before the baptism of their youngest daughter Mary in Bickington on 4 November 1828 (DSF 15).

Joseph Lovecraft probably departed before his bankruptcy proceedings in England transpired in September–October–November 1831 (DSF 15–16). It is possible that some of his children traveled separately—it seems natural to suppose that one or more of his sons, perhaps Joseph, Jr., who arrived in

---

30. Squires kindly informed me that his source for the date of Joseph Lovecraft, Jr.'s arrival in Rochester was a newspaper obituary (DSF 14n54).

Rochester, New York, as early as 24 May 1831, went out first to reconnoiter before their parents, well beyond mid-life, sailed for America. (Joseph Lovecraft, baptized in Woodland on 20 November 1774, had celebrated his fifty-sixth birthday during the fall of 1830, while his wife Mary (Full) Lovecraft, baptized as Mary Full in Denbury on 10 September 1782, had celebrated her forty-eighth birthday during the summer of the same year.) One daughter, Eliza, baptized in Woodland parish on 11 August 1820, is not known to have accompanied her parents; it is possible that she died in England before they emigrated or that she remained with friends or relatives in England or that she emigrated to America at another time than her parents (DSF 18).

Overall, my considered opinion is that the likeliest time for the emigration of Joseph and Mary Lovecraft was the second quarter (April–May–June) of 1831. Finding them (or their children) in ship passenger lists would be the next step. The possibility that they may have arrived first in Canada (see Lovecraft's letter to Moe of 4 April 1931 [*MWM* 294]) and may possibly have traveled using assumed names should be borne in mind in conducting such an investigation.[31]

The Development of H. P. Lovecraft's Knowledge of His Paternal Ancestry

Lovecraft's knowledge of his paternal ancestry appeared to be considerably less in 1915–16 than it was in 1927–31. For example, on 1 January 1915 he wrote to Maurice W. Moe: "My paternal grandfather, George by name, (whom I never saw),

---

31. Docherty, Searles, and I speculated that the Lovecrafts probably traveled from Torquay in Devon to Quebec when they emigrated (DSF 15n57). We also speculated that the family may have traveled under an assumed name (or names) to escape their creditors because they were leaving England in advance of Joseph Lovecraft's bankruptcy proceedings in September–October–November 1831 (DSF 16).

emigrated to Rochester N.Y. in the first half of the nineteenth century" (*MWM* 43). He refined this account somewhat when he wrote to Rheinhart Kleiner on 16 November 1916: "My father was the son of an Englishman who came from Devonshire to the state of New York in 1847 on account of a loss of fortune" (*RK* 61). In these two passages Lovecraft appears to be referring to his grandfather George Lovecraft (1815–1895), who married Helen Allgood at Grace Episcopal Church in Rochester, New York, in 1839, as the original emigrant to America (Squires 30). Squires writes that George Lovecraft was about seventeen when he arrived in Rochester (30).[32] For that matter, George's eldest brother John Full Lovecraft (1806–1877) married Elinor Gaskin at St. Luke's Church in Rochester as early as 8 June 1833 (Squires 14, 51). The first Rochester directory (1834) included Joseph Lovecraft and his sons John Full Lovecraft, Joseph Lovecraft, Jr., and William Lovecraft (Squires 11). (Joseph's two youngest sons George Lovecraft and Aaron Lovecraft were still minors when this directory was published.) Perhaps Lovecraft did not bother to consult his 1905 copy of the Allgood chart when he wrote to Moe and Kleiner a decade later in 1915–16. It is also possible that he obtained additional information concerning his paternal ancestry during the decade 1917–27 from correspondence with other surviving Lovecraft family members.

Another possibility is that Lovecraft did consult his 1905 copy of the Allgood chart when he corresponded with Moe and Kleiner in 1915–16, but decided to describe his grandfather George Lovecraft, rather than his great-grandfather Joseph Lovecraft, as the original emigrant to America because he wished to conceal the 1831 bankruptcy of Joseph Lovecraft. He may have decided to describe his paternal ancestry more accu-

---

32. Squires gives George Lovecraft's year of birth as 1814 (30). George Lovecraft was baptized in Woodland parish on 9 February 1815 (DSF 13).

rately when he corresponded with Long in 1927 and with Moe in 1931. To the best of my knowledge, Lovecraft never did disclose that his great-grandfather Joseph Lovecraft had a bankruptcy—in fact, he blamed his family's financial ruin on his putative 2×-great-grandfather Thomas Lovecraft (*MWM* 193–94), rather than upon his great-grandfather Joseph Lovecraft.

Rather than hypothesizing an attempt by Lovecraft to conceal his great-grandfather's 1831 bankruptcy, I believe it is preferable to assume that Lovecraft's knowledge of his paternal ancestry gradually improved, with the assistance of one or more family informants, especially after his friend Wilfred B. Talman reawakened his interest in his family history in 1927. This thesis of gradually improving knowledge seems likelier to me than any deliberate attempt by Lovecraft to (1) minimize the role of the emigrant Joseph Lovecraft, (2) shift responsibility for the financial ruin of the family to Joseph's putative father Thomas Lovecraft, and (3) conceal Joseph's 1831 bankruptcy. In fact, Lovecraft may never have been aware of his great-grandfather Joseph Lovecraft's bankruptcy, rediscovered by Chris J. Docherty about 170 years after the original bankruptcy proceedings transpired in September–October–November 1831 (DSF 15–16).

Possible Family Informants in America

Lovecraft's younger aunt Mary Louisa (Lovecraft) Mellon (1855–1916) had died in Mount Vernon, New York, in 1916, leaving her nephew a legacy of $2000 (de Camp 156). However, his elder aunt Emma Jane (Lovecraft) Hill (1849–1925), her husband Isaac Hill (1849–1932), their daughter Ida (Hill) Lyon (1874–1951), and their son-in-law David Lyon (1874–1945) all lived in Pelham, New York. About 1921, Lovecraft assigned his interest in his paternal grandfather George Lovecraft's lot in Woodlawn Cemetery in the Bronx to his aunt Emma Jane

(Lovecraft) Hill. There is no indication that any financial consideration was involved; perhaps Lovecraft simply decided after the death of his mother in May 1921 that he wanted to be buried with his parents in Swan Point Cemetery in Providence and would not have any use for a burial place in the Lovecraft lot in Woodlawn Cemetery.

Lovecraft is not known to have met his Hill and Lyon relatives when he lived in New York in 1924–26, but he did write to his aunt Lillian D. Clark of exploring the Mt. Vernon–Pelham area (located immediately north of New York City and readily accessible by public transportation) for ancestral homes c. 1925, so it is possible that he met the Hills or the Lyons. (He did look up a friend of his aunt Lillian.) In any case, he could have obtained additional information by correspondence with the Hills or the Lyons without ever meeting any of them in person.

There were also other American relatives, more distant than his aunts Emma Jane (Lovecraft) Hill and Mary Louisa (Lovecraft) Mellon, with whom Lovecraft could have corresponded after 1915–16, among them: Josephine (Lovecraft) Jordan (1842–1933) (Squires 20, 51), daughter of John Full Lovecraft (1806–1877); Bertha Avis (Andrews) Ratcliffe (1866–1928) and Harriet Eliza Andrews (1871–1957) (Squires 21–22, 52–53), granddaughters of William Lovecraft (1808–1882); George Elliott Lovecraft (1866/67–1932) (Squires 28–29, 54; LSHL), grandson of Joseph Lovecraft, Jr. (1810–1879); Florence Veazie (Lovecraft) Salmons (1861–1950)[33] (Squires 44, 56), daughter

---

33. Florence Veazie (Lovecraft) Salmons was the sister of the next most famous family member after HPL, Frederick Aaron Lovecraft (1850–1893), whose New York City suicide in 1893, followed by the suicide of his mistress May Brookyn and the contest of his will by his family in the following year, received national newspaper coverage. Squires (36–44) provides an extended treatment of Frederick Aaron Lovecraft. In 2013 journalist David Acord published an electronic book devoted to Frederick Aaron Lovecraft,

of Aaron Lovecraft (1817–1870); George Francis Myers (1865–1937) (Squires 35–37, 56), grandson of Aaron Lovecraft; and Robert Bell Brown (1862–1934) (Squires 46, 57), son of Mary Lovecraft (1828–1907) and her husband James Brown (1806–1889). Of these, all were female line relatives except for George Elliott Lovecraft.

It is difficult to speculate over which of these relatives, if any, might have imparted additional family data to Lovecraft. Robert Bell Brown and his wife Helen (Morgan) Brown honored the Lovecraft family name with the middle name that they chose for their son Gordon Lovecraft Brown (1901–1975). Gordon Lovecraft Brown and his wife Sarah S. (Bickford) Brown in turn named their own son Gordon Lovecraft Brown, Jr. (1927–2003) (Squires 57). Perhaps the consciousness of the Lovecraft family name was highest among the descendants of Aaron Lovecraft (1817–1870), whose line also included the other famous Lovecraft, Aaron's son Frederick Aaron Lovecraft (1850–1893), whose 1893 suicide, combined with the suicide of his mistress May Brookyn and the contest of his will by his family in 1894, received national newspaper coverage (Squires 38–44; Acord).

Possible Family Informants in England

John Lovecraft (1840–1911), apparently the last male bloodline Lovecraft in England, died in the first quarter of 1911. It is possible that the c. 1911 Lovecraft chancery court case in London mentioned by Lovecraft in his 1931 letter to Moe (*MWM* 294?) involved the estates of William Lovecraft (1803–1883), son of the Broadhempston tailor William Lovecraft (1776–1855), and his second wife Elizabeth Whithear (Knowles) Lovecraft (1809–

The Other Mr. Lovecraft: A True Story of Tragedy and the Supernatural from H. P. Lovecraft's Family Tree. The cover of Acord's work reproduces contemporary portraits of Frederick Aaron Lovecraft and May Brookyn.

1893). This chancery court case may have attracted some attention to the Lovecraft family name in England. A transcription of the 1901 UK census recorded two elderly Lovecroft sisters, Ellen, age seventy-one, and Henrietta, age sixty-six, in Lichfield, Staffordshire; but based upon earlier records relating to the sisters, Chris J. Docherty concluded that their surname was actually Laverock or Loverock and was transcribed incorrectly in the 1901 census transcription (DSF 35–36).

There were female line descendants of the Broadhempston tailor William Lovecraft still living in England in 1911. For example, William's daughters Elizabeth (b. 1819) and Jane (b. 1823) had had a double wedding with George Kerby, Jr. and Bernard John Muller, respectively, at Old Church, St. Pancras, London on 31 March 1844 (DSF 2.30). Two daughters of Bernard and Jane (Lovecraft) Muller were living with their widowed father Bernard John Muller in Islington, London, at the time of the 1881 UK census. Muller's spinster sister-in-law Sarah Lovecraft (1800–1889), sister of William Lovecraft (1803–1883), was also living in his household at the time (DSF 34). The estate of George Lovecraft Kerby (1859–1918), born in Hackney, London,[34] and probably the son of George Kerby, Jr. and Elizabeth (Lovecraft) Kerby, was in probate in 1919. It is unlikely that Lovecraft corresponded with female line relatives in England; in his 1931 letter to Moe, he wrote: "If I can ever get over to Devon I may try to see what sort of cousin I can unearth there aside from those planted beneath and around the parish churches of the Newton-Abbot region" (*MWM* 294). He would probably not have used these words if he had already been in correspondence with a Lovecraft family informant in England.

---

34. George Lovecraft Kerby was still living in Hackney, London, in 1893–95 (see the London Electoral Register for those years). He was residing in Low Leyton, Essex, by the time of the 1901 and 1911 UK censuses.

Possible Family Informants in Australia

An Australian informant is also possible, albeit unlikely. William Lovecraft (1850–1867), the grandson of the tailor William Lovecraft (1776–1855) of Broadhempston and the son of tailor John Lovecraft (1813–1875) of London, emigrated to Australia. The male Lovecraft bloodline in Australia ended when William Lovecraft died in Bankside, Bankstown, West Liverpool, New South Wales, on 24 September 1867, aged only seventeen. Tailor William Lovecraft's daughters Eliza (b. 1810; married Charles Scott) and Ann (b. 1811; married [1] Hugh Montgomery and [2] Charles Scott, her sister's widower) also emigrated to New South Wales, Australia (DSF 2.30). At least Ann (Lovecraft) Scott (1811–1897) had descendants.

Could Lovecraft's Informant Have Been a Family Friend in New York?

Lovecraft did have correspondents in England [e.g., Arthur Harris (1893–1966)[35]], Australia [e.g., George William Sidney Fitzpatrick (1884–1948)[36]], and New Zealand [e.g., Robert George Barr (1906–1975)[37]], so international postage was no barrier for his correspondence. We cannot say whence he drew his enhanced knowledge of his paternal family history by 1927. Per-

---

35. Arthur Harris was the longtime publisher of the amateur magazine *Interesting Items*. For HPL's letters to Harris, see *RK*.
36. George William Sydney Fitzpatrick was a pioneering Australian public relations executive. He was also a book collector and corresponded with HPL about bookplates. Fitzpatrick was identified by David Haden in his paper "Additions and Corrections for 'Lovecraft's 1937 Diary,'" *Lovecraft Annual* No. 7 (2013): 180–81. My original paper "Lovecraft's 1937 Diary" is included in this volume. Haden succeeded in identifying many of the obscure correspondents whom I failed to identify or identified inaccurately or incompletely in my paper.
37. Robert George Barr's amateur journalism collection was donated to the National Library of New Zealand in 1977.

haps he simply studied his 1905 copy of the Allgood chart(s) more carefully than he had done when he corresponded with Moe and Kleiner about his family history in 1915–16. Or he may have benefited from conversation or correspondence with a family source at present still unknown to us.

Langley Searles's maternal uncle Nelson William Rogers (b. 10 March 1878, d. 6 August 1951) was introduced to Whipple V. Phillips and his family in Providence when he was only six or eight months old (late 1878). He became the particular friend of Whipple's daughter Sarah Susan (Susie) Phillips, who married Winfield S. Lovecraft in June 1889. Rogers visited Susie Lovecraft in her home at 598 Angell Street in Providence on Saturday, 10 February 1912, but Susie's son Howard was too ill to awaken to greet their visitor. Susie and her son shortly thereafter wrote to Rogers to acknowledge his visit, in letters dated Saturday, 17 February and Wednesday, 21 February 1912, respectively (for Lovecraft's letter, see *LFF* 1005).

Rogers had spent most of his life in Mount Vernon, New York, where Susie's father-in-law George Lovecraft (1815–1895) had also lived, but lived in Peekskill, New York, by the time he married Searles's aunt Sophie in 1940. He had had an earlier marriage that produced four children and ended in divorce. Rogers and Searles's aunt Sophie met through a mutual interest in political topics. He was a graduate of Cooper Union and had lectured on scientific topics earlier in his life (Searles 182).

Rogers himself gave Searles the boyhood photograph of Lovecraft (aged six years six months) in a sailor suit (first published in *Fantasy Commentator* for Spring 1945 and reprinted as the frontispiece for *Something about Cats* [Arkham House, 1949]). Rogers's widow later gave her nephew the 1912 letters written to Rogers by Susie and Howard, a photograph of Lovecraft aged eight and one-half months (probably taken early May

1891), a photograph of his mother Susie, and a photograph of his maternal grandfather Whipple V. Phillips[38] (Searles 179).

New York City Lovecraft collector Jack Grill[39] owned an early (c. 1891-92) family group photograph containing Susie, Howard, and Winfield Lovecraft, reproduced as the frontispiece for *The Shuttered Room* (Arkham House, 1959) and a photograph (c. 1895) of the family home at 454 Angell Street including Lovecraft's grandparents, his mother,[40] and his younger aunt (reproduced in the same volume opposite page 48), both of which he may possibly have obtained from Rogers, although Lovecraft's first cousin Ida (Hill) Lyon (1874–1951) of Pelham, New York, or relatives in Rochester, New York, are other possible sources.

Conclusion

Whether Lovecraft's informant was Nelson Rogers, Emma Jane (Lovecraft) Hill, Ida (Hill) Lyon, or some other person, or whether he simply was motivated by his friend Wilfred B. Talman to study his 1905 copy of the Allgood chart(s) more closely than he had when he corresponded with Moe and Kleiner in 1915–16, we can be grateful that Lovecraft shared his enriched (or refreshed) knowledge of his paternal ancestry with us in his 1927 letter to Long and his 1931 letter to Moe. Despite the in-

---

38. Searles published these three photographs in *Fantasy Commentator* for Spring 1948.
39. For Grill's collection see Mark Owings and Irving Binkin, *A Catalog of Lovecraftiana: The Grill/Binkin Collection* (Baltimore: Mirage Press, 1975). The c. 1891-92 family photograph is item 532 and the c. 1895 home photograph is item 536 in this book (both p. 57). Both photographs are reproduced in the photographic plate section of the book although the home photograph is mislabeled as item 534. The family photograph was earlier reproduced in *Fresco* for Spring 1958.
40. I have contended that HPL's pet cat Nigger-Man is held by his mother in this photograph, but Sean Donnelly and Donovan K. Loucks have questioned this identification.

accuracies undoubtedly contained in Lovecraft's accounts of his paternal ancestry, he provides a wealth of detail that has already brought forth books from Richard D. Squires (1995); Chris J. Docherty, A. Langley Searles, and me (2003); and David Acord (2013). The effectiveness of Lovecraft's fiction is strongly dependent upon his carefully constructed settings and chronologies, both of which are informed by his interest in family history (QAT 14). The study of Lovecraft's ancestry will continue to influence the study of the man and his work. New resources and new technologies that become available in the future will probably provide future students with a much fuller knowledge of Lovecraft's ancestry than we have today. It is possible that future students will even have the benefit of a nearly complete Lovecraft family genealogy—something of which we can only dream today.

Works Cited

Acord, David. *The Other Mr. Lovecraft: A True Story of Tragedy and the Supernatural from H. P. Lovecraft's Family Tree.* 2013. An electronic book available for purchase from Amazon.com.

Beckwith, Henry L. P., Jr. *Lovecraft's Providence and Adjacent Parts.* West Kingston, RI: Donald M. Grant, 2nd ed. 1986.

de Camp, L. Sprague. Lovecraft: A Biography. Garden City, NY: Doubleday, 1975.

Docherty, Chris J., A. Langley Searles, and Kenneth W. Faig, Jr. *Devonshire Ancestry of Howard Phillips Lovecraft.* Glenview, IL: Moshassuck Press, 2003. [DSF] (An electronic version of this title is available on familysearch.org. Go to familysearch.org/catalog-search/ and search for call number 929.273 L941.)

———. "Lovecraft, Lovecroft and Allied Families." Unpublished manuscript (2004), John Hay Library, Brown University. [DSF 2]

Evans, Rev. H[enry] R[ichard]. "Broadhempston." *Transactions of the Devonshire Association* 90 (1958): 62–126. [EVB]

———. "Woodland." *Transactions of the Devonshire Association* 92 (1960): 158–232. [EVW]

Everts, R. Alain. "The Lovecraft Family in America." *Xenophile* 2, No. 6 (October 1975): 7, 16.

Faig, Kenneth W., Jr. *George Elliott Lovecraft: Lost Scion of the House of Lovecraft*. Glenview, IL: Moshassuck Press, 2010. [LSHL] (An electronic version of this title is available on familysearch.org. Go to familysearch.org/catalog-search/ and search for call number 921.73 L941.)

———. "The Impact of the Fulford Will on Lovecraft's Claims of Fulford Ancestry." *Moshassuck Review* [Glenview, IL: Kenneth W. Faig, Jr.; published for the Esoteric Order of Dagon Amateur Press Association] (August 1996): 1–3. [IFW] (Contains a reproduction and a transcription of Rev. Francis Fulford's Prerogative Court of Canterbury will [1772].)

———. *Lovecraft's Pillow and Other Strange Stories*. New York: Hippocampus Press, 2013. [LP]

———. "Quae Amamus Tuemur: Ancestors in Lovecraft's Life and Fiction."[41] In Faig's *The Unknown Lovecraft*. New York: Hippocampus Press, 2008. 14–49. [QAT] (An electronic version of the Moshassuck Press printing of this essay is available on familysearch.org. Go to https://familysearch.org/ catalog-search/ and search for call number 929.273 L941)

Hanks, Patrick, and Paula Hodges. *A Dictionary of Surnames*. Oxford: Oxford University Press, 1988.

Joshi, S. T. *The Assaults of Chaos*. New York: Hippocampus Press, 2013.

---

41. HPL provided the Lovecraft family motto ("Quae Amamus Tuemur") in his letter to Richard F. Searight dated 14 November 1934 (*EHP* 335). S. T. Joshi translates it as "We Defend the Things We Love" (QAT 14).

Mellor, Moira. *Looking Back: People and Places in Broadhempston*. Totnes, UK: Broadhempston Society, 2006.

Orme, Nicholas. *The Saints of Cornwall*. Oxford: Oxford University Press, 2002.

Searles, A. Langley. "Recollections: VIII: Family Matters." *The Annex* [Bronxville, NY: A. Langley Searles; published for the Esoteric Order of Dagon Amateur Press Association] (Summer 2007): 175–84.

Sneyd, Steve. "Hunting for Lovecraft's Ancestors." *Ibid* [Teaneck, NJ: Benjamin P. Indick; published for the Esoteric Order of Dagon Amateur Press Association] (January–March 1999): 2–3.

Squires, Richard D. *Stern Fathers 'neath the Mould: The Lovecraft Family in Rochester*. West Warwick, RI: Necronomicon Press, 1995.

Franklin C. Clark (1847–1915)

For S. T. Joshi

Franklin Chase Clark was born in Barrington, Rhode Island, on 26 May 1847, the son of Edward Taylor Clark (1816–1849) and Mary Ann (Chase) Clark (1814–1906). Edward Taylor Clark and Mary Ann Chase were married at the First Baptist Church in Providence, R.I., on 21 January 1841, by the Rev. Alexis Caswell. Only eleven days later, on 1 February 1841, Rosina Child Chase (1823–1909), the younger sister of Mary Ann, and the noted portrait painter James Sullivan Lincoln (1811–1888) were also married by the Rev. Caswell. Mary Ann Chase had been admitted to the First Baptist Church by letter on 12 June 1834. Her younger sister Rosina Child Chase had been admitted to the church by baptism on 1 April 1838. Both sisters remained on the rolls of the church for the remainder of their lifetimes, and Rosina's daughter Ellen D. Lincoln (1843–1910) was baptized there on 28 March 1869.

By profession, Edward Taylor Clark was a druggist,[1] which may have influenced his son's choice of a medical career. The

---

1. In his article "A History of the Drug Business in Providence," *Narragansett Historical Register* 5 [1886–87]: 345–62), Oliver Johnson has this to say of Edward T. Clark: "John H. Taylor at one time had a drug store on North Main Street, as did also Drs. George Capron, and Lloyd B. Brayton. The store of the latter was opposite the First Baptist Meeting House. Dr. Capron was a judicious and careful physician, and continued to occupy a high position to the time of his death, which occurred in 1881. Drs. Capron & Brayton were succeeded by Edward T. Clarke [*sic*], and he by William B. Blanding, who still has a store near by in addition to another on Weybosset street" (360). On p. 361 of his article, Mr. Johnson also lists Edward T. Clarke [*sic*] among the druggists listed in the 1843 Providence city directory. I wonder whether the John H. Taylor men-

1841, 1843, and 1847/48 Providence city directories list Edward T. Clark as a druggist at 59 North Main Street. His residence in the 1841 and 1843 directories is listed as 53 George Street; in the 1847/48 directory, as the Franklin House Hotel on Market Square. In the tax book *City Tax for* 1847 (Providence: H. H. Brown, 1847), Edward T. Clark was assessed a tax of $12.15 based on $2 real property and $25 personal property. His mother Alice (Taylor) Clark was assessed a tax of $46.35 based on $60 real property (the family home at 9 Thomas Street) and $43 personal property.

But Edward T. Clark's young family was not to remain together for long, for he died on 12 September 1849, not yet three months past his thirty-third birthday. His mother Alice (Taylor) Clark had purchased a family lot at Swan Point Cemetery (lot 327, First Unitarian Society) on 15 May 1849—whether in anticipation of her son's demise I know not—and Edward was the first burial therein four months later. It seems likely that Dr. Clark had little personal recollection of his father. The narrator of Dr. Clark's novel *Susan's Obituary*, Dr. Jenckins, writes of his reunion with his old mentor Dr. Joe in the

Franklin Chase Clark, Brown University Class Photograph (1869). *Courtesy Martha L. Mitchell, Brown University Archives*

---

tioned in Mr. Johnson's article may have been a relative of Edward T. Clark's maternal grandfather, Deacon Edward Taylor (1751–1832).

eleventh chapter: "My eyes were also dim; and my heart beat with love for the kindly old man [Dr. Joe] who loved me with the affection of a father—a parent whose affection I had never known, so soon after my birth had he left my good mother a widow."

Franklin Chase Clark was the only child of the marriage of Edward Taylor Clark and Mary Ann (Chase) Clark to survive to adulthood. The first volume of the *Alphabetical Index of the Births, Marriages and Deaths Recorded in Providence* (Providence: Sidney S. Rider, 1879) records (424) the deaths of two unnamed children of Edward Clark: a daughter [7:168], age one day, who died 1 December 1843, and a son [8:29], age not stated, who died 10 February 1845. Unless there was another Edward Clark in Providence during this period,[2] these two children were probably early-deceased siblings of Franklin Chase Clark. In *Susan's Obituary*, Dr. Joe tells his young acquaintance Dr. Jenckins: "I had no brothers and sisters of my own to my knowledge; that is they died before I was born and I was in consequence indulged to death."

The birth of Dr. Clark was recorded in Providence [3:146 and 4:417], but Dr. Clark's death certificate and the questionnaire he completed for the Keeper of the Graduate Records at Brown University on 28 November 1903 state that he was born in Barrington, R.I.

Considering the early death of his father, it seems likely that Dr. Clark spent many of his early years on the farm of his maternal grandfather Darius Chase. Perhaps Dr. Clark was recalling his own carefree years on his grandfather's farm in the following words of the narrator Dr. Jenckins in *Susan's Obituary:* "The scenes took me back to my boyhood days when I used to roam about my grandfather's farm, and the surrounding country in hunting and nutting,

---

2. Contemporary Providence city directories list no Edward Clark other than Dr. Clark's father.

though the latter pursuit came somewhat later on."

In the 1860 federal census, young Franklin Clark was enumerated in the Barrington, R.I., household of Darius and Elizabeth (Winslow) Chase, along with his mother Mary A. Clark, aged 45, and her sisters Elizabeth Chase, aged 48, and Adeline Chase, aged 28. In the same household were Darius Chase's son-in-law, the portrait-painter James Sullivan Lincoln (1811–1888) and his granddaughter Ellen D. Lincoln (1843–1910), along with the 21-year-old farmhand Edward Seyler, an immigrant from Ireland. For some reason, Mr. Lincoln's wife, Darius's daughter Rosina Child (Chase) Lincoln (1823–1909), was absent from the household at this time. Darius and Elizabeth (Winslow) Chase had a number of additional children, probably at least nine in all.

Dr. Clark took seriously his Christian duties as a good Samaritan and took at least two of his aged Chase aunts into his own home and cared for them. Elizabeth Winslow Chase, the eldest daughter, never married and died of chronic bronchitis and catarrhal pneumonia in Dr. Clark's home at 186 Benefit Street on 5 November 1886, aged 75 years, 7 months, and 25 days. Another aunt, Adeline Amalia, the youngest daughter of Darius and Elizabeth (Winslow) Chase, had married Benjamin F. Bucklin in Providence on 8 December 1873, but was left a widow by 1900 and lived with Dr. Clark and his mother at 80 Olney Street in 1900–02. Upon the marriage of Dr. Clark to Lillian Delora Phillips in April 1902, Adeline Bucklin took up residence with her elder sister Rosina Child (Chase) Lincoln (1823–1909), widow of James Sullivan Lincoln, in her home at 38 Barnes Street. Upon the death of Mrs. Lincoln in 1909, this became the home of Franklin and Lillie (Phillips) Clark, who cared for Adeline Bucklin until her death, aged 82 years, 6 months, and 11 days, of influenza and senile debility on 17 April 1912.

In addition to his Chase aunts, Dr. Clark and his mother also cared for and lived with his paternal grandmother Alice (Taylor) Clark at 9 Thomas Street in her final years, until she died on 14 March 1883, of sheer old age. Dr. Clark and his mother Mary Ann (Chase) Clark also doubtless had much to do with the care of his maternal grandmother Elizabeth (Winslow) Chase, the widow of Darius Chase. Following the death of Darius Chase in 1863, Mary Ann (Chase) Clark and her mother Elizabeth (Winslow) Chase made common household at 139 Congdon Street, where they lived together through at least 1870. Elizabeth (Winslow) Chase died there of on 29 August 1878, aged 92 years and 3 months. From 1874 onward, Dr. Clark's mother Mary Ann (Chase) Clark appears to have lived with her son, continuing to do so even after his marriage to Lillie Phillips in 1902. Mary Ann (Chase) Clark died of senile debility at the home of her son and daughter-in-law at 161 Benefit Street on 17 May 1906, aged 92 years, 2 months, and 24 days.

Franklin Chase Clark and "Auntie Chase" [Probably Elizabeth Winslow Chase (1811–1886)]. From a Spicer Family Album. *Courtesy William Arnold Spicer, 3rd*

It may thus be said without exaggeration that Dr. Clark devoted a major portion of his life to the care of elderly female family members. We may perhaps forgive the author of *Susan's Obituary* for lapsing a bit into autobiography when he attributed to the beloved Dr. Joe of Rowport the words: ". . . I was generally from my youth the favorite of old ladies, as I am now." It may well be that Dr. Joe's moving account of the hope he instilled in a dying nonagenarian may reflect the care he provided for one of his own family. Dr. Clark also served as a physician for the Home for Aged Women at East and Tockwotton Streets in 1883–84. The *Annual Reports* of the Home for Aged Women for 1883 and 1884 list Charles Value Chapin and Clarence M. Godding, respectively, as physicians; perhaps Dr. Clark served in the interim between the two reports or assisted these physicians. Dr. Clark never cared for preferment or notice, but he did what he saw as his duty as a physician and a Christian. In a tender note bearing on his own family, Dr. Clark wrote in his 1909 paper "The Problem of Centenarianism" in the *Providence Medical Journal:*

> A hundred years is a great age to live. It was my privilege to see two grandmothers and my mother live beyond ninety. With the exception of one grandmother, they all retained their faculties nearly to the last. But in all of them, as they reached ninety and passed that age, a gradual failure of the physical strength was noted, somewhat greater than that observed when they were in their eighties.

Dr. Clark was graduated from Brown University with the degree of A.B. in 1869. At least six other men among the fifty-nine members of Brown's Class of 1869 went on to become physicians: Joseph Harris Cowell (1847–1920), Saginaw, Michigan, M.D., University of Michigan, 1871; George Hurlburt Felton (1846–1943), New Orleans, Louisiana, M.D., University of the City of New York, 1878; George Dallas Hersey (1847–1919),

Providence, Rhode Island, M.D., University of the City of New York, 1874; Charles Hitchcock (1848–1923), New York City, New York, M.D., College of Physicians and Surgeons (subsequently Columbia University), 1872; Nelson Perrin (1846–1915), Providence, Rhode Island, M.D., Harvard University, 1873; and Wallace Winfield Potter (d. 1923), Spokane, Washington, M.D., Bellevue Hospital Medical College, 1871. Of these six physicians, Dr. Hitchcock was Dr. Clark's fellow student not only at Brown but also at the College of Physicians and Surgeons in New York City. Dr. Hersey served as editor of the *Providence Medical Journal* between 1899 and 1910 and printed Dr. Clark's article "The Problem of Centenarianism" in 1909. Many other members of the Class of 1869 went on to become prominent clergymen, attorneys, educators, and businessmen, including historian and political scientist John Bates Clark (1847–1938) (the only other Clark of the Class of 1869), clergyman and missionary David Downie (1838–1927), and educator and antiquarian Ray Greene Huling (1847–1915).

Following his graduation from Brown University, Dr. Clark attended Harvard Medical School in Cambridge, Massachusetts, in 1869–70. While at Harvard Medical School, Dr. Clark received special instruction from Oliver Wendell Holmes (1809–1894), Park Professor of Anatomy and Physiology at Harvard between 1847 and 1882. Dr. Clark's obituary, published in the *Providence News* for 27 April 1915, recorded: "His first year after graduation [from Brown University] was spent in studying special courses with the celebrated poet, Oliver Wendell Holmes."

Dr. Clark pursued his studies at the College of Physicians and Surgeons (now part of Columbia University) in New York City and received the degree of M.D. in 1872. Marvin J. Taylor, Head of the Special Collections of the Health Sciences Library at Columbia University wrote to me on 16 April 1993:

Unfortunately, our records for students from the College of Physicians and Surgeons prior to 1900 are scant. We do have one grade book for the year 1872 that includes grades for Franklin Clark who graduated in that year. He received 'aye' grades in all subjects, including his thesis. No thesis title is given.

In the same year, 1872, Dr. Clark received the degree of A.M. from his alma mater, Brown University.

The bustling metropolis of New York City, with all its grandeur and squalor, left a lifelong impression on Dr. Clark. Undoubtedly, his youthful exposure to New York City confirmed him in his decision to return to Providence immediately after securing his degree—and there he remained until his death in 1915, after some forty-three years of medical practice. Interestingly enough, his nephew Howard P. Lovecraft also spent two years of his adult life (1924–26) in New York City, only to return to his native Providence for the rest of his life. But while Lovecraft grew to hate the teeming masses of New York City, Dr. Clark came away with a renewed respect for the suffering of his fellow men. One recollection that remained particularly vivid for him was of a Thanksgiving spent at the Mission House in Five Points, one of the worst slums of New York City, in 1871. Wrote Dr. Clark in his article "A Royal Thanksgiving" in *The Providence Press* for 23 November 1875:

> The scenes of this Thanksgiving come to my mind most vividly at its every anniversary; and I see again before me in a great trembling mass, those almost naked, starving children, pressing anxiously forward with shouts of joy, to a dinner, to which the greatest feasts of royalty itself dare not bear comparison.

Dr. Clark undoubtedly told his nephew Howard P. Lovecraft, who grew up amidst wealth and privilege on the prosperous East Side of Providence, of this memorable Thanksgiving in New York City. Lovecraft and his mother Sarah Susan (Phillips)

Lovecraft (1857–1921), the sister of Dr. Clark's wife Lillian Delora (Phillips) Clark (1856–1932), were left in reduced circumstances following the death of the family patriarch Whipple Van Buren Phillips in March 1904. Over the ensuing decade, the gifted young man and his mother doubtless enjoyed numerous Thanksgiving feasts of their own at the cheerful home of Lillie and Franklin Clark. In fact, Lovecraft's multi-volume *Selected Letters,* as published by Arkham House, begin with a 1911 missive in poetry directed to his mother, asking to be excused from the Thanksgiving festivities at Lillie's.

After attaining his medical degree at the College of Physicians and Surgeons, Dr. Clark returned to Providence to commence practice. The Providence city directories record his movements, first listing him in 1872 as a physician boarding at 9 Thomas Street, the home of his paternal grandmother Alice (Taylor) Clark. His business address is listed in the 1873–78 directories as 15 Meeting Street. In 1873, he resided at the same address; in 1874, he moved his residence to 40 Barnes Street, and in 1875 to 34 Benevolent Street. In 1877–79 he practiced and resided at 81 Broadway, during the same period that his future father-in-law Whipple V. Phillips (1833–1904) resided at 276 Broadway. In 1880–85 he practiced and resided again at 9 Thomas Street, the home of his paternal grandmother Alice (Taylor) Clark, who died there on 14 March 1883.

Between 1886 and 1898, Dr. Clark resided and practiced at 186 Benefit Street. He removed to 80 Olney Street in 1899 and remained there through 1903. In 1904 only, Dr. Clark was listed at 11 Camp Street; between 1905 and 1909, he resided and practiced at 161 Benefit Street. From 1910 until his death on 26 April 1915, he resided at 38 Barnes Street. In 1910–12 he practiced at 75 Westminster Street; from 1913 until his death he practiced from his home. He died at his home at 38 Barnes

Street on 26 April 1915, aged 67 years and 11 months, as a result of a cerebral hemorrhage and chronic Bright's disease, and was buried in the lot owned by his paternal grandmother Alice (Taylor) Clark at Swan Point Cemetery in Providence, Rhode Island (First Unitarian Society, Magnolia Path, lot 327). Interred there with him are his wife Lillian Delora (Phillips) Clark, his parents Edward Taylor and Mary Ann (Chase) Clark, and his paternal grandmother Alice (Taylor) Clark.

At this removal in time we can recover only small snippets of Dr. Clark's busy medical career. The fullest listing of his professional accomplishments appears in his biography in the *Historical Catalogue of Brown University 1764–1914* (Providence: Brown University, 1914):

> CLARK, FRANKLIN CHASE, A.B., A.M., M.D. College of Physicians and Surgeons, Columbia College, 1872; physician and surgeon, Providence, R.I.; surgeon, outpatients department R.I. Hospital 1876–83; physician, Providence Dispensary and Home for Aged Women 1883–84; acting secretary, R.I. State Board of Health 1890–91; acting police surgeon 1896; author of various contributions to periodicals. Address 38 Barnes St., Providence, R.I.

Dr. Clark was also a fellow of the Rhode Island Medical Society and a member of the American Medical Association. The journal of the American Medical Association reported his death in its issue dated 15 May 1915 (p. 1672).

In a Brown University questionnaire that he dated 28 November 1903, from 11 Camp Street, Dr. Clark described his publications as "various articles in newspapers, periodicals and magazines (literary, medical & scientific) too numerous and unimportant to mention." Nevertheless, on the verso of the form he mentioned as his most important works "Prenatal Education" (*Fifth Annual Report of the State Board of Health of the State of Rhode Island* . . ., Vol. 3, 1881, pp. [229]–54.), "Travels of Intermittent Fever in Rhode Island" (State Board of Health *Reports*, 1886), "Parks and Open Spaces in Cities" (*Fifth Annual Report of the State Board of Health of the State of Rhode Island . . .* Vol. 5, 1883, pp. [303]-07.), "Song of the Cicada" (*American Naturalist,* ca. 1875), "Red Snow" (*American Naturalist,* March 1875), and "Experiments in Hypnotism" (*Popular Science Monthly,* 1876). Dr. Clark also published substantial works in the *Medical Library and Historical Journal* and other medical periodicals. A substantial collection of his published articles and manuscripts, including the corrected typescript of *Susan's Obituary,* is held in the University Archives in the John Hay Library at Brown University.

It is difficult to form a reliable judgment concerning Dr. Clark's scientific, literary, and antiquarian work. His scientific and medical works bespeak a lively intellectual curiosity and commitment to the profession of healing. It remains true today that only an exceptional medical practitioner contributes both to the practice of healing and to the literature of the profession. While the majority of Dr. Clark's medical and scientific papers are of a technical nature, ranging from the medical properties of various compounds to the treatment of urethral chancroids and cerebro-spinal meningitis, a principal theme that reverberates in his more popular medical writings for the newspaper press is a commitment to public health measures. That Dr. Clark should have labeled among his most important medical papers "Open Spaces in Cities" and "Prenatal Education" bespeaks the nature of his interests. Among his surviving manuscripts at the Rhode Island Historical Society is an unpublished work, *History of the Development of Sanitary Science in Rhode Island,* consisting of a preface and nine chapters. While now somewhat dated, this specialized work would still merit publication and constitutes the most extensive of Dr. Clark's surviving scientific and medical writings.

Like his fellow reformer and antiquarian Sidney S. Rider (1833–1917), Dr. Clark had a lively interest in public sanitation measures and was an early and lively advocate of the public parks movement. His article "Open Spaces in Cities" in the *Providence Press* for 20 October 1882 indicates some of these interests:

> We have a "Common Street," but no common. Blackstone Park has been encroached upon, and all that broad expanse of country to the north has been "staked out" into house lots without the thought of open space. The land once used for burial purposes, the West Burying Ground, has shared the same fate. The broad, airy common upon Federal Hill has followed its example. Now the extension of trade demands the extinction of the Cove basin; and when that goes, only the Dexter Training Ground will be left us as a large open space. But there may, perhaps, be found some flaw, some *legal* irregularity, in its charter, so to speak, to give that park likewise to the ever-grasping maw of trade.

On 26 April 1883, Dr. Clark addressed the Park Association at the Franklin Lyceum Hall on "The Evils of Overcrowding." His talk was originally to have been on the Cove, then being threatened by the railroads that eventually destroyed it to build their central terminus. Like many before and after him, Dr. Clark loved the old Cove basin. He even broke into verse on the subject in the *Rhode Island Press* for 29 March 1884:

> The Old Cove Park
>
> Aye, blot it from the face of day!
> Too long has it been saved;
> Too long has been a hallowed spot;
> Too many storms has braved.
> The hearts are mingled with the dust
> That beat in rapture there—
> Why need we care for heroes dead

Who framed our freedom fair?
That liquid plain, where wild-fowl played,
Trees with soft verdure crowned,
Where gentle zephyrs hailed the morn,
And coolness breathed around,
No more shall cannon there proclaim
The triumph of the free:
A Vandal hand has dared profane
Its ancient sanctity.

Oh! better far its scarred face
Should sink beneath the sea,
And Ocean once more o'er it roll,
Once more resume his sway!
Let billows dark upon it beat—
No vestige let remain—
Till Time and Space shall be no more,
And Chaos there hold reign!

F. C. C.

Perhaps Dr. Clark himself had once courted in the Old Cove Park. With his wide antiquarian reading, he knew all its associations with Providence's storied past and could therefore experience special grief upon its demise in the pursuit of commercial interests and modernization. The final stanza of his poem bespeaks a "cosmic" viewpoint that would doubtless have pleased his more famous nephew.

The love for tradition and common sense in his own profession was another hallmark of Dr. Clark's professional writings. His 1908 series "Some Oldtime Physicians," which appeared in the *Providence Sunday Journal*, bespeaks a love for the practitioners of an earlier generation who preceded him in medical practice in Providence. Perhaps he could not help but think of his own early-deceased father, the druggist Edward Taylor Clark, of whom he probably had no personal memory, since the elder Clark died before his son was two and a half years old. It is doubtful that Dr. Clark had even a photograph of his father, since the latter died before photography became commonly available. Harkening back to an even earlier generation of medical practice, Dr. Clark wrote of his great-grandfather Dr. Ebenezer Winslow (1742–1833) in a letter to the editor of the *Providence Sunday Journal* for 22 March 1904, published under the title "Common Sense in Medicine":

> There was an old physician, a member of the writer's family, who practiced in the state of Massachusetts for nearly 70 years, till his death, in 1833. He is reputed to have attached more value to the healing properties of brown bread pills and soap and water than to those of actual drugs. He employed to a great extent rest, cleanliness, diet in his prescriptions and whatever contributed to the comfort of mind and body. To be sure his materia medica was very meager, but, so far as can be learned, he was as successful as similar country practitioners are today, who are provided with all modern appliances. He married twice and brought up 15 children and lived well for those times.

The cheery, devoted country practitioner "Dr. Joe" in *Susan's Obituary* was probably based on Dr. Clark's own knowledge of contemporary country practitioners and on his secondhand knowledge of the practice of his ancestor Dr. Ebenezer Winslow. In the end, the young protagonist of *Susan's Obituary* is sorely tempted to forego his more metropolitan opportunities to become Dr. Joe's successor in humble Rowport.

What can we say in the final analysis of Dr. Clark as a medical practitioner? He did much to relieve the sufferings of his fellow men and women—which is the first and most important thing to say of any physician. He valued the ethical standards of his profession more than worldly wealth and preferment. He knew the importance of soundness both of mind and of body and recognized the value of good cheer, good food, and healthful surroundings. Perhaps he was a "whole person" or holistic practitioner before his time, although one suspects the best of general practitioners have always practiced thus. He added to the literature of his profession, especially in the fields of public health, sanitation, and health education. He valued the traditions of his profession and helped preserve the memory of its past practitioners. He devoted a major part of his life to caring for his own elderly relatives. While none of Dr. Clark's medical papers are likely to be of more than historical interest for current practitioners, they remain tangible evidence of a useful career that doubtless benefited many hundreds if not thousands of human beings.

At least one published testimony of Dr. Clark's skill as a physician and surgeon remains, contributed by his nephew Howard P. Lovecraft. The story begins with Lovecraft's youthful interest in chemistry, narrated in his letter to Rheinhart Kleiner dated 16 November 1916:

> In 1899 a new interest began to gain ascendancy. My predilection for natural science, fostered by my Aunt Lillian, took form in a love of chemistry. A friend of ours is Prof. John Howard Appleton [1844–1930], the venerable professor of chemistry at Brown, & author of many books on the subject. He presented me with his own book for beginners—*The Young Chemist*, & before many months had elapsed, I was deep in experimental research, having a well-equipped laboratory in the cellar, which my grandfather [Whipple V. Phillips, 454 Angell Street] had fitted up for me. (*RK* 68)

On 4 March 1899, Lovecraft commenced "publication" of a hectographed chemical journal, entitled *The Scientific Gazette,* which he produced in "editions" of a half-dozen or fewer copies for eight years. Many issues of this journal and its companion, *The Rhode Island Journal of Astronomy,* are preserved in the Lovecraft Collection in the Brown University Special Collections Department. But let Lovecraft continue the story in his letter to Alfred Galpin dated 29 August 1918:

By 1901 or thereabouts I had a fair knowledge of the principles of chemistry and the details of the inorganic part—about the equivalent of a high-school course, and not including analysis of any kind. Then my fickle fancy turned away to the intensive study of geography, geology, anthropology, and above all *astronomy,* after which came a revival of classicism, Latinity, etc. Not until 1906 did chemistry come into my life again. In that year I encountered *physics* in high-school, which reawakened my dormant laboratory instincts, and led me back to the study of matter, its constitution and properties. I increased my chemical library by fully twenty volumes—to say naught of the physics textbooks I bought—and obtained a plenitude of new instruments. I was now in a smaller house [598 Angell Street], with a smaller laboratory, but the new room was ample for the purpose. In 1907 I took chemistry in high-school, but since I knew all the course before, had more fun than instruction in the class room. I left high school certified in physics and chemistry, and intended to specialise in those subjects at college; but just then my nervous system went to pieces, and I was forced to relinquish all thought of activity. Yet at home I continued my chemical studies, dabbling in a correspondence course which helped me in matters of *analysis* and *organic chemistry,* hitherto neglected by me. But in the mean time literature had been on the increase once more, and I found my interest centering more and more in old-fashioned scribbling. By 1912 I had practically ceased to be active in chemistry, and have since partially dismantled my laboratory, owing to my mother's nervousness at having deadly poisons, corrosive acids, and potential explosives about the place. One tangible memorial of my hobby remains—a bulky manuscript entitled *A Brief Course in Inorganic Chemistry,* by H. P. Lovecraft, 1910. There is also a physical memorial—the third finger of my right hand—whose palm side is permanently scarred by a mighty phosphorus burn sustained in 1907. At the time, the loss of the finger seemed likely, but the skill of my uncle—a physician—saved it. It is still a bit stiff, and aches in cold weather—as no doubt it always will. During the bandage and splint days I had to pick out my verses and articles with my left forefinger on the typewriter. (*AG* 210–11)

Lovecraft's aunt Lillie had taken chemistry courses during her time at Wheaton Seminary (now Wheaton College) in Norton, Massachusetts, in the early 1870s, and Dr. Clark doubtless encouraged his nephew in his scientific and literary interests following his marriage to Lillie Phillips in 1902. In his published letters, Lovecraft has left us a permanent record of Dr. Clark's skill as a physician and surgeon. We ought not to forget the second part of that title—surgeon—for in the résumé submitted for the *Historical Catalogue of Brown University* Dr. Clark mentioned his service as a surgeon at Rhode Island Hospital in 1876–83 and as acting police surgeon in 1896. Many of his medical publications deal with surgery, including the lengthy survey "A Brief History of Antiseptic Surgery," which appeared in the *Medical Library and Historical Journal* in 1907, the very year he saved his young nephew's finger.

It is equally difficult for me to attempt to assess the literary work of Dr. Clark. Suffice it to say that his primary strength was doubtless as a keen observer of human nature, as witness the many vivid character portraits he paints in *Susan's Obituary*. Dr. Clark's traditional verse may be very much out of fashion, but it often has a touch of wistful humor that redeems it from the charge of being merely mechanically competent work. That he had an eye for female beauty and the enviable gaiety of youth can be seen from his early parody of Edgar Allan Poe's "Bells," entitled "Sledging," first published in the *Providence Press* for 23 January 1879:

> Sledging (After E. A. Poe)
>
> See the sledges with the belles!
>   Happy belles!
> What a burst of pleasure wells
> From the palpitating belles!
> How they shriek out their delight

In their swift and airy flight!
   Oh, the belles, belles, belles!
   And the swells, swells, swells.

How each voice with laughter rings!
How it rises! How it flings
   About its echoes on the snow!
Keeping time, time, time
In spite of killing rime,
   As they go!
   Oh, the belles, belles, belles!
   And the swells, swells, swells.

How the bells do tink and tinkle,
And the belles do prink and prinkle
   For the swells!
See the prancing of the horses!
Hear the shouting of the bosses!
   And the yells!
   See the belles, belles, belles!
   And the swells, swells, swells!

How the breath and pulses quicken, and a glow
Too of pleasure lights up every cheek and brow
Of the belles, belles, belles, belles of the belles,
Responsive to the tinkling and jingling of the belles!

                      F. C. C.

Perhaps knowledge of his own classmates of the Brown University Class of 1869 inspired Dr. Clark when he took up his pen to write "On Going to College" for the *Providence Journal* on 8 February 1904:

        On Going to College

Some go to college just for fun;
And some go there for reasons none,
Some matriculate to be
Mighty men in dignity.
Some for family motives go,

Though nothing else they have to show;
Some go to play ball, or foot or base,
And be the winners in the race.
Some would their reputation make
Of boxer there, or sport, or rake,
Some go to seek their fortune there,
In hopes to win a wealthy fair.
Some go there to make a splurge
And from obscurity emerge.
Some go there for a short sojourn;
But some go there, we hope, to learn.

          F. C. C.

A thin booklet of the best of Dr. Clark's humorous poetry might even now make enjoyable reading. He could even tease the members of his own profession, in such works as "A Meeting of the County Medical Society." His most substantial endeavor in verse, however, was undoubtedly his translation of Virgil's *Aeneid*. Not having had the benefit of reading the eight surviving books (V–XII) of his translation owned by the Brown University Archives, I must forego comment in favor of the doubtless biased judgments of Dr. Clark's nephew Lovecraft as printed later in this essay. It seems doubtful that Dr. Clark's translation would merit publication today. It is only a pity that his nephew had no opportunity to revise and edit it for publication in an era when it might have made a significant impact on classical studies. Of Dr. Clark's fiction, only *Susan's Obituary* seems to survive. I hope that Dr. Clark's vivid portraits of New England character contained therein will more than justify its publication by Moshassuck Press in 1996. I like to think with what pride Howard P. Lovecraft might have held the 1996 Moshassuck Press edition by his scholarly uncle in his own hands. Indeed, it is a pity that *Susan's Obituary* appeared in 1996, not 1936, when this might have been reality. Hopefully, that "alternative universe" publishing house of 1936 would have had the prescience to contract with Howard P. Lovecraft to write the introduction for his uncle's work.

Dr. Clark's prowess as an antiquarian is attested by the regard in which he was held by men like Zachariah Allen, James Newell Arnold, John Osborne Austin, John Russell Bartlett, Thomas Williams Bicknell, and Amos Perry. Some of Dr. Clark's able antiquarian writings appeared in his friend James Newell Arnold's *Narragansett Historical Register,* a magazine whose diversity Dr. Clark must have loved. He also published at least one article in Sidney S. Rider's famous *Book Notes.* He could write ably on such obscure subjects as the history of Rhode Island shell fishery law and candlelight in colonial times. Having lived in the immediate Benefit Street area for most of his life, he knew the detailed history of virtually every lane and dwelling place in the neighborhood. Much of this he doubtless imparted to his young nephew Lovecraft, who also had an antiquarian bent.

It is difficult to resist finding word-portraits of Dr. Clark in the elderly scholars of Lovecraft's own fiction: Dr. Elihu Whipple in "The Shunned House," Dr. Marinus Bicknell Willett in *The Case of Charles Dexter Ward,* and Dr. George Gammell Angell in "The Call of Cthulhu," to cite only a few examples. Much of the rich antiquarian background used in Lovecraft's Providence masterpiece *The Case of Charles Dexter Ward,* particularly the detailed topography and history of the Stampers' Hill area, undoubtedly came to Lovecraft from Dr. Clark. Dr. Clark's knowledge of the Benefit Street area also undoubtedly contributed to Lovecraft's story "The Shunned House." Dr. Clark's poem "The Old Cove Park" bespeaks the love he felt for the ancient places of his beloved native city—a love he succeeded in imparting to his young nephew, whose own favorite place in the city was Prospect Terrace Park, which still overlooked the old Cove when it was originally dedicated.

We must avoid, however, viewing Dr. Clark only in the reflected light of Lovecraft's fame. Probably the strongest literary precedents Dr. Clark set for his nephew were as an occasional writer for the newspaper press and as a poet.[3] Lovecraft began to write for the Providence newspaper press as early as 1906, and Dr. Clark doubtless encouraged him in his endeavors over the ensuing decade. Dr. Clark's early "Microscopial" columns reporting on the activities of the microscopy department of the Providence Franklin Society are mirrored by Lovecraft's own astronomical articles in the Providence newspaper press (1906–08, 1914–18).

Like his uncle, Lovecraft also contributed poetry to the newspaper press, beginning in 1912. However, we must avoid the error of identifying the work of uncle and nephew too closely, for their viewpoints were markedly different—Clark the believer, Lovecraft the atheist; Clark the optimist, Lovecraft the pessimist; Clark the patriot, Lovecraft the loyalist; Clark the advocate of the common man, Lovecraft the aristocrat. While Lovecraft believed that foreign immigrants were destroying the traditional Yankee culture, Clark believed that in fact the foreigners were being exploited financially by the old Yankees and would even-

---

3. The only newspaper press contributor on the maternal (Phillips) side of Lovecraft's family was his distant cousin Casey B. Tyler (1819–1899), who published his *Historical Reminiscences of Foster, Rhode Island* in the *Pawtuxet Valley Gleaner* in 1884 and again in 1892–93. Tyler was a close friend of Lovecraft's maternal grandfather Whipple V. Phillips (1833–1904); the two were cosigners of a defaulted note which cost Whipple Phillips most of his first fortune, amassed at Greene, R.I., at the hands of a speculator in 1869. Lovecraft himself stated that he published a "miscellany" of articles in the *Pawtuxet Valley Gleaner* in 1906–08, but only the issues of 1906, containing exclusively astronomical articles from his pen, appear to survive.

tually become fully Americanized. Contrast Lovecraft's early poem "On the Creation of Niggers" with Clark's views in this poem, published in the *News* in April 1900:

> The White Man's Answer
>
> O listen to his cries,
> Which now ascend to heaven
> To make it of less size!
> Regard the awful duties
> Imposed against his will.
> For money's sake, consider
> One who meant nothing ill.
>
> Take off the white man's burden!
> A dreadful lord it lies—
> And lay it on another
> Who different color is;
> On brown or red or yellow,
> On sooty hottentot—
> But on some other fellow
> Whoe'er will mind it not.
> Take off the white man's burden!
>
> Remember what is done
> To the poor Anglo-Saxon—
> 'Twas surely meant in fun.
> Take off that heavy burden,
> His peaceful mind restore,
> And give him back the freedom
> He boasted of from yore.
>
> Take off the white man's burden!
> Release a suffering race;
> Forget not that forgiveness
> Should hold the foremost place,
> O lift the white man's burden!
> And when he comes to die
> His ghost shall never haunt you
> In dim futurity.

On 10 April 1902, Dr. Clark married Lillian Delora Phillips, born 20 April 1856 at the old Tyler Store in Foster, R.I., the eldest child of Whipple Van Buren Phillips (1833–1904) and Robie Alzada (Place) Phillips (1827–1896). Lillian Phillips had attended classes at the Wheaton Seminary in Norton, Massachusetts, and at the Rhode Island Normal School in Providence. Unlike her close friend Nabby Emogene (Tyler) Kennedy (1854–1945) (Mrs. Alvero A. Kennedy), however, Lillian never graduated from the Normal School. Before her marriage she taught school and helped her mother keep house. Her father purchased a handsome home on the northwest corner of Angell Street and Elmgrove Avenue on the East Side of Providence in 1881 (demolished 1960). Lillian was also a painter in oils. Her younger sisters Sarah Susan Phillips (1857–1921) and Annie Emeline Phillips (1866–1941) had married Winfield Scott Lovecraft (1853–1898) and Edward Francis Gamwell (1869–1936), in 1889 and 1897, respectively. The Rhode Island author Howard P. Lovecraft (1890–1937) was the only child of the first of these marriages. The two children of the marriage of Edward F. Gamwell and Annie E. (Phillips) Gamwell, Phillips Gamwell (1898–1916) and Marion Rhoby Gamwell (1900–1900), died in childhood. The Phillips sisters had one brother, Edwin Everett Phillips (1864–1918) (who married Martha Helen Mathews and died without issue), in business with his father Whipple V. Phillips for most of his career, and one sister, Emeline Estella Phillips (1859–1865), who died in childhood. Whipple V. Phillips and Robie A. (Place) Phillips came from old Foster, R.I. families and had made a first fortune in Greene, R.I. before settling in Providence in 1874.

Howard P. Lovecraft felt a strong attachment to the intellectual pursuits of his uncle Dr. Clark. As early as 1 January 1915, he wrote to his friend Maurice W. Moe:

> My two uncles-in-law, Dr. Clark and Mr. Gamwell, both Brown University men, stimulated my intellectual activities immensely. Dr. Clark is a physician and student of the highest type, whose articles have had a wide circulation in medical journals, whilst Mr. Gamwell[4] is an editor and all-around literary man of very thorough scholarship. (*MWM* 46)

Writing more expansively to his friend Rheinhart Kleiner on 16 November 1916, Lovecraft stated:

> It was about this time that Dr. Franklin Chase Clark, a distant relative who had become closer kin through marriage to my aunt, began to influence my intellectual development. He was a man of vast learning—a graduate of Brown, Harvard Medical School, & Columbia College, bearing the degree of A.M. besides his ordinary A.B. & professional M.D. He was an author of medical treatises, & an authority on medical ethics; but besides all this there was another separate side to his life—the classical side. He translated Homer, Virgil, Lucretius, & Statius into excellent English verse, & composed reams of original material. *Purely by coincidence,* he was an old-fashioned poet of my own beloved school & he did much to correct & purify my faulty style. He likewise worked wonders with my prose. I regarded, & still regard, his level as unattainable by myself; but I was so desirous of his approbation, that I would labour hours with my work to win a word of praise from his lips. I hung upon his conversation as Boswell hung on Dr. Johnson's; yet was ever oppressed by a sense of hopeless inferiority. His historical attainments were likewise immense. After his death last year, the R.I. Historical Society took over his unpublished manuscripts. (*RK* 71–72)

A fellow student of the classics, Lovecraft cherished his uncle's copy of Liddell & Scott's *Greek-English Lexicon* (*LFF* 1015). He also cherished a copy of the 1702 London first edition of Cotton Mather's *Magnalia Christi Americana*—probably the single most valuable book in his library—which he had inherited from Dr. Clark. Dr. Clark himself had inherited the Mather

---

4. Readers curious about Edward F. Gamwell may refer to my essay "Edward Francis Gamwell and His Family" (*Lovecraftian People and Places* 72–107).

book from his relation Walter Raleigh Danforth (1787–1861), an attorney who served as mayor of Providence, whom Lovecraft states to have been "own cousin" (i.e., first cousin) of Dr. Clark's father Edward Taylor Clark (1816–1849) (*ET* 75). Danforth was a notable antiquarian in his own right, whose own account of Providence was edited by Clarkson A. Collins III and published posthumously in *Rhode Island History* in 1951–52 under the title "Pictures of Providence in the Past, 1790–1820." Dr. Clark would doubtless have relished this choice of title, because of the coincidence of the dates with the lifetime of his own paternal grandfather Henry Finney Clark. Perhaps young Franklin Clark may even have met Walter Raleigh Danforth.

Lovecraft instructed his literary executor, Robert Hayward Barlow (1918–1951), to give his treasured Danforth-Clark copy of *Magnalia* to his dear friend, fellow amateur journalist and kinsman James Ferdinand Morton, Jr. (1870–1941), curator of the Patterson, New Jersey, museum.

Toward the end of his life Lovecraft wrote to his young friend Richard F. Searight.

> My late uncle Dr. Clark made a pentameter blank verse translation of the Aeneid & Georgics, but died before getting at the Eclogues. It has never been published, but I have the typed Ms. Wish I could publish it some day—finishing the Eclogues myself. (*EHP* 377)

> As for my uncle's translation—it is closer to Virgil than Dryden, but not so vigorous as English poetry. The Eclogues were not translated when FCC died. If I ever had an opportunity for getting it published, I'd take it—perhaps trying to fix up a version of the Eclogues in a similar style myself. (*EHP* 385)

Perhaps Lovecraft's admiration and love for his uncle Dr. Clark is best capsulized by the brief recollection he offered to his correspondent Searight on 4 November 1935:

Long before that, my uncle had had Dr. Holmes as a teacher in the Harvard Medical School, & I still have a letter which Holmes wrote him—congratulating him on an article in a medical journal. Very few people seem to realize that Holmes was a really eminent physiologist as well as a literary man. (*EHP* 397)

Lovecraft had himself met Dr. Oliver Wendell Holmes as an infant. His parents Winfield Scott and Sarah Susan (Phillips) Lovecraft were boarding at the Auburndale, Massachusetts, home of poetess Louise Imogen Guiney (1861–1920) and her mother in 1892 when Dr. Holmes came to visit.[5] While Lovecraft had no personal recollection of the event, his mother told him that the elderly Dr. Holmes rode him on his knee. The letter from Dr. Holmes to Dr. Clark must have been doubly dear to Lovecraft because of this personal association.

Another letter to Searight (*EHP* 371) cites Dr. Clark's connection with the firm that published the *Book of Knowledge* encyclopedia. This is apparently the work listed in *Lovecraft's Library* as item 750:

> *People's Cyclopaedia: A Complete Library of Reference Containing the Exact Knowledge of the World* [etc.], under the chief editorship of Charles Leonard-Stuart and George J. Hagar, New York: Syndicate Publishing Co. (1914), 5 vols.

---

5. I have recently discovered that HPL and his parents could not have been the May–July 1892 boarders in the Guiney home in Auburndale referenced in Guiney's correspondence to Frederick Holland Day (1864–1933) owned by the Library of Congress, first cited in this regard by L. Sprague de Camp in his 1975 biography of Lovecraft. In the letter to Day dated 4 June 1892, Guiney identified these boarders as Germans. Nor are there references to additional boarders in the Auburndale household in Guiney's copious letters to Day for the period through Winfield Scott Lovecraft's hospitalization at Butler Hospital in Providence in April 1893. Nevertheless, I continue to believe that there was an association between the Lovecrafts and the Guineys, based probably (as Lovecraft asserts) upon a friendship between his mother and Guiney dating from the period (1874–79) when Guiney attended the Elmhurst Academy directed by the Sacred Heart Sisters in Providence.

The extent of Dr. Clark's labors on this work are unknown to me. If the articles are initialled, it may be that the extent of Dr. Clark's contributions may be determined from an examination of the work itself.

The principal collection of Dr. Clark's articles and manuscripts resides today in the Brown University Archives, where they have been ably organized by Archivist Martha L. Mitchell. The general collections of the Rhode Island Historical Society contain a selection of Dr. Clark's printed works and some manuscript material including notes on the Finney family, an index to Staples's *Annals of Providence,* and three volumes of indexed newspaper cuttings with great emphasis upon developments affecting the Cove basin. A small group of important manuscripts is held in the Manuscript Division of the Rhode Island Historical Society Library. The RIHS *Collections* 12, No. 1 (January 1919) noted: "Mrs. Franklin C. Clark has presented to the Society some of the manuscript notes and papers of her late husband; thus making accessible to students the vast fund of material collected by that diligent antiquarian" (14).

A useful guide to the Franklin C. Clark papers at the Rhode Island Historical Society has been prepared by the Society's manuscript curator Rick Stattler. The Clark manuscripts preserved there include antiquarian works treating life in old-time Providence, the Providence town house, and the history of circuses and taverns in the city, and a history of Rhode Island fisheries. Also included are Dr. Clark's two most extensive surviving works, *History of the Providence Fire Department 1754–1904* (1905)[6] and *History of the Development of Sanitary Science in Rhode Island* (1893; rev. 1904).

---

6. Dr. Clark's history of the Providence fire department is full of rich detail available nowhere else and still merits attention by students of the subject despite the subsequent publication of an excellent illustrated volume by Patrick T. Conley and Paul R. Campbell, *Firefighters and Fires in Providence: A Pictorial History of the Providence Fire Department 1754–1984* (Providence:

As noted in the RIHS *Proceedings* 1905–06 (Providence: Rhode Island Historical Society, 1908), Dr. Clark had been elected a member of the Rhode Island Historical Society at the quarterly meeting held on 4 April 1905—a signal honor that during this era was accorded only to the cream of Rhode Island society and the most distinguished scholars. In the *Proceedings* 1903–04, the Librarian's Report (p. 28) noted the gift of a map of the original Providence home lots north of Olney Street drawn by Dr. Clark.

Lovecraft was certainly not alone in his admiration for Dr. Clark. His fellow antiquarians and genealogists were especially generous in their admiration for his work. In the introduction to the very first volume of his *Vital Record of Rhode Island 1636–1850* (Providence: Narragansett Historical Publishing Co., 1891), James Newell Arnold (1844–1927) wrote: "To Dr. F. C. Clark, of Providence, we have been indebted for many valuable suggestions which we have carried out in this compilation." Lovecraft's own library (item 77) contained a copy of John Russell Bartlett's *Dictionary of Americanisms* (Boston: Little, Brown, 4th ed. 1877) inscribed by the author to Dr. Clark on 17 December 1877. Bartlett (1805–1886) was a bookseller, bibliographer, and librarian who compiled notable historical, genealogical, and literary reference works and who also served as Rhode Island Secretary of State between 1855 and 1872.

Catalog 218 (4 May 1985) issued by California Book Auction Galleries described as Item 584 a copy of John Osborne Austin's

---

Rhode Island Publications Society/Donning Co., 1985). Regrettably, the bibliographical essay contained in Conley and Campbell's work does not mention Dr. Clark's work, unless their reference to "Captain Charles E. White (ed.), *Fire Service in Providence 1754–1904* (1905), a lengthy unpublished typescript at the Rhode Island Historical Society" is actually a miscitation of Dr. Clark's work. That the authors were aware of Dr. Clark's work is certainly evident from their reference to "fire historian Franklin C. Clark" on page 69 of their work.

The Journal of William Jefferay Gentleman: A Diary That Might Have Been (Providence: E. L. Freeman, 1909) containing a presentation letter from the author to Dr. Clark and Lovecraft's signature and bookplate.[7] Austin (1849–1918) was a pioneering Rhode Island Genealogist whose most notable work was undoubtedly his *Genealogical Dictionary of Rhode Island*.[8]

Of the antiquarians of this era, Dr. Clark undoubtedly also knew the prolific Sidney S. Rider. While Dr. Clark's associations with James Newell Arnold and John Osborne Austin were surely preoccupied by antiquarian and genealogical matters, Dr. Clark shared with Mr. Rider, in addition to these interests, a strong interest in public health and the parks movement. I once wrote a story ("A Pair of Old Shears") in which the young Lovecraft gathered information about his Phillips family forebears at a get-together including Arnold, Austin, and Rider at the Clark home on Barnes Street. Whether any such meeting ever took place must be left for speculation. Dr. Clark would be pleased to know that his final residence at 38 Barnes was subsequently, for many years, the home of one of Brown University's great classics professors. It was probably young Rhode Island Historical Society librarian Howard Millar Chapin who described Dr. Clark as "that diligent antiquarian" in the 1919 RIHS *Collections*.

By his will dated 8 October 1913, Dr. Clark named his wife Lillian Delora (Phillips) Clark as his sole heir and executrix. Sidney F. Adams, a grocer residing at 10 Thomas Street; George E. Bliss, a clerk residing with Dr. A. T. Jones, surgeon, at 214 Benefit Street; and William F. Brooks, residing at 144 Lafayette Street, Pawtucket, R.I., served as witnesses. The principal clauses of Dr. Clark's apparently self-written will were as follows:

---

7. This book is also recorded in *LL* as item 64.
8. Albany, NY: Joel Munsell's Sons, 1887; rpt. Baltimore: Genealogical Publishing Co., 1969, 1982, 1995.

First, I declare and direct that all my just debts and funeral expenses be paid out of my estate.

Second, I desire that my lot at Swan Point Cemetery be put under perpetual care and markers be set up wheresoever necessary in the lot and the said lot be transferred to the Corporation of the said cemetery.

Third, I give, devise and bequeath all my property, wheresoever found, both personal and real, and wheresoever situate, including my books, pamphlets, and manuscripts, to my wife Lillie D. Clark, to be for her use and behoof.

Fourth, I hereby appoint my said wife to be the sole executrix of this my last Will and Testament, without bonds or other securities.

This will was admitted to probate following Dr. Clark's death in 1915, and Mrs. Clark was duly appointed the executrix of her husband's estate. "Lillie" Clark, as she was called by the family, lived on until 3 July 1932, surviving her husband by more than seventeen years. From 1926 until her death, Mrs. Clark and her nephew Lovecraft both had rooms at 10 Barnes Street, only a few doors from where Dr. Clark had spent his final years. Except when he was traveling, Lovecraft habitually spent several hours every evening with his elder aunt; and during these times they must have shared many memories of Franklin Chase Clark. Many letters written to Mrs. Clark by her nephew while he was living in New York City in 1924–26 grace the Lovecraft Collection in the Brown University Library Special Collections in the John Hay Library, only a stone's throw from the site of the residence Lovecraft and his younger aunt Annie E. (Phillips) Gamwell shared at 66 College Street beginning in May 1933. Dr. Clark and his wife lie buried today in the Clark lot at Swan Point Cemetery under stones which bear only their initials: "F.C.C." and "L.D.C."

On 29 April 1915, Lovecraft published his poetic tribute to Dr. Clark in the *Providence Evening News,* where his own astronomical articles appeared between 1914 and 1918:

An Elegy on Franklin Chase Clark, M.D.

Died April 26, 1915

Can learned Clark in truth have ceased to be
    As Reason's bitter voice hath coldly said?
Can vibrant intellect, of earth so free,
    Like peasant clay be lost among the dead?

But yesterday the lustre of his mind
    Had force to pale obscurity away.
In its stern glare the folly of mankind
    Shrunk, like the shadows of the noon of day.

A changing world of strife about him seeth'd,
    Ideals less'ning and the pure disdain'd;
But his soul untainted wisdom breath'd,
    And linger'd round him whilst his form remain'd.

A fleeting fame, or momentary praise,
    How little wish'd he, and how nobly scorn'd.
How oft were Learning's richer, deeper ways
    Sought out by him, and by his hand adorn'd.

Whilst empty multitudes in frenzy crave
    The glitt'ring gold or honours of a lord,
In quiet he his best endeavour gave
    Content to serve; unthinking of reward.

Let lesser men display the laurell'd brow,
    And beg for homage to the world beneath.
In silence he's a greater master now,
    E'en though his laurel be his funeral wreath.

Say not that in the void beyond death's door
    The mighty and the lowly are the same;
Can boorish dust, in life but little more,
    Equality with mental essence claim?

His voice is still'd, his body run its course:
    But have those waves of intellect decay'd?
Can subtle energy, eternal force,
    As mortal flesh within the tomb be laid?

> Have not these waves, sent forth by matchless mind,
>   An endless path in boundless space to run?
> To flow unseen, alive but undefin'd,
>   But never, like the body, to be done?
>
> Who can declare that such unbody'd thought,
>   Sent forth by sages of an earlier time,
> Through other, living, bodies hath not wrought
>   The good of ev'ry age and ev'ry clime?
>
> So tell me not that he no more remains,
>   Whose silent form no word responsive gives;
> His body sleeps, reliev'd of earthly pains,
>   But he, the guiding soul, immortal lives!

Some of Lovecraft's critics, perhaps disliking its reflections concerning the immortality of human intellectual achievements, have found Lovecraft's poetical tribute to his deceased uncle rather wooden. It does, however, capture both Dr. Clark's considerable intellectual accomplishments and his personal modesty and disregard for worldly honors. In a letter to his friend and fellow amateur journalist George W. Macauley, cited by Macauley in his article "Lovecraft and the Amateur Press" (*Fresco* 8, No. 3 [Spring 1958]: 44), Lovecraft offered some of the same reflections in prose:

> His [Dr. Clark's] influence on me from childhood upward was very strong and any precision which my English may possess is due largely to his training. His retiring nature kept him from wider fame. . . . He is one who will not easily be replaced.

In Memoriam: Ethel Phillips Morrish (1888–1987)

Fifty winters have now passed since Howard Phillips Lovecraft was laid to rest in Swan Point Cemetery on the banks of the Seekonk River in Providence, R.I., on 18 March 1937.

Apart from those attending in a professional capacity (Horace B. Knowles' Sons, funeral directors), there were present four persons. The principal mourner was surely Lovecraft's beloved aunt, Annie Emeline Phillips Gamwell, the widow of Edward F. Gamwell, with whom Lovecraft had shared housekeeping at number 66 College Street since May 1933. Now past her seventieth birthday, Annie Gamwell had hoped for the company of her beloved nephew for the rest of her lifetime. Bereft of her only son, Phillips Gamwell, on 31 December 1916, at the tender age of eighteen, Annie's ties to her nephew were undoubtedly far stronger than those normally subsisting between aunt and nephew. She alone of all persons living shared with her nephew the vivid memory of her father Whipple V. Phillips's household at 454 Angell Street on the fashionable East Side, which the family had lost following the death of Whipple Phillips on 28 March 1904. All the rest of the immediate family were long gone: her only brother Edwin E. Phillips so long ago as November 1918; and then her sister Sarah Susan Phillips Lovecraft, Howard's mother, in May 1921; and finally her eldest sister, Lillian Phillips Clark, in July 1932.

The link between Lovecraft and his aunts Lillian and Annie was close and longstanding. Lillian's husband, Dr. Franklin Chase Clark (1847–1915), a Providence physician and antiquarian, was probably Lovecraft's strongest role model after the death of his grandfather Whipple Phillips. The only other close male relatives, Whipple's brother James W. Phillips (1830–1901) and his son Jeremiah W. Phillips (1863–1902), died even before grandfather Whipple, while Lovecraft was still a boy.[1] Uncle Edwin E. Phillips would seem to have lost a considerable sum of Sarah Susan Phillips Lovecraft's inheritance through poor investments about 1911, and Lovecraft has virtually nothing to say about his uncle in his published letters. But aunts Lillie and Annie returned very visibly to Lovecraft's life in March 1919, when they assumed household management of the 598 Angell Street residence on the East Side where Lovecraft and his mother had lived since 1904, upon the hospitalization of Sarah Susan at Butler Hospital on the banks of the Seekonk River, the same institution in which her husband Winfield Scott Lovecraft (1853–1898) had spent the final six years of his life. She never emerged, and the 598 Angell Street household did not break up until Lovecraft eloped to New York City to marry Sonia H. Greene in March 1924. The marriage was not happy, and by January 1925 Sonia had parted company with Lovecraft to take a job in the Midwest, while he was installed in a rented apartment at 169 Clinton Street in Brooklyn. Though Sonia wished to preserve the marriage, one believes very much that aunts Lillie and Annie were instrumental in the return of Lovecraft to his native Providence on 17 April 1926.

From his return to Providence until his move to 66 College Street in May 1933, Lovecraft lived in a second-story one-room apartment with alcove at 10 Barnes Street, where his elderly aunt Lillie also lived on the ground floor. Following the death of Lillie in July 1932, Lovecraft and his surviving aunt Annie, who was also living in Providence, sought more commodious quar-

---

1. Another son Walter Herbert Phillips (1854–1924) lived longer.

ters, and were fortunate to find the marvelous second-floor flat at 66 College Street, a stone's throw from the John Hay Library where Lovecraft's literary papers are now preserved through the wise intervention of R. H. Barlow and S. Foster Damon. Here was the scene not only of a happy reunion between Lovecraft and his aunt Annie but also a liberation from storage of many prized family artifacts from the author's happy childhood years at 454 Angell Street. From the southwest study that was Lovecraft's, the doomed Robert Blake pondered the mysterious goings-on at the Starry Wisdom Church on distant, looming Federal Hill, in "The Haunter of the Dark," Lovecraft's last substantial work of fiction. Here he and his aunt Annie greeted the admirers and correspondents who came to visit in increasing numbers toward the end of his life. Here he cared solicitously for Annie during several serious illnesses that incapacitated her for lengthy periods.

Annie was not Lovecraft's favorite among his aunts: the intellectual Lillie most certainly had the claim to that position. But Annie was the last of the immediate family of Whipple V. Phillips to which he belonged; and in the bosom of their mutual affection and the shared artifacts of earlier days and dear family members they shared the crowning years of Lovecraft's life at 66 College Street from May 1933 until his death in March 1937. The first harbinger of the end was Annie's discovery of her nephew's "Instructions in Case of Decease" on his desk in the autumn of 1936. Then came a more serious and enduring bout of the winter "grippe" than her nephew had ever experienced before, leaving him fully incapacitated by the end of January 1937. Grave illness and more marked incapacity followed throughout the month of February; and in the early days of March, the diagnosis of intestinal cancer was finally made, and Lovecraft was removed to the Jane Brown wing of Rhode Island Hospital on 10 March. Annie's pathetic wire to young Barlow following Lovecraft's death early on the morning of 15 March stated: "nothing to do."

18 March 1937: Lovecraft is laid to rest at Swan Point Cemetery and Annie is the principal mourner. Only a few lonely years remain for her, fraught with concern over whether she had acted rightly in allowing young R. H. Barlow to take charge of her nephew's literary affairs. Finally, family attorney Albert A. Baker (1862–1959), the man who served as guardian for Lovecraft during his minority and for his father during his incapacity, was able to achieve an amicable resolution of the disputes, and Annie had the joy of receiving the Arkham House omnibus volume of her nephew's best work, *The Outsider and Others,* dedicated to her by editors August Derleth and Donald Wandrei, in December 1939. It was to be her last Christmas at 66 College Street—a tradition that she and her nephew had preserved in spite of his yearly pilgrimage to New York City to join the holiday reunions of the erstwhile Kalem Club. Sometime in 1940 Annie Gamwell was confined in a sanatorium in Newport, where Lovecraft's friend Edward Cole visited her in 1940. By the end of January 1941, she, too, had passed, of cancer, like her nephew.

Of the other three persons in attendance at Swan Point Cemetery that winter day of 18 March 1937, Edward Cole was one. He was, in fact, the only one of Lovecraft's personal and literary friends to learn of his death in time to attend. So dear a friend as Frank Belknap Long learned of Lovecraft's death from the "trailer" item that newspapers nationwide (including the *New York Times,* where Long saw it) picked up from the obituaries in the Providence newspapers, which described how Lovecraft had chronicled a history of his illness for his physicians. (This story has been disputed as apocryphal.) Neither Moe nor Morton nor Kleiner nor Cook learned of the death of their friend in time to attend. Barlow, notified immediately by a telegram sent by Annie, arrived by bus several days after the funeral, to take up residence at the downtown YMCA while sorting Lovecraft's literary papers during the day. Far off in Wisconsin and Minnesota, Derleth and Wandrei, who were to perpetuate Lovecraft's worldwide literary reputation, had yet to learn of the death of their friend and correspondent. Derleth, who bore the major labor of publishing Lovecraft's work over the years, was never to meet his friend, correspondent, and mentor in person.

Edward Cole (1892–1966) memorialized Lovecraft in his *Olympian* in 1940 and contributed a recollection for George T. Wetzel's *Lovecraft Collectors Library* in the 1950s. A correspondent of Lovecraft from the latter's advent to amateur journalism in 1914, Cole, like Moe, was a high school teacher by profession. His letters from Lovecraft came to the Lovecraft Collection at Brown University in the early 1970s. How fitting that at least one personal and literary friend was able to mourn H. P. Lovecraft in person that winter day of 18 March 1937. And how fitting that that friend came from the world of amateur journalism, which sustained Lovecraft through the lean and lonely years during which his failure to find a career and his rejection by the military must have left him discouraged from time to time.

The crowning reward of this association with amateur journalism was the finding of his wife Sonia H. Greene, and the crowning tragedy the eventual conflict of Sonia's practicality and Lovecraft's idealism. Into the bosom of Providence and his aunts he fled, after some fifteen months among his Kalem Klub acquaintances in Brooklyn in 1925–26. Reconciliation failed definitively in 1928, and matters proceeded to the granting of a decree of divorce on the grounds of desertion in 1929, which, however, Lovecraft failed to finalize. "A gentleman does not divorce his wife without good cause": but Sonia would not have a marriage by correspondence only, and the aunts would not have her work for a living in Providence, even if it were possible. When she went to Europe in the early thirties, Sonia showered her ex-husband with postcards of places with historic or literary associations. They met once more, for a day only, in Wethersfield, Connecticut, in 1932. Sonia only learned of Lovecraft's death from Wheeler Dryden in the 1940s. By then she had married Dr. Nathaniel Davis. So Annie Gamwell and Edward Cole were left the principal representatives of family and friends on 18 March 1937.

The remaining two persons in attendance that day were more properly representatives of the friends and family of Annie Gamwell than of H. P. Lovecraft personally. Edna Winsor Lewis (1868–1955) was a friend of Annie who came to mourn. A close friend she must have been, for when Annie wrote her will in 1940, she left her estate, apart from the royalties from *The Outsider and Others,* in equal parts to Edna Lewis and the final attendee. One imagines a lady of the old school, of the genteel New England stock whose clinging to conservatism and traditional values Lovecraft had come to scorn by his final years.

In his last participation in the electoral process Lovecraft had voted for Franklin D. Roosevelt, while the old conservatives of the Hope Club had feared for the nation should Alf Landon be defeated. A virtual convert to the socialism of many of his literary friends by his later years, Lovecraft nevertheless never lost his respect for family, decorum, and other traditional things of aesthetic merit. That at least one other representative of the "old school" to which Annie and by implication Lovecraft himself belonged should have come to mourn on 18 March 1937 was entirely fitting and proper.

Known in fact to but a few of the most thorough students of Lovecraft's life, the final mourner on 18 March 1937 came close to seeing the fiftieth anniversary of the sad event. This mourner stemmed not from the line of Whipple V. Phillips (1833–1904),

Lovecraft's grandfather, which was extinguished with the deaths of Lovecraft himself and Annie Gamwell, but from the line of Whipple's elder brother James W. Phillips (1830–1901). Both James and Whipple were sons of Jeremiah Phillips (1800–1848) and his wife Robie Rathbone (1797–1848), the other children being a son Wheaton, who apparently died young, and sisters Susan (1827–1850) and Abbie E. (1839–1873). Jeremiah Phillips was the son of Asa or Asaph Phillips (1764–1829) and his wife Esther Whipple (1767–1842), one of eight children. He succeeded his father as a farmer in the town of Foster, R.I., and in the 1830s acquired a grist mill on the Moosup River in the same town. Here his life was to end tragically in November 1848, when he was crushed to death in the gearing of his mill.

The year 1848 left the young children of Jeremiah Phillips and Robie Rathbone orphans: their mother Robie Rathbone died in July, and the tragic death of their father Jeremiah followed in November. Whipple spent a year (1852–53) with his uncle James Phillips (1794–1878), another son of Asa and Esther, in Delavan, Illinois, but returned to Rhode Island and took up teaching in the rural schools and minding store. As L. Sprague de Camp related in his biography of Lovecraft, when the Phillips boys, James and Whipple, decided to take the Place cousins, Jane and Robie, to wife, it was James who elected to stay on the farm of his father Jeremiah and Whipple who decided to seek his fortune elsewhere. This he accomplished to a moderate degree by developing sawmill and real estate interests in the village of Greene in Coventry, R.I., until he suffered a setback through standing security for someone indebted to a speculator called Hugog around about 1870. His daughters Lillie and Sarah Susan were born in Foster in 1856 and 1857, respectively, and Edwin and Annie followed in Greene in 1864 and 1866. A fourth daughter, Emeline, was born in 1859 and died as a child in Greene in 1865.

In losing only one child before adulthood, Whipple and his wife Robie were spared much of the tragedy that could mar the mid-lives of Victorian couples. In various business endeavors, some of which took him to Europe, Whipple gradually recouped the wealth lost to Hugog in 1870 and bettered it. The year 1874 saw his removal to Providence, and the year 1881 his establishment at 454 Angell Street (then numbered 194) on the fashionable East Side. In the 1880s he formed the Owyhee Land and Irrigation Company (initially called the Snake River Company) to develop mining and agricultural interests in the Snake River Valley of Idaho. Whipple, his own son Edwin E. Phillips (1864–1918), and Jeremiah W. Phillips (1863–1902), the younger son of his brother James Phillips, were all involved with this endeavor at one time or another.

For the long years of the 1850s, 1860s, 1870s, and 1880s, few tragedies, apart from the loss of their daughter Emeline in 1865, were to mar the lives of Whipple, Robie, and their family. The older generation naturally passed, with uncles Benoni Phillips (1788–1850) and Whipple Phillips (1797–1856), both sons of Asaph Phillips and Esther Whipple, dying in Providence in the 1850s. Benoni Phillips and his wife Lucy Fry Phillips (1794–1884) left a family of eleven children, one of whom, Jeremiah B. Phillips (1828–1907), joined his uncle James Phillips (1794–1878), yet another son of Asaph and Esther, in Delavan, Illinois. Both James and his nephew prospered in Delavan, and Jeremiah B. Phillips had a son Frank Phillips and a daughter Nina Phillips Kimmler, the latter of whom I believe to have been the Illinois family member with whom Annie Gamwell corresponded. Altogether, four sons survived Asaph Phillips and are named in his 1828 will: Benoni (1788–1850), James (1794–1878), Whipple

(1797–1856), and Jeremiah (1800–1848). Asaph was also survived by three daughters named in his 1828 will: Betsey (b. 22 August 1789), who married Judge Daniel Howard, Jr. (1793–1879); Anne or Anna (b. 6 February 1804), who married Gardner Lyon; and Esther (b. 20 June 1807), who was unmarried at the time Asaph wrote his will in 1828. An eighth child of the marriage of Asaph Phillips and Esther Whipple is reflected on the Foster vital record: Waite (1791–1883) and her brother Benoni had married Fry siblings in a double wedding

While many of these branches stemming from Asaph Phillips and his wife Esther Whipple had descendants, none so far as I know were on a particularly intimate basis with Whipple Phillips and his family. Probably the most prominent descendant from Asaph and Esther was Theodore Winthrop Phillips (1836–1904), the son of Asaph's and Esther's son Whipple Phillips (1797–1856). Theodore Winthrop Phillips married Sarah M. Lawton in 1861 and became prominent in the steam engine industry in Providence. He was a member of the Rhode Island Historical Society from 1873 and anticipated Whipple Phillips by five years in building a home on the far reaches of the fashionable East Side of the city, at what eventually became 612 Angell Street, where he lived out the rest of his life until his own death and the death of his wife, a few months apart, in 1904. It was, however, with the family of his brother James W. Phillips (1830–1901) that Whipple Phillips (1833–1904) and his family had the closest connections.

While Whipple went into business, James W. Phillips and his wife Jane Place, exactly one year his elder, took up the family farm on Johnson Road (formerly Moosup Valley North Road) in Foster and kept it through the end of the century, dying in Providence at the age of seventy on 9 February 1901. The family of James Phillips and his wife Jane Place consisted of two sons:

an elder, Walter H. Phillips, born 7 November 1854, and a younger, Jeremiah W. Phillips, born 5 July 1863. Jeremiah W. Phillips appears to have resided for most of his life in Johnston, R.I., although he is listed with business connections as a salesman and treasurer in Providence directories from the 1890s. Of the two sons of James W. Phillips, Jeremiah Phillips appears to have had the closer relationship with Whipple Phillips, serving as secretary-treasurer of the Snake River Company following its organization in 1887. (Whipple, of course, was president.) Jeremiah does not appear among the officers or directors of the Owyhee Land and Irrigation Company following its reorganization under that title in 1889.

Jeremiah married Abigail or Abbie Ryan, born May 1865 in Wisconsin. The story of their meeting I do not know. The 1900 Soundex index of the Rhode Island Census, combined with the published vital statistics of the City of Providence, give a picture of their family during its early years. The published vital statistics of Providence record the birth of an unnamed daughter to the couple on 15 May 1888, and the death of a son, Harry R. Phillips, aged three years, on 7 January 1890. The 1900 Soundex index shows Jeremiah W. Phillips and his wife Abby M. Phillips living at 11 Franklin Avenue in Cranston, R.I. (RI Vol. 10 E.D. 188 Sheet 11 Line 79), with four living daughters: Ethel M., born May 1888; Helen M., born January 1891; Rachel A., born December 1892; and Dorothy J., born November 1896. From the Providence directories we know that Jeremiah W. Phillips died at the early age of thirty-nine on 17 December 1902. His daughter Ethel M. Phillips, born 15 May 1888, in Providence, was the final mourner at the funeral of H. P. Lovecraft on 18 March 1937.

Ethel M. Phillips died the widow of Roy A. Morrish, Sr., at the home of her daughter, Mrs. Elizabeth A. Drew, 39 Forsythia

Lane, Cranston, R.I., on 17 January 1987, in her ninety-ninth year. Her obituary may be found at page C-10 of the *Providence Sunday Journal* for 18 January 1987. Her wake was held in West Warwick on Monday, 19 January, and her funeral took place at the Meshanticut Park Baptist Church in Cranston, of which she was an honorary life deacon, on Tuesday, 20 January, followed by burial the same day in Highland Memorial Park in Johnston. She was an elementary school teacher in the Providence school system before retiring, and, according to the *Sunday Journal* obituary, was "the last relative of author H. P. Lovecraft." She was survived by three daughters: Mrs. Dorothy M. Harrall of Cranston, R.I.; Mrs. Marjorie P. Arthur of Mandeville, Louisiana (born 24 March 1919 in Providence, according to the Providence vital records); and Mrs. Elizabeth A. Drew of Cranston (born 25 January 1930 in Providence, according to the Providence vital records), with whom she made her home.

At the time of her death, Ethel Phillips Morrish had lived in Cranston for forty-three years. She left twelve grandchildren, including Robert Harrall, deputy administrator of the Rhode Island court system, and eighteen great-grandchildren at the time of her death. She was preceded in death by a son, Roy A. Morrish, Jr., also a resident of Cranston, R.I., who died on 15 February 1986, at the age of seventy (see *Providence Sunday Journal*, 16 February 1986, page C-28). Mr. Morrish was a veteran of World War II and the Korean War, commander of the 743rd Ordnance Unit of the Rhode Island National Guard, a member of the Meshanticut Park Baptist Church, and of Doric Lodge 38, Fraternal and Ancient Order of Masons. He had also been district chairman of the Cranston area for the Narragansett Council, Boy Scouts of America. He was superintendent of the E. E. Weller Company, of Providence, for twenty years before his retirement in 1981. Like his mother, he was buried in Highland

Memorial Park in Johnston, Rhode Island. He left a wife, the former Mamie Droitcour, and two daughters, Mrs. Judith Kjaer of Alabama and Mrs. Paula Wagenfeld of Woodbridge, Virginia.

Much more might undoubtedly be said of this family, but I have made no effort to invade their privacy apart from what is related in published obituaries and vital records. One will recall the membership of Robie Place and her daughters Lillian, Sarah Susan, and Annie in the First Baptist Church of Providence; and it is pleasant to note the Baptist connection of the family continuing with Ethel Phillips Morrish and her son Roy A. Morrish, Jr. Why Whipple V. Phillips never affiliated with the First Baptist Church of Providence, I do not know; he and his wife had been members of the Rice City Baptist Church in the 1870s. Perhaps he simply did not wish to surrender old connections with western Rhode Island. Just as pleasing to note is the association of Roy A. Morrish, Jr., with masonry. Whipple V. Phillips was a prominent local mason with important political connections (he suffered his fatal apoplectic stroke on 27 March 1904, while conferring with Providence alderman Gray), and Roy A. Morrish, Jr. is also associated with masonry. We know from a photograph published by R. Alain Everts in his *Arkham Sampler* that Whipple's son Edwin E. Phillips was also associated with masonry; and it is probable that his brother James W. Phillips (1830–1901) and his nephew Jeremiah W. Phillips (1863–1902) were also so affiliated.

The bare facts I have recorded concerning Ethel M. Phillips Morrish provide little picture of the woman who was indeed the last close relative of H. P. Lovecraft who had any significant degree of personal association with the writer. (Whether any of the children of Ethel and Roy Morrish met Lovecraft, I do not know.[2]) It is clear that she was a very dear friend and relative of

---

2. Mrs. Elizabeth A. Drew later recalled to me visiting at 66 College Street as a child.

Annie E. Phillips Gamwell (1866–1941), her cousin, and L. Sprague de Camp, one of the few Lovecraftian researchers who interviewed her, wrote of her visits to Annie and Lovecraft at 66 College Street. School teaching reflects an intellectual predilection with which Lovecraft would naturally have sympathized, and he and his aunt Annie undoubtedly found Ethel among the most welcome occasional visitors at 66 College Street.

Why Ethel alone of the four daughters of Jeremiah W. Phillips and Abigail Ryan Phillips who were living to be enumerated in the 1900 census should have formed a firm and fast friendship with Annie Gamwell, I cannot explain. Some of the other daughters—Helen M., Rachel A., and Dorothy J.—may have moved away. Others may not have lived to adulthood.[3] In any case, following the death of Lillian D. Clark on 3 July 1932, Ethel was the one close relative of Annie E. Gamwell in Providence. Though several of Annie's letters mention her relatives in Illinois, presumably descendants of Jeremiah B. Phillips (1828–1907), son of Benoni Phillips (1788–1850), Ethel M. Morrish and Edna Lewis were her closest relative and her closest friend, respectively, as evidenced by her will of 1940.

For decades and decades the graves of Howard Phillips Lovecraft and of his mother Sarah Susan Phillips Lovecraft (1857–1921) remained unmarked apart from the inscriptions on the central monument of Whipple Phillips's lot in Swan Point Cemetery. Through the efforts of Dirk W. Mosig and other devotees of Lovecraft's work, and with the consent of Mrs. Morrish and her family, memorial stones, in the same design as that placed to mark the grave of Winfield Scott Lovecraft following his death on 19 July 1898, were eventually placed on the graves of Lovecraft and of his mother in the 1970s.

---

3. In fact, daughter Rachel died in childhood.

How fitting and congruent, however, to end our essay by noting that stones were placed not only for Lovecraft, but also for his mother, a talented, artistic woman who in my opinion has suffered unduly from the biographers of Lovecraft. Should it not be enough that, setting aside the tragic end of the marriage of Sarah Susan Phillips and Winfield Scott Lovecraft, she gave birth to a genius whose works have enthralled millions? Should it not also be enough to note that after his father's early disability Lovecraft and his mother were taken back under the wing of Whipple V. Phillips, and that these childhood years at 454 Angell Street were among Lovecraft's happiest memories? How glorious a conclusion to an all too brief life, those years at 66 College Street with Annie Gamwell and many of the treasured relics of 454! How fitting that Lovecraftians placed stones not only for Lovecraft but also for his mother in the 1970s. (This may have been dictated more by cemetery regulations than by choice of the donors, but it was nevertheless a happy outcome.)

As that day of 18 March 1937, when H. P. Lovecraft was laid to rest, fades from the domain of memory to the domain of history, it is pleasing to note that, despite the shock with which the news of his death was received by many friends and correspondents, a small coterie of friends and relatives were able to accompany him personally to his grave. Annie Gamwell, surely, was the principal mourner. Edward Cole, for the literary friends and associates from amateur journalism. Edna Lewis, the friend and supporter of Annie Gamwell. And, finally, Ethel M. Phillips Morrish, the representative of Lovecraft's and Annie Gamwell's remaining family in Rhode Island. Already a woman of forty-eight years at the time of Lovecraft's death, older than the decedent himself, Ethel lived almost to see the fiftieth anniversary of that final farewell on 18 March 1937. It is fitting that I and my readers, be they few or many, now note her departure, barely short of her one hundredth year and of the fiftieth anniversary of Lovecraft's death. Surely she met few Lovecraftians during her long lifetime (Arthur S. Koki and L. Sprague de Camp among them), and she left, to my knowledge, no published recollection of Lovecraft. Her importance to Lovecraftians is her relationship to the author.

In an article in *Fantasy Review* on the subject of August Derleth and Arkham House, Jack L. Chalker remarked that Lovecraft's surviving relatives, after the death of Annie Gamwell in 1941, had no connection with books or fantasy. Whether true or untrue, this statement is hardly relevant. To enjoy the work of Lovecraft, one need know nothing of the man's life and family; and I have often thought that it is better to know nothing than a little, since the little that consists of the thumbnail sketch of an eccentric recluse of nocturnal habit is so deceiving. If we would know of the man—and many have found the man as fascinating as his work—our knowledge should ideally be as complete as competent research can make it. To me, those four mourners of 18 March 1937 are essential. To read the *Selected Letters* effectively, you must appreciate those four and their antecedents.

Lovecraft broke with the religion of his ancestors early in life, and with their predominant political philosophy late in life. (In defense of his support of Roosevelt it might be noted that his great-uncle James Phillips was a lifelong Democrat and that Asaph Phillips, his yeoman great-great-grandfather of Foster, R.I., was very probably of this political persuasion as well.) Frankly, I find the religious separation taken early in life the more difficult to account for, intellectually and emotionally, than the political separation. Unlike most Lovecraftians, I believe that there is some evidence pointing toward an attempt by Lovecraft to make some kind of religious adjustment as a young adult; perhaps the views of some of the literati in amateur journalism eventually swung him toward agnosticism, although, to be fair, he certainly also encountered a number of deeply religious individuals in amateur journalism, perhaps most notably Maurice W. Moe, with whom he debated such matters endlessly. These separations in religion and politics, however, do not separate him one jot from his bloodlines and their traditions, as anyone reading Lovecraft's western Rhode Island travelogues of 1926 and 1929 knows well. None of this involves fantasy or books (goodness knows yeoman Asaph Phillips probably did not own many books beyond a Bible, if indeed he was not himself illiterate), but that does not affect the matter in hand at all.

If you would know of Lovecraft the man—and his life is a fascinating subject—you must stray into the reality that fantasy and books strive to make more livable for those lucky enough to enjoy them. I fancy that the four mourners of 18 March 1937 knew far more of books, and perhaps even more of fantasy, than we might imagine. Certainly, Edward Cole, teacher of English, was a man of books. Annie Gamwell knew enough of the important strains in Lovecraft's life and literary work to see that the Providence newspaper obituaries of 1937, even from the perspective of fifty years, were prescient and fair. Edna Lewis and Ethel Morrish have so far left little mark on our picture of Lovecraft, although I suspect that little may be more significant than we yet know. The mourners of 18 March 1937 are by definition relevant for the study of Lovecraft the man. Now that they have all passed from this life, I hope that we shall eventually know more of them and of their connection with Lovecraft. Even if their relationship to Lovecraft's works of genius was small, their relationship to the man was certainly great, as evidenced by their personal attendance upon the occasion of his wake and burial.

Did any minister of religion offer sentiments of consolation to the mourners at Lovecraft's wake and burial? I have not read a full enough account of that sad day to make a judgment on this question. Despite their nominal membership on the rolls of the First Baptist Church of Providence, an Episcopal clergyman and friend of the family performed such a function when Sarah Susan Phillips Lovecraft and Lillian D. Phillips Clark died in 1921 and 1932, respectively. Of Whipple Phillips's three daughters who survived to adulthood, Annie was probably the most conventionally religious; she would undoubtedly have had abundant need for consolation resulting from the deaths of her daughter Marion Rhoby as an infant (1900) and of her son Phillips Gamwell as a youth of eighteen (1916) and from the failure of her marriage to Edward F. Gamwell (1869–1936) and their resulting separation. Annie is described as the widow of Edward F. Gamwell, so apparently their marriage of 1897 was never dissolved.

Whether Lovecraft himself would have sanctioned the speaking of any sort of words of consolation by a minister of religion at his wake or at his funeral is a subject on which I cannot opine. Suffice it to say that he sanctioned such a role when the deaths of his mother and his elder aunt occurred. In my opinion, the consent of the author to the speaking of any such words, with the principal aim of offering consolation to his survivors, and the subsidiary aim of departing this earthly existence in a manner congruent with ancestral traditions and societal norms, would not to any degree have lessened his commitment to the philosophical stance of an atheist, a stance he claimed in correspondence he shared with his elder aunt Mrs. Clark.

How much of her nephew's work did Annie Gamwell ever read? Did she care for it? Did Ethel Morrish know Lovecraft's work as well? We shall probably never know the answers to these and similar questions. To have read any of Lovecraft's New England stories with their special insight into the author's family background would surely have been a unique experience—

although, perhaps, sometimes one too close for entire comfort. We can never duplicate that. We can only attempt to approximate it, if we wish to study the man as well as his work. Let us now give the man all due honor for his works of genius and his many kindnesses, whatever his faults. And let us spare a few moments of reflection for these four mourners, the last of whom has now departed from among us.

At the centennial of Lovecraft's birth on 20 August 1990, the boy-editors of fandom who corresponded with him so voluminously in the 1930s will be men in their seventies. In another fifty years from 15 March 1987, all who ever knew H. P. Lovecraft in the flesh will surely have passed from among us. Yet I predict that our knowledge of the man and his work will grow greater and greater as the years pass and new resources become available for research. Let us then not forget those four mourners. They have each added to that knowledge and that perception which now only the ages will perfect. Reflect only on the great good that Annie Gamwell accomplished in letting the brilliant young Barlow take charge of Lovecraft's literary papers and secure them a fine home in the John Hay Library of Brown University; upon the great addition that Edward Cole's correspondence from Lovecraft made to that collection in the 1970s; upon the priceless family recollections and mementos that Ethel Morrish shared with Lovecraftian researchers over the years; upon the friendship of Edna Lewis that consoled Annie Gamwell in the difficult period following Lovecraft's death. All these mourners have done their part in preserving and perpetuating the memory of Lovecraft and of his work.

The work of H. P. Lovecraft is read worldwide by more readers than ever. His work has been republished in new, corrected editions from Arkham House, and these texts will surely find their way into all the paperbound editions and translations as the years go by. Who will continue the work of pioneer researchers on Lovecraft—like Winfield Townley Scott, Francis Towner Laney, George Townsend Wetzel, Randal Alain Everts, Dirk W. Mosig, and S. T. Joshi—in the years to come is yet to be seen. One hopes that a number of Lovecraft's close personal friends—like Frank Belknap Long, Donald Wandrei, E. Hoffmann Price, Fritz Leiber, Robert Bloch, Willis Conover, and so many others—will be living to join in the celebration of Lovecraft's centennial on 20 August 1990.[4] The four mourners of 18 March 1937 have now all joined the man whose passing they commemorated on that day. They are now a part of the history that is our picture of the man Lovecraft. I hope that generations and generations, including now and then a Phillips or Lovecraft family descendant, will benefit in their lives from the body of literary, biographical, and other research which has grown around H. P. Lovecraft and his work.

Lest I be accused of attempting to write and to publish a sermon on the semi-centenary of the death of Howard Phillips Lovecraft, I now bring my labors to a close. With every good wish to my patient readers, I give them this small portrait of Lovecraft and his four mourners of 18 March 1937: *in memoriam*.

---

4. In fact, Wandrei and Price died before the Lovecraft centenary.

EDUCATORS

Abbie Ann Hathaway (1852–1917)

Lovecraft's Teacher at Slater Avenue Primary School

For Chris Perridas, who so ably traversed these paths before me[1]

Abbreviations: US XXXX = U.S. census for the year XXXX; RI XXXX = Rhode Island state census for the year XXXX; MA XXXX = Massachusetts state census for the year XXXX; PD XXXX = Providence Directory for the year XXXX; PHD XXXX = Providence House Directory for the year XXXX. USPS abbreviations are used for the states.

Note: Abbie A. Hathaway clearly preferred Abbie as the spelling of her first name. Abby also occurs, especially in early records. I presume that her actual given name was Abigail.

At the corner of University Avenue and Slater Avenue stood the Slater Avenue Primary School,[2] where Lovecraft first attended school in 1898–99 and 1902–03 (*IAP* 71). His teacher there was Abbie Ann Hathaway. He at first declined to address his graduating class in June 1903, but finally spoke about the as-

---

1. Chris Perridas has six separate posts mentioning Abbie A. Hathaway, of which the most extensive is his post of 7 February 2010: chrisperridas.blogspot.com/2010/02/time-traveling-chrispy-in-search-of.html.
2. The school building of HPL's time has been replaced by a modern school building (address 220 University Avenue) used by School One, a private high school founded in Providence in 1973. The original Slater Avenue Primary School House was built of wood in 1890 and contained four rooms. The total cost was $13,072.85 (*Financial Report of the City of Providence, Rhode Island* [1896], 255). HPL wrote to Rheinhart Kleiner on 16 November 1916 (*RK* 67) that the Slater Avenue Primary School was to be abandoned by the Providence Public Schools in 1917, after only twenty-seven years of use.

tronomer Sir William Herschel (*IAP* 89; *RK* 70–71). He presented Miss Hathaway with a copy of his poem "C.S.A. 1861–1865: To the Starry Cross of the SOUTH," knowing that her father had fought for the Union in the Civil War (*IAP* 114). After being tutored by Arthur P. May in 1903–04, Lovecraft entered Hope Street High School in the fall of 1904. He proclaimed to a correspondent:

> The Hope Street preceptors quickly *understood* my disposition as "Abbie" never understood it, & by *removing all restraint*, made me apparently their comrade & equal; so that I ceased to think of discipline, but merely comported myself as a gentleman among gentlemen. (*RK* 72)

It's clear that the disciplinarian Abbie Ann Hathaway made an impression—albeit not a favorable one—on the young Lovecraft. So it is not unnatural for us to try to discover a few facts concerning her. She and Lovecraft did remain friends after he ceased to be her pupil. He wrote to Rheinhart Kleiner on 16 November 1916:

> At school I was considered a bad boy, for I would never submit to discipline. When censured by my teacher for disregard of rules, I used to point out to her the essential emptiness of conventionality, in such a satirical way, that her patience must have been quite severely strained; but withal she was remarkably kind, considering my intractable disposition. Her name is Abbie A. Hathaway, called "Abbie" behind her back by the boys. She is now retired on a pension, having been rather elderly even in my time. She still takes an interest in my work, & I chat pleasantly with her (more pleasantly than of yore) whenever I meet her. I managed to excel in studies at Slater Avenue, which perhaps reconciled her to my outrageous deportment. In history classes we used to have thunderous debates, for while "Abbie" was the daughter of a Union veteran, the Munroe boys[3] & I were Confederate sympathizers.

---

3. HPL met Chester P. Munroe (1889–1943) and Harold B. Munroe (1891–1966) during his first term at Slater Avenue School in 1898–99 (*RK* 67).

How we used to annoy her with our "compositions"—all flaming with love & glorification of the South! (*RK* 69–70)

Abbie Ann Hathaway was one of three daughters of Franklin Lafayette Hathaway (1824–1902) and his wife Alice Ann Freeborn (1827–1909), who married on 10 September 1847. Abbie Ann was the middle daughter: her elder sister Mary Esther Hathaway (who like Abbie Ann never married) was born in Fall River, Mass., on 26 September 1849. Abbie Ann was born in Fall River on 16 June 1852.[4] The youngest of the three sisters, Lena Franklin Hathaway, was born in Providence on 18 October 1871. Lena was the only one of the Hathaway sisters to marry. On 23 September 1896 she married William C. Sutherland (1872–1966), the son of Angus W. Sutherland and Esther (Forbes) Sutherland. Franklin and Alice Hathaway, all three of their daughters, and their son-in-law William C. Sutherland are buried in Swan Point Cemetery in Providence.

The Hathaways may have moved to Fall River to join the family of Alice Ann (Freeborn) Hathaway, who resided there. The birth record of their daughter Mary Esther Hathaway described her father as a housewright (i.e., house carpenter[5]). US 1850 enumerated the Hathaway family in Fall River: Franklin L. Hathaway, age 26, carpenter, born MA; Alice A. Hathaway, age 24, born RI; and Mary E. Hathaway, age 8 months, born MA. By the time MA 1855 was enumerated, the family had moved to Somerset, Bristol County MA: Franklin L. Hathaway, age 31, carpenter, born Freetown MA; Alice A. Hathaway, age 27, born Portsmouth RI; Mary E. Hathaway, age 4, born Fall River MA;

---

4. US 1900 gives her month and year of birth as June 1853. In my experience, one-year month and year of birth misstatements are very common in US 1900.

5. A house carpenter was skilled in the erection of house frames as opposed to more general carpentry work.

and Abby A. Hathaway, age 3, born Fall River MA. The family remained in Somerset MA when US 1860 was enumerated: Franklin L. Hathaway, age 35, carpenter, born MA, $400 personal estate; Alice A. Hathaway, age 32, born RI; Mary E. Hathaway, age 10, born MA; and Abby A. Hathaway, age 8, born MA.

The greater commercial opportunities available in Providence probably induced Franklin L. Hathaway to move his family from Somerset to Providence. The family of Franklin and Alice Hathaway was already in Providence (at 110 John Street) when RI 1865 was enumerated: Franklin L. Hathaway, age 40, born MA, gunsmith; Alice A. Hathaway, age 37, born Portsmouth RI; Mary E. Hathaway, age 15, born MA; Abby A. Hathaway, age 12, born MA; Abby S. Hambly, age 28, born MA, tailoress; Ellen A. Lake, age 17, born MA, jewelry worker. PD 1866 listed Franklin L. Hathaway, gunsmith, with house at 110 John Street. PD 1867 listed Franklin L. Hathaway, foreman, Providence Tool Company's Armory, with house at 110 John Street. PD 1868 listed Franklin L. Hathaway, pattern maker, with house at 158 Wickenden Street.

PD 1869 was the first to announce the partnership of Franklin L. Hathaway and William Douglass in the firm of Hathaway & Douglass, carpenters, with office at 109 Waterman Street. Franklin L. Hathaway continued to reside at 158 Wickenden Street in 1869. In 1870, Franklin L. Hathaway remained in partnership with William Douglass, but removed his household to 278 Wickenden. The family resided in Providence Ward 2 when US 1870 was enumerated: Franklin Hathaway, age 45, carpenter, born MA; Alice A. Hathaway, age 43, housekeeper, born RI; Mary E. Hathaway, age 20, clerk, born MA; and Abbie A. Hathaway, age 18, at school, born MA.

Franklin L. Hathaway continued in partnership with William Douglass in the firm of Hathaway & Douglass, carpenters, in

PD 1872, PD 1874, PD 1879, PD 1882 and PD 1885. In these directories the house address for Franklin L. Hathaway was Butler Avenue near President Avenue.[6]

Abbie A. Hathaway graduated from the Rhode Island State Normal School in Providence in 1873 and began teaching. It appears that her first position was in Cranston, R.I. When RI 1875 was enumerated, Abbie A. Hathaway, age 23, born MA, school teacher, was a boarder in the Cranston household of Henry and Eunice Gardiner. She was still working as a teacher in the Cranston Public Schools in 1877 (*Annual Report of the Board of* Education [1877], 5). However, Abbie became an employee of the Providence Public Schools and remained so until her retirement. PD 1878 listed Abbie A. Hathaway as assistant teacher at the Julian Street Primary School[7] in Providence.

US 1880 enumerated the family of Franklin and Alice Hathaway on Slater Avenue in Providence: Franklin Hathaway (head), age 56, carpenter, born MA of MA-born parents; Alice A. Hathaway (wife), age 52, housekeeper, born RI of RI-born parents; Mary E. Hathaway (daughter), age 30, milliner, born MA of MA-born father and RI-born mother; Abbie A. Hathaway (daughter), age 28, schoolteacher, born MA of MA-born father and RI-born mother; Lena F. Hathaway (daughter), age 8 years 8 months, at school, born RI of MA-born father and RI-born mother; John H. Freeborn (brother[-in-law]), age 55, carpenter, born RI of RI-born parents.

When RI 1885 was enumerated, Abbie Hathaway, age 33, born MA, public school teacher, was a member of her parents' household (district 4, family 42, six total persons). Perhaps there

---

6. Later numbered as 115 Butler Avenue.
7. The Julian Street Primary & Intermediate School was built of wood in 1875. The total cost of the two-story structure, including furnishings, was $11,003.95 (*Report of the City Auditor* [1889], 129).

was one servant in the household in addition to Abbie, her two sisters, and their parents. (Abbie's maternal uncle John Hambly Freeborn, who boarded with the family, had died in 1884.) PD 1885 listed Franklin Hathaway as residing on Butler Avenue, near President Avenue. PD 1887 listed Miss Abbie A. Hathaway as a teacher at the Coville Street School.[8] She boarded in her parents' home at 115 Butler Avenue; her father continued in his business partnership with William Douglass. *Directory of the Public Schools* (1886) identified the staff at Coville Street Intermediate School:

> Nellie F. Crocker, Principal, room 1, residence 6 Kepler Street; Mary C. Devanaux, Assistant, room 1, residence 48 Willow Street; Julia A. Dunham, Assistant, room 2, resident 34 Armington Avenue; Abbie A. Hathaway, Assistant, room 3, residence Butler Avenue; Mary J. Kenney, Assistant, room 4, residence 46 Penn Street (67).

I have not been able to determine just when Abbie received her final assignment to Slater Avenue Primary School. I suspect she may have become principal when the school was first opened in 1890. The *City Manual* for 1893, 1897, 1899, and 1901 identifies Abbie A. Hathaway as principal and Sabrina P. Prouty as assistant at Slater Avenue Primary School. Beginning with 1901, the Providence directories identified Abbie A. Hathaway as a teacher at Slater Avenue School.[9]

No later than 1896, Franklin Hathaway and his family were residing at 97 Blackstone Boulevard in Providence. Abbie Hathaway would have had a very comfortable short walk from her residence on Blackstone Boulevard to Slater Avenue Primary School on the corner of University Avenue and Slater Avenue

---

8. The Coville Street School House was built of wood in 1886. The cost of the two-story structure was $14,908.73 (*Report of the City Auditor* [1889], 130).

9. In the primary and grammar schools, principals were both administrators (being supervisors of the assistants) and teachers.

(address 220 University Avenue). By 1902–03, when Lovecraft re-enrolled, Slater Avenue School had been expanded to include more grades. The 1907–08 *Directory of the Public Schools* identified the following staff at Slater Avenue Primary School: Abby A. Hathaway, Principal, room 1, grades 5A and 6B; Katherine H. Hurley, room 2, grades 3B and 4B; and Josephine Bishop, room 4, grades 1B and 2B. I presume that students in grades 7–8 would go on to one of the grammar schools before entering high school for grades 9–12.

In 1896, Abbie's younger sister Lena married William C. Sutherland. The entire extended family was enumerated at 97 Blackstone Boulevard in US 1900: Franklin L. Hathaway (head), born September 1824 MA of MA-born parents, age 75, married for 53 years, contractor; Alice M. Hathaway (wife), born September 1827 RI of RI-born parents, age 72; Mary E. Hathaway (daughter), born September 1849 MA of MA-born father and RI-born mother, age 50, milliner; Abby A. Hathaway (daughter), born June 1853 MA of MA-born father and RI-born mother, age 47, teacher; William C. Sutherland (boarder), born March 1872 RI of Nova Scotia-born parents, age 28, painter; Lena F. Sutherland (wife), born October 1871 RI of MA-born father and RI-born mother, age 28; Franklin C. Sutherland, born May 1899 RI of RI-born parents, age 1; Sarah A. Hands (servant), born May 1879 Ireland of Irish-born parents, age 21.

The Hathaway sisters lost their father in 1902 and their mother in 1909. US 1910 enumerated the following reduced household at 97 Blackstone Boulevard: Abbie Hathaway (head), age 57, single, born MA of MA-born father and RI-born mother, public school teacher; Mary E. Hathaway (sister), age 50, single, born MA of MA-born father and RI-born mother; William C. Sutherland (brother-in-law), age 38, born RI of Canadian-born parents, decorator & paper hanger, in first marriage for

13 years; Lena H. Sutherland (sister), age 38, born RI of MA-born father and RI-born mother, in first marriage for 13 years, 1 child borne, 1 child living; Franklin C. Sutherland (nephew), age 10, born RI of RI-born parents, at school.

By the time RI 1915 was enumerated, William C. Sutherland had become the head of household at 97 Blackstone Boulevard: William C. Sutherland (head), age 42, born US of Canadian-born parents, painter & decorator; Lena F. Sutherland (wife), age 43, born US of US-born parents, no occupation; Mary E. Hathaway (sister-in-law), age 65, born US of US-born parents, manufacturer (art books); Abbie A. Hathaway (sister-in-law), age 62, born US of US-born parents, own income; Franklin C. Sutherland (son), age 15, born US of US-born parents, no occupation. PD 1914 had listed Abbie A. Hathaway as a teacher at the Slater Avenue School, so I think we can infer she retired sometime between the compilation of the data for PD 1914 and the enumeration of RI 1915.

Abbie did not enjoy a long retirement. She died on 14 October 1917 in Providence and was buried with her parents in Swan Point Cemetery. Her elder sister Mary Esther Hathaway lived on until 1928, when she died and joined her sister and their parents at Swan Point Cemetery. Identified as a clerk in US 1870, Mary was identified as a milliner as early as US 1880. In PD 1901, she was identified as a milliner with her place of business at 335 Westminster Street, room 1. PD 1906, PD 1908, PD 1910, PD 1912, and PD 1914 did not list any occupation for Mary E. Hathaway, who continued to board at 97 Blackstone Boulevard. However, RI 1915 identified her work as manufacturer (art books). PD 1916 listed her occupation as "fancy work," and this listing was continued in PD 1922, PD 1924, and PD 1928. Perhaps she sold her work through one of the fashionable gift shops in the Wayland Square neighborhood.

William C. Sutherland and his wife Lena Franklin (Hathaway) Sullivan continued to live at 97 Blackstone Boulevard for many years. William was still living there in 1960, the year of his wife's death. The Sutherlands lived long lives, but also had to mark the sad occasion of the death of their son Franklin Channing Sutherland in 1946.

Abbie Ann Hathaway doubtless believed in discipline in her classroom. Whether she was an adherent of "spare the rod, spoil the child" the surviving record does not indicate. Perhaps the teachers at Hope Street High School handled Lovecraft differently, but they also had to deal with his nervous tics and apparent seizures. In the end he was withdrawn from school and did not receive his high school diploma.[10] Perhaps Abbie Hathaway had to exercise considerable restraint when Lovecraft placed a poem lauding the Confederacy on her desk. Having chosen him to address his graduating class in 1903, she doubtless recognized that he was a student of unusual promise, albeit difficult to manage. She was probably relieved to hand him along to the attention of tutor Arthur P. May in 1903–04 and to the Hope Street High School faculty in 1904–08. Whatever her difficulties with her pupil may have been, Lovecraft's fame has succeeded in shining at least a dim light upon his erstwhile preceptress.

Lovecraft did indicate that a photograph of the Slater Avenue Primary School class of 1903 was taken. Perhaps there remains hope that a copy of this photograph will yet be found. Perhaps it contains the images not only of Lovecraft and his classmates but also of their teacher Abbie Ann Hathaway.

---

10. It is possible that he obtained his diploma in evening high school, but records have been lost. The Providence Amateur Press Club had several members who were evening high school students, so that it is not impossible that HPL met some of them when he himself was attending evening high school. However, the standard account is that Edward H. Cole introduced Lovecraft to the Providence Amateur Press Club in 1914.

Hathaway family home at 97 Blackstone Blvd., Providence. Abbie's brother-in-law William C. Sutherland still lived here in 1960. Credit: Google Maps.

Abbie Ann Hathaway (1852–1917)

Rhode Island State Normal School. This postcard dates 20+ years after Abbie Hathaway's graduation (1873) since the State Capitol Building (in rear) was not erected until 1895.

222

Slater Avenue Primary School House, built in 1890, of wood, four rooms, and cost for building and furnishing, $13,072.85. This lot was bought of Henry L. Aldrich, December 26, 1887, and cost $2,500, being lot No. 179 on plat 39, and contains 15,000 square feet. The lot is located on the easterly side of Slater avenue, between Irving and Lloyd avenues, and measures 100 feet on Slater avenue and extends back 150 feet. Assessors' valuation of land, $1,800; building, $10,000; total, $11,800.

Financial Report of the City of Providence, Rhode Island (1896), 255. Where Abbie Hathaway taught until her retirement in 1914–15.

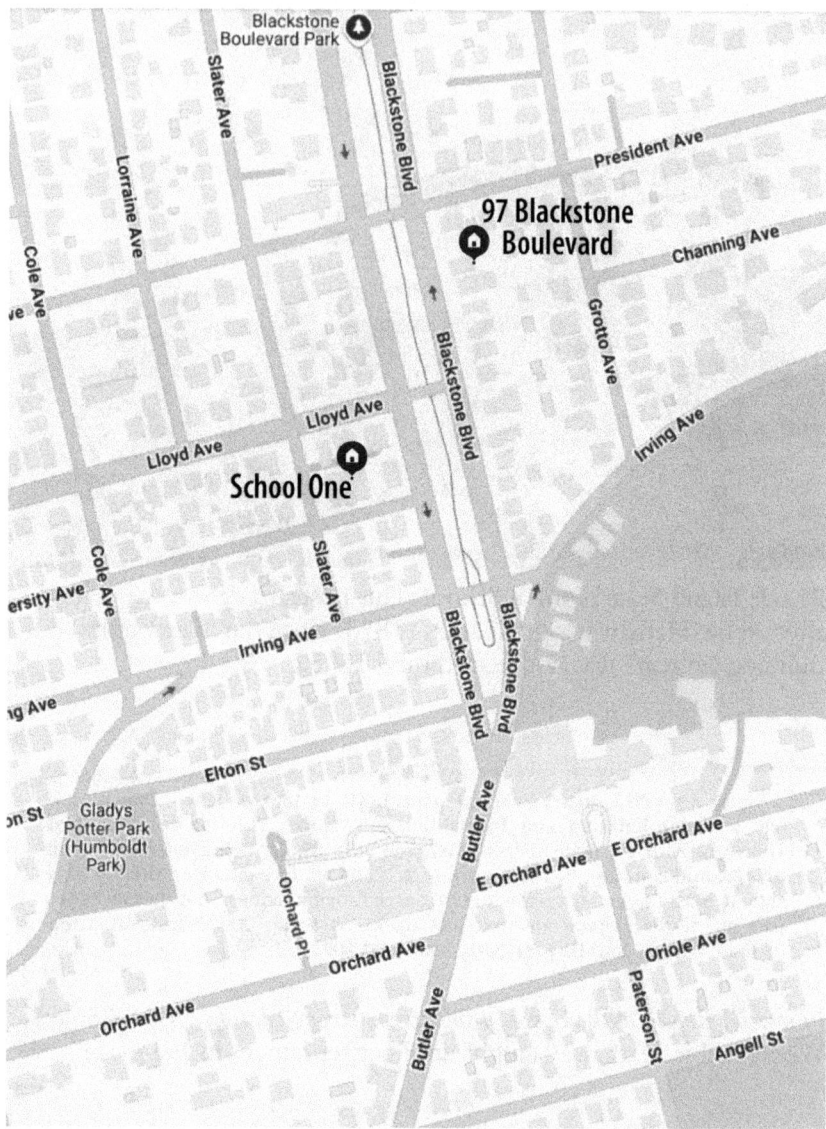

Abbie Hathaway would have had a short walk from her home at 97 Blackstone Blvd. (arrow) to Slater Avenue Primary School (marked as School One) at University Avenue & Slater Avenue. If she took the Butler Avenue trolley to do shopping in Wayland Square or downtown, Lovecraft's 1904–24 home at 598 Angell (Butler Avenue & Angell Street) would have been along the way. Note: I believe Butler Avenue originally continued north where Blackstone Blvd. was later developed.

School One, 220 University Avenue (corner of University Avenue & Slater Avenue), Providence. Former site of Slater Avenue Primary School. Credit: Google Maps.

Arthur Palmer May (1880–1941) Lovecraft's Tutor

The author is grateful to the Rhode Island State Archives for assistance. All opinions and any errors contained herein remain the sole responsibility of the author.

Abbreviations: RI XXXX = Rhode Island state census for the year XXXX US XXXX = United States census for the year XXXX PD XXXX = Providence directory for the year XXXX. USPS abbreviations are used for states.

In 1903–04, after he had left Slater Avenue Primary School in the spring of 1903 and before he entered Hope Street High School in the fall of 1904, Lovecraft had private tutors. S. T. Joshi remarks of one of them:

> We know the name of one such tutor, A. P. May, although Lovecraft did not have a very high opinion of him. There is an unwontedly sarcastic ad for this person in the January 3, 1904 issue of the *Rhode Island Journal*, proclaiming May as a "10th rate Private Tutor" who is offering "Low Grade Instruction at High Rates"; the ad concludes: "HIRE ME. I CAN'T DO THE WORK BUT I NEED THE MONEY." Perhaps May was teaching Lovecraft things he already knew. Years later he spoke of May a little more charitably, if condescendingly, as "my odd, shy private tutor Arthur P. May—a theological student whom I loved to shock with my pagan materialism . . ."[1] (*IAP* 87)

Arthur Palmer May was born in Somerset, Bristol County MA on 26 February 1880, the son of Frank [Francis] A. May and Amelia Baker (Hood) May. US 1900 enumerated the following

---

1. Joshi cites this quotation to Lovecraft's letter to Maurice W. Moe dated 27–29 July 1929.

household in Somerset MA: Amelia B. May (head), born September 1850 MA of MA-born parents, age 49, widow, boarding house keeper; Arthur P. May (son), born February 1880 MA of MA-born parents, age 20, single, clerk (broker's); Mary J[ennie] (daughter), born August 1882 MA of MA-born parents, age 17, single; Mary E. May (boarder),[2] born November 1841 MA of MA-born parents, age 58, single.

When he enrolled as a freshman at Brown University in 1901, Arthur's home was still in Somerset MA. He resided at 155 Lippitt Street during his freshman year at Brown.

Arthur still listed his home address as Somerset MA when he was a senior in 1904–05, but his local residence was 68 Olney Street, where his mother Amelia B. May and his sister Jennie May (b. August 1882 MA), a clerk, also resided in PD 1903 and PD 1904. I suspect that Arthur's attendance at Brown University brought the family from Somerset MA to Providence. Arthur was elected to Phi Beta Kappa in his senior year. Here is his photograph from the 1905 *Liber Brunensis:*

Arthur Palmer May
"May"

Born at Somerset, Mass., 1880. Prepared at Colby Academy, New London, N.H. Expects to teach for a few years and later study theology.

"They also serve who only stand and wait."

---

2. Mary E. May (1841–1911) was a sister of Francis A. May.

I have to admit that Arthur's photograph reminds me a bit of photographs of his pupil as a young man. His *Liber Brunensis* write-up confirms Lovecraft's assertion that May intended to study theology.

PD 1906 still listed Mrs. Amelia B. May and her daughter Jennie May, clerk, at 68 Olney Street, but indicated that Arthur P. May had removed to Gladstone MI. Gladstone is a small city in Delta County on the Michigan Upper Peninsula, founded in 1877. Its population was 3,380 in 1900 and 4,211 in 1910. I assume that Arthur went there to teach rather than to study theology, unless he had arranged to have private lessons with a local clergyman.

Arthur had returned to Providence by the time the data for PD 1908 was compiled. Mrs. Amelia B. May was householder at 92 Olney Street, with her children Arthur P. May, apprentice, and Jennie May, bookkeeper, 297 Plain Street, as boarders. The listing was the same in PD 1909, except that Arthur had now advanced from apprentice to bookkeeper.

In fact, Arthur had apprenticed and gone to work at the Gorham Manufacturing Company, where he worked for most of the rest of his life. US 1910 enumerated the following household at 53 Norwich Avenue in Providence: Amelia B. May (head), age 59, widow, born MA of MA-born parents, three children borne, two children living, own income; Arthur P. May (son), age 30, single, born MA of MA-born parents, bookkeeper (silversmith); and M[ary] Jennie May (daughter), age 27, single, born MA of MA-born parents, bookkeeper (market).

PD 1910 recorded Mrs. Amelia B. May as the householder at 53 Norwich Avenue, with her children Arthur P. May, clerk at Gorham's, and Jennie May, bookkeeper at 297 Plain, as boarders. Mrs. May remained at the same address in PD 1911 and PD 1912, with her son Arthur P. May, clerk at Gorham's, as a boarder. Then PD 1914 listed Amelia B. May as householder at 53 Norwich Avenue, with her children Arthur P. May, clerk at Gorham's, and Jennie May, bookkeeper at 18 Richmond, as boarders.

Arthur's sister Mary J[ennie] May married on 16 December 1914 (RI) Eugene Haven Randlett (1858–1940), the son of Haven Randlett and Mary J. (——) Randlett. It was a first marriage for Jennie but a second marriage for her husband. He had earlier married 24 December 1885 (Norwood MA) Edith Maud (Achorn) Gilman (1860–1909), the daughter of Caspar F. Achorn (1837–1914) and Augusta (——) Achorn (1834–1920). It was a first marriage for Eugene and a second for Edith. Both bride and groom were residents of Norwood MA at the time of their marriage. Eugene worked as a coachman.[3]

RI 1915 enumerated Amelia May, age 64, no occupation, and her son Arthur P. May, age 35, bookkeeper (silversmiths) at 53 Norwich Avenue in Providence. In PD 1916, Amelia B. May, widow of Frank, had moved into her son-in-law's home at 149 Messer. Her son Arthur P. May, clerk at Gorham's, remained as a boarder at 53 Norwich Avenue. However, a big change affecting their lives happened in that year: on 14 July 1916 Arthur married Gladys Clarke Spink (1891–1934), the daughter of William A. Spink (1843–1898) and Belle Clark (1867–1949). Gladys Spink and her sister Irene had worked as milliners before Gladys married.

The marriage was, alas, not long-lasting and ended in divorce. When Arthur P. May registered for the draft on 12 September 1918, he named his mother Amelia B. May, of 57 West Friend-

---

3. US 1900 enumerated Eugene H. Randlett and his wife Edith M. Randlett at 64 South Street in Lynn MA. Eugene was then working as a transformer winder. His wife told the census enumerator that she had borne four children, of whom none were then living.

ship Street in Providence, as his nearest relative. He was working as a cost accountant for the Gorham Manufacturing Company and boarding at 748 Broad Street in Providence:

PD 1918 listed Amelia B. May, widow of Frank, as a boarder in the home of her daughter and son-in-law at 322 Killingly Street, and Arthur P. May, clerk at Gorham's, with house at 748 Broad. Arthur was to remain at this address—a boarding house—through at least Apr. 15, 1930. US 1920 enumerated

Arthur, cost accountant at Gorham Manufacturing Company, at 748 Broad, and PD 1920 listed him there, too.

The next big change in Arthur's life was the death of his mother Amelia Baker (Hood) May, age 71, of a cerebral hemorrhage on 4 December 1921. She was buried with her husband in Palmer Street Cemetery in Somerset MA. Arthur's Providence directory listings remained unchanged in PD 1922, PD 1924, PD 1925, and PD 1928. US 1930 enumerated Arthur P. May, age 49, divorced, bookkeeper (silver manufacturer), in the boarding house of Henry H. Jackson at 748 Broad Street in Providence. Arthur's last day of employment by the Gorham Manufacturing Company was 12 July 1930 (letter from former employer dated 8 December 1941). PD 1931 listed Arthur P. May, bookkeeper, residing in the home of his sister and his brother-in-law at 322 Killingly Street.

When he was enumerated in RI 1935, Arthur P. May was still residing with his sister and brother-in-law at 322 Killingly Street. His employment was recorded as bookkeeper for a jewelry shop. He stated his marital status as divorced. Curiously, he stated his date of birth as 21 January 1874—perhaps he wanted to become eligible earlier for the newly enacted Social Security program. PD 1939 listed Arthur P. May as a resident of his sister's and brother-in-law's home at 322 Killingly Street, with no employment indicated.

When US 1940 was enumerated on 1 April 1940, Arthur P. May, age 60, single, was recorded as an inmate (i.e., patient) at the Rhode Island State Infirmary in Howard, Cranston RI. He stated that he had resided in Providence on 1 April 1935. He died at the State Infirmary in Howard, Cranston RI at 10 A.M. on 2 October 1941 of a spontaneous coronary occlusion, with epilepsy and latent [hues?] as contributing causes. He was buried in Highland Cemetery in Somerset MA.

Lovecraft's "odd, shy" tutor seems to have lived a correspondingly modest life after a promising beginning as a Phi Beta Kappa student at Brown University. The Gorham Manufacturing Company was the only employer I discovered for him. That his sole venture into matrimony was a failure was probably a severe blow for him. He spent the entire 1920s living in a boarding house on Broad Street in Providence. When he became ill, he could not afford a private hospital, but had to become a patient at the State Infirmary in Cranston.

I wish that I could add photographs of Arthur Palmer May's parents, sister, and brother-in-law to his handsome photograph in *Liber Brunensis* for 1905. As things stand, we are probably lucky to have the *Liber Brunensis* photograph. While Arthur May may not have had much to impart to Howard P. Lovecraft, I think that his own life may have much to teach us. Arthur was one of those whose mission was to "stand and wait." That greater opportunities never came his way—or never came within grasping distance—is probably a circumstance with which the great majority of humanity can empathize.

Helpers and Neighbors

Delilah Townsend (ca. 1868–1944)

With Jason C. Eckhardt

Jason C. Eckhardt and Donovan K. Loucks (proprietor of the hplovecraft.com website) independently discovered that Mrs. Delilah Townsend was the occupant of the dwelling at 6 Olney Street in the 1927–28 Providence House Directory. During the period 1926–32, Mrs. Townsend, a black woman, provided housekeeping, laundry, and attendance services for Lovecraft's aunt Lillian D. Clark (1856–1932) at 10 Barnes Street. Mrs. Townsend also worked for Mrs. Clark at prior addresses, including 115 Waterman Street and 598 Angell Street. Her ex-husband William Townsend may have helped Lovecraft and his aunt with some heavier work, including possibly Lovecraft's removal from 10 Barnes Street to 66 College Street in May 1933. The following passage from *The Case of Charles Dexter Ward* thus provides additional identification of the dwelling at 6 Olney Street as the inspiration for Joseph Curwen's abode (emphasis added):

> The discovery was doubly striking because it indicated, as the newer Curwen house built in 1761 on the site of the old, a dilapidated building still standing in Olney Court and well known to Ward in his antiquarian rambles over Stampers' Hill. The place was indeed only a few squares from his own home on the great hill's higher ground, and was now the abode of *a negro family much esteemed for occasional washing, housecleaning, and furnace-tending services.* (CF 2.270–71)

Numerous letters from Lovecraft to his aunt Mrs. Clark refer to her housekeeper "Delilah" but it is only Lovecraft's letter to Mrs. Clark dated 1 August 1924 which provides her surname: "On this occasion I met for the first time the Michigan amateur

Clyde G. Townsend (no relative of Delilah's, but a fine Nordic specimen with yellow hair and blue eyes!)."[1] In his letter to Mrs. Clark dated 22–23 December 1925, Lovecraft appears to suggest that Delilah Townsend may have been employed by the Phillips family as early as the first decade of the twentieth century:[2]

> Yes indeed—I certainly wish that you could be a Wendell heir, so that you might be here for the Christmas dinner; or that *I* could be; so that 454 Angell St. might be the home of both, & the dinner prepared by Norah or Delia (sober, I trust) or Svea or Jennie or Bridget under your own direction, & served by honest Delilah in proper uniform & apron! (*LFF* 515)

In his correspondence with Mrs. Clark, Lovecraft's references to Delilah Townsend range from openly appreciative to the blatantly racist. He wrote of Delilah's "effective aid in the locomotive process" when Mrs. Clark was afflicted with arthritis. As Mrs. Clark was then in the process of removing from 598 Angell Street to 115 Waterman Street, Lovecraft advised her: "Don't work too hard at your moving—remember that Delilah is on hand to do all the heavy lifting" (HPL to LDC, 20 October 1925; *LFF* 451). When Mrs. Clark suffered another spell of illness, Lovecraft wrote to his friend Frank B. Long: "For some time in the evening the faithful old negress Delilah comes in to supply my place as I go home to collect my mail and eat my dinner" (HPL to FBL, 20 May 1926, *SP* 301). On the other hand, he could write to his aunt Mrs. Clark of her faithful helper Delilah Townsend: "She certainly is a valuable nigger, & ought to bring a good $900 or $1000 in any fair market north of Savannah" (HPL to LDC, 7 November 1925; *LFF* 476).

---

1. The authors are indebted to David E. Schultz for all quotations from the letters of H. P. Lovecraft referring to "Delilah."
2. Lovecraft and his mother had to remove from 454 Angell Street following the death of his grandfather in March 1904.

Recounting his reading of Gertrude Selwyn Kimball's *Providence in Colonial Times* (Houghton Mifflin, 1912) at the New York Public Library to his aunt, he mentioned casually the alleged haunting of the Halsey mansion:

> In the last chapter of the Kimball book I learnt of the spectre which haunts the Halsey Mansion in Prospect St. It is a *thing* which plays the piano during the sinister small hours.... & there is a bloodstain on the floor which cannot be washt out. Niggers from the neighbouring darktown will not pass the place after dark—or at least, would not at one time. Ask Delilah about it. (HPL to LDC, 27 September 1925; *LFF* 414)

Today of course we can take a more enlightened view of Delilah Townsend. The 1900 U.S. census of Providence, R.I., found her and her family residing at 46 Thayer Street on the East Side on 1 June 1900:

> Townsend, William, head, negro, male, born May 1872, age 28, married for 6 years, born New Bedford MA of NY-born father and MA-born mother, occupation: day laborer, can read & write, speaks English, rents;
> Townsend, Delilah, wife, negro, female, born December 1872, age 28, married for 6 years, mother of 2 children (1 living), born VA of VA-born parents, can read & write, speaks English;
> Townsend, William, son, negro, male, born March 1896, age 4, single, born RI of RI-born father [*sic*] and VA-born mother, at school.

There is no notation that Delilah Townsend might then have been a domestic employee of Whipple V. Phillips at 454 Angell Street. William Joseph Townsend was born in New Bedford MA on 6 May 1872, the son of Robert H. and Sarah (Ferguson) Townsend of New Bedford MA. The 1880 U.S. census recorded Robert Townsend as MA-born of MA-born parents and his wife Sarah as VA-born of VA-born parents; Robert was employed as a sailor. There were three children in their household in that year: Robert H., age 12, Martha M., age 10, and William J., age 7. The earlier history of William's wife Delilah is less certain but we believe she can be identified in the following household in the 1870 U.S. census of Pine Top, Middlesex County VA:

> Robinson, George,[3] age 25, male, negro, farmer, born VA, cannot read or write;
> Robinson, Amanda, age 22, female, negro, keeping house, born VA, cannot read or write;
> Robinson, Lelia F., age 2, female, negro, at home, born VA;
> Robinson, Mary A., age 4 months, female, negro, at home, born VA.

Amanda Robinson was apparently widowed or separated from her husband when her household was enumerated in the same place in the 1880 U.S. census:

> Robinson, Amanda, black, female, age 28, born VA, keeping house;
> Robinson, Lelia F., black, female, age 12, daughter, born VA, at home;
> Robinson, Mary E., black, female, age 10, daughter, born VA, at home;
> Robinson, Annie B., black, female, age 8, daughter, born VA;
> Robinson, George W., black, male, age 5, son, born VA.

The 1905 Rhode Island state census recorded Delilah Townsend in a household of four persons at 46 Thayer Street in Providence. She was illiterate and her marital status was recorded as divorced. She had been born in 1870 in Virginia of Virginia-born parents. She had been a resident of Rhode Island for ten years.[4] She worked as a private family laundress and was a Baptist. Her former husband William Townsend resided at 185 North Main in Providence and recorded his marital status as married. His usual occupation was a fishery laborer, but he had been idle for eighteen months. In the 1914 Providence Directo-

---

3. Most records indicate that the name of Amanda Robinson's husband was Henry Robinson. Perhaps her husband George as enumerated in the 1870 U.S. census was also known as Henry, or perhaps Henry Robinson was a second husband of Amanda Robinson.
4. She had married William Joseph Townsend on 9 February 1895 in Lincoln, Rhode Island. Her marriage record gave her maiden surname as Robertson.

ry, William J. Townsend, a clerk at 169 South Water Street, resided at 42 Wickenden Street. Tragically, Delilah's and William's son William Joseph Townsend [Jr.], then residing at 91 Bates Street, died on 21 July 1915, aged only 19 years 4 months 20 days.[5] His cause of death was recorded as angina pectoris. He had been working as a chauffeur at the time of his death. He was buried in Grace Church Cemetery.

We next encounter Delilah Townsend with her sister and her mother at 7 Olney Street (southeast corner of Olney and North Main) in the 1920 U.S. census on 7 January 1920:

> Townsend, Lila, rents, female, negro, age 45, widow, cannot read or write, born VA of VA-born parents, occupation: laundress-private family;
> Robinson, Mary, sister, female, negro, age 54, single, cannot read or write, born VA of VA-born parents, no occupation;
> Robinson, Amanda, mother, female, negro, age 72, widow, cannot read or write, born VA of VA-born parents, no occupation.

By 1927–28, Delilah and her family had removed a few doors to 6 Olney Street to be recorded in the Providence House Directory. In the 1930 U.S. census, Delilah and her family were recorded nearby at 474 North Main Street on 17 April 1930:

> Townsend, Delilah, head, rents ($22/month), female, negro, age 50, divorced, cannot read or write, born VA of VA-born parents, occupation: none;
> Robinson, Mary, sister, female, negro, age 54, single, cannot read or write, born VA of VA-born parents, occupation: cook-private family;
> Robinson, Amanda, mother, female, negro, age 80, widowed, cannot read or write, born VA of VA-born parents, occupation: none;
> Johnson, Sarah, lodger, female, negro, age 52, widowed, cannot read or write, born VA of VA-born parents, occupation: laundress-private family.

---

5. The inferred date of birth for William Joseph Townsend, Jr. (1 March 1896) agrees with his month and year of birth as stated in the 1900 U.S. census.

Mary Robinson, age given as approximately 50, born Halifax County VA, daughter of Henry and Amanda Robinson, died of uremia and diabetes on 14 January 1934, and was buried in Grace Church Cemetery. She was residing with her sister Delilah Townsend at 473 North Main Street at the time of her death. She had continued to work at her occupation as a private family cook until ten days before her death. Her mother Amanda Robinson, age given as "120 years according to family," born Halifax VA, daughter of VA-born Benjamin Robinson and VA-born Lucinda Johnson, died at home at 481 North Main Street of pneumonia on 5 March 1941, and was buried in Grace Church Cemetery. If her identification in the 1870 U.S. census is correct, she was more probably 92 or 93 than 120 at the time of her death.

Delilah Townsend herself followed her sister and her mother in death on 21 November 1944, aged 74 according to her death certificate. She was buried three days later in Grace Church Cemetery in Providence.[6] Her last residence had been 45 East Transit Street in Providence, but she spent the last eleven days of her life in the State Infirmary in Cranston, R.I. She was listed as the widow of William Townsend and the daughter of Henry and Amanda Robinson. Her birthplace was given incorrectly as North Carolina.

Of her erstwhile husband William Townsend we can find a few records. In the 1915 RI Census, 43-year-old William Townsend and his wife 37-year-old Mary Townsend were recorded at 42 Wickenden Street. William was working as a fish cleaner at a fish market and his wife Mary as a private family cook.[7] In the 1925 RI census, William Townsend, male, black, age 52, born MA, was recorded alone at 42 Wickenden Street. William

---

6. Her mother, sister, and son were all also buried in Grace Church Cemetery.

7. It is possible that William took Delilah's sister Mary, who worked as a private family cook, as his second partner.

Townsend married Sarah J. Johnson in Providence on 26 October 1930. His bride was probably the same Sarah Johnson who resided in the household of his former wife Delilah Townsend at 474 North Main Street in the 1930 U.S. census. It seems likely Sarah Johnson was a niece of Amanda Robinson, whose mother's name was Lucinda Johnson. In the 1935–36 RI Census, William Townsend, born 6 May 1872 MA, residing at 185 North Main Street, was recorded on 12 May 1936. His occupation was given as fishery laborer. Also recorded in his household at 185 North Main Street was Sarah Townsend, born 22 October 1889 VA, unemployed. William Townsend died in Cranston on 6 August 1966, at the great age of ninety-four. He left his body to medical science.

We know that Lovecraft explored the Stampers Hill neighborhood with James F. Morton and Clifford M. Eddy on 27 December 1923. It seems likely that he renewed his acquaintance with the neighborhood after his return to Providence in April 1926, since it would have been only a short walk down the hill from his home at 10 Barnes Street. During most of the period of Lovecraft's residency at 10 Barnes Street (1926–33), Delilah (Robinson) Townsend was still performing housekeeping and attendance duties for his aunt Lillian D. Clark. During all this period, Delilah lived in the immediate neighborhood of 6 Olney Street, at the actual address itself in 1927–28. It is possible that Lovecraft paid occasional visits to the neighborhood to drop off laundry parcels or conduct other business.

We will allow other writers to discuss the significance of Lovecraft's relationship with Delilah Townsend. We suspect that Delilah was grateful for the income which she derived from her services to Mrs. Clark. Her interactions with Lovecraft were more limited. How she might have reacted to Lovecraft's reference to her as a slave in his private correspondence with Mrs.

Clark is of course unknown. He surely never intended to make any statement about slavery in Delilah's presence. We are doubtful that Lovecraft was ever rude or insulting to her in person. Whether she would agree with "vicious racist" as a proper label for Lovecraft is unknown. Perhaps she might say he had always treated her well and that as for his beliefs they were probably no worse and no better than those of most of his fellow white citizens. Delilah Townsend was a hard worker who helped to make life easier for Mrs. Clark and to a lesser degree for Lovecraft. Therefore, we hope that our readers will hold her and her family in grateful memory regardless of their own beliefs.

Mariano De Magistris (1862–1939)

Lovecraft's Mortgagor on the Manton (Violet Hill) Quarry in Providence

For All the Members of the De Magistris Family

Ralph De Magistris (1896–1956) and his family.
Credit: R. Alain Everts.

In correspondence with friends, Lovecraft bemoaned the fact that the Lovecraft family had ceased to be members of the "landed gentry" when Minster Hall, near Exeter, Devon was lost in 1823 as part of the financial disintegration resulting from the imprudent lifestyle of his alleged ancestor Thomas Lovecraft (1745–1826) (*MWM* 293–94). Whether Thomas Lovecraft was his ancestor or not, his great-grandfather Joseph Lovecraft (1774–1850) did pack his bags and emigrate to Rochester, New York, in 1831 to escape a bankruptcy proceeding. Joseph

Home of Mariano and Carmela (Di Meo) De Magistris, 23 Baltimore Street, Providence Credit: Google Maps.

brought his family of five sons and one daughter along with him. His son George Lovecraft (1815–1895) spent most of his working career in the nursery business and died in Mount Vernon, New York. George's son Winfield Scott Lovecraft (1853–1898), named for the famous Mexican War general, held various jobs including blacksmith and barkeeper, but ended as a salesman for the Gorham Manufacturing Company of Providence, R.I. Just how he met Sarah Susan Phillips (1857–1921), the daughter of Whipple V. and Robie A. (Place) Phillips, is uncertain, but they were married at St. Paul's Cathedral in Boston in 1889. Their son Howard Phillips Lovecraft was born on 20 August 1890 in the home of his maternal grandparents in Providence.

Grandfather Phillips died in 1904, and Howard and his mother moved several blocks eastward to a flat, where he remained until his marriage in 1924. Just how Lovecraft acquired a $500 mortgage secured by the quarry operated by Mariano De Magistris on Violet Hill in the Manton section of Providence is uncertain.[1] It seems probable that Susie's brother Edwin E. Phillips (1864–1918) was providing her with financial advice at this time. He advertised in the Providence directory as a dealer in mortgages, so perhaps he helped Mariano De Magistris (1862–1939) acquire the property necessary to begin operating his quarry on Violet Hill in the Manton section of Providence ca. 1906. Having begun as a teamster and a grocer after his arrival from Italy in 1891, De Magistris had been working for some years as a mason and a contractor. By 1906 he was operating the quarry from his home at 44 Leander Street. Whether Edwin had a role in helping De Magistris to assemble the property for his quarry or not, he may have directed Susie's attention to the

---

1. David Haden (www.jurn.org/tentaclii/2013/02/) asserts that the mortgage was inherited by HPL. HPL did receive an Allgood bequest in 1908, which might have facilitated his acquisition of the mortgage.

availability of the mortgage.² Payments were due semi-annually in February and August and were probably at a generous rate proportionate to the business risks involved.

However, there is evidence that Lovecraft's recollection in 1927 that he had held the quarry mortgage for about twenty years is inaccurate.³ The inventory of Lovecraft's estate, dated 6 May 1937, listed just one asset:

> Three (3) promissory notes dated February 1, 1911, balance due thereon cannot be determined, if any, secured [*sic*] by mortgage deed of real estate recorded in Office of Recorder of Deeds of City of Providence, State of Rhode Island in Mortgage Book No. 305 at page 482.⁴

The original inventory from 1937 does not seem to be among the documents reproduced by Chris J. Karr. The summary page for Lovecraft's estate (no. 37854), as reproduced by Chris J. Karr, contains these notations at lines 5 and 6:

Karr also reproduces a document filed by executor Albert A. Baker on 24 March 1937 that stated that Lovecraft had left a widow and estimated the value of his personal estate as $1380:

---

2. HPL referred to the amount of the mortgage as "my modest thou" in his letter to James F. Morton dated 19 May 1927 (*JFM* 137). The $500 valuation reflected in the summary page for the Lovecraft estate (see *infra*) may reflect either (or both): (1) amortization of the original $1,000 mortgage principal or (2) non-payment by the mortgagor after some point (i.e., non-performing status).

3. For the assertion see HPL to James F. Morton, 19 May 1927 (*JFM* 137).

4. Quoted by L. Sprague de Camp, *Lovecraft: A Biography* (Garden City, NY: Doubleday, 1975), 429. De Camp states that the inventory was erroneously dated 6 May 1957 (475n2).

Estate of Howard P. Lovecraft

Died testate March 15, 1937
domiciled in said City of Providence

No. 37854

March 24, 1937

Your petitioner being ~~a~~—the executor named prays that the accompanying instrument dated the twelfth day of August, 1912, ~~respectively~~

may be admitted to probate as the last will and testament of the deceased and that letters testamentary may be issued to the executor.

Deceased left a ~~husband~~ widow and the following heirs at law who would inherit had deceased died intestate: Personal estate estimated at $ 1380.00

Name. Residence. Relationship.

Perhaps this estimation was made before the diminished value of the promissory notes was ascertained—for example, to determine the appropriate bond to be posted by the executor. Lovecraft's executor Albert A. Baker (1862–1959) continued to practice law until nearly the end of his long life. Mariano De Magistris son Ralph had died in 1956, and perhaps the discharge of the mortgage was part of the wrap-up of the financial affairs of Providence Crushed Stone & Sand Company in the wake of his death. The quarry property could not have been sold without discharging the mortgage.

In any case, Lovecraft became, if not a landed gentleman, at least a mortgage holder in 1911. If he was the original mortgagee (and not a successor or assign), it might be noted that the 1 February 1911 promissory notes were dated a little over six months before he attained his legal majority on 20 August 1911. Perhaps some rearrangement of his assets was deemed prudent at that time.

Lovecraft continued to collect the semi-annual interest payments of $37.08[5] throughout his entire remaining lifetime. Based on a principal amount of $1,000, semi-annual payments of

---

5. For the amount of the semiannual payment, see HPL to Lillian D. Clark, 2 February 1925 (*LFF* 241) and *IAP* 306, 574, 687.

$37.08 would represent an interest rate of about 7.4% ($74.16/$1000), assuming that Lovecraft received only interest on the outstanding balance.[6] It is possible that the payments constituted both principal and interest, in which case the effective interest rate would have been less. The following table examines the semiannual payment amount and the outstanding balance at the end of twenty-six years (1937–1911 = 26) for a thirty-five-year mortgage originating on 1 February 1911 (and maturing 1 February 1946):

Interest Rate[7]	Balance As Of Feb. 1, 1937	Semiannual Payment
5.00%	$436	$30.40
5.50%	$454	$32.34
6.00%	$472	$34.34
6.50%	$490	$36.37
6.67%	**$496**	**$37.08**
6.75%	*$499*	*$37.41*
7.00%	$507	$38.46
7.40%	$521	$40.16

Note that an annual rate of 6.67% (in bold) produces the closest match to a semi-annual mortgage payment (consisting of principal and interest) of $37.08, while an annual rate of 6.75% (in bold italics) produces the closest match to an outstanding balance (as of 1 February 1937) of $500.[8] Of course, a thirty-

---

6. This would have represented a so-called "balloon" mortgage, with no diminution of the outstanding principal over the term of the mortgage and the entire original principal balance due at maturity.

7. Annual nominal rate. Semi-annual effective rate = annual nominal rate divided by two.

8. See Kenneth A. Snowden, *Mortgage Banking in the United States, 1870–1940* (Research Institute for Housing America, n.d.), at papers.ssrn.com/sol3/papers.cfm?abstract_id=2349189. Table 8 (page 32) shows an average interest rate for farm mortgages in New England in 1910 as 5.7%. A

five-year term is only an assumption. It is possible that the mortgage became non-performing after Lovecraft's death and that the $500 approximate outstanding principal balance as of his death was eventually used to clear the debt. The mortgage was not finally paid off until 1957, when Lovecraft's executor Albert A. Baker used the principal to pay off Lovecraft's still unpaid funeral expenses.[9] Without knowing the exact terms and conditions of the three promissory notes dated 1 February 1911, it is not possible to be more specific.

These facts would all be among the not very significant minutiae of Lovecraft's life if it were not for the fact that his friend James F. Morton, Jr. (1870–1941) became curator of the Paterson, New Jersey, museum in 1925—a position he occupied for the rest of his life.[10] Morton became a self-educated authority on the subject of rocks and minerals, and once he became aware that his friend Lovecraft held a mortgage on a quarry noted for its foliated talc and other minerals, it wasn't too long before he induced Lovecraft to take him to visit the quarry,[11] where he met Mariano De Magistris and the two sons principally involved with helping him to operate the business, Ralph De Magistris (1896–1956) and Carl De Magistris (1899–1992).

The Providence Crushed Stone & Sand Company, Inc. was founded in 1911 by Frank (Francesco) Ricci. However, Mariano

---

mortgage loan on quarry property would probably have been appraised as a riskier endeavor than a loan on farm property. For one thing, the value of quarry real estate would be subject to diminution as recoverable rock and minerals were reduced by ongoing quarrying operations.

9. See www.aetherial.net/static/lovecraft/hpl-probate.pdf on Chris J. Karr's "Black Seas of Copyright" website.

10. For accounts of Morton's visits to the De Magistris quarry, see *JFM* 100, 137, 146, 156, 159–60, 171, 172, 232–33, 235–37, 241–42, 288–90, 291–92, 300–301, 327, 416–18.

11. When he wrote to Morton on 19 May 1927, HPL had yet to visit the quarry (*JFM* 137).

De Magistris was already functioning as the company's manager in 1914, as witnessed by the Providence directory of that year:

> **PROVIDENCE COUNTY SAVINGS BANK**
> 216 Main Pawtucket—see page 1005
> " Cricket Club 200 Reservoir av
> " Crushed Stone and Sand Co Mariano De Magistris mgr 645 Manton av

PD 1914, PD 1916, and PD 1918 all listed Mariano De Magistris as the company's manager. A full-page display advertisement for the company appeared in PD 1924:

> *Contractors*
> ADVERTISING DEPARTMENT 1339
>
> # Providence Concrete Architectural Stone Works
>
> OPERATED BY
> **Providence Crushed Stone and Sand Co.**
> MARIANO De MAGISTRIS, Proprietor
>
> Waterproof Concrete Products
> Archi-Orna Concrete Products
> *Monuments*
> Marble and Granite Finished Building Stone
> Stucco and Plaster
> Mosaics and Tiles, Etc.
>
> ## CONCRETE BRICK
>
> GARDEN AND LAWN FURNITURE
>
> Ornamental Concrete Work of all Description
> *In fact all Concrete Work a Specialty*
>
> OFFICE AND WORKS
> **647 Manton Avenue   Providence, R. I.**
>
> TELEPHONE { Office West 0781
>   Residence West 1118-W

Lovecraft took the visiting James F. Morton and Donald Wandrei to see the quarry on Friday, 22 July 1927. S. T. Joshi recounts:

> Morton then dragged Lovecraft and Wandrei to the rock quarry on which Lovecraft still held the mortgage, and for which he was still receiving his pittance of a payment ($37.08) every six months. The owner, Mariano de Magistris, set his men to hunting up specimens, while his son drove them home in his car. "That's what I call real Latin courtesy!" Lovecraft remarked in a rare show of tolerance for non-Aryans. (*IAP* 687)

Joshi cites Lovecraft's letter to Maurice W. Moe dated 30 July 1927, in which Lovecraft recounted their visit more fully:

> This time, through a singular coincidence, the designated territory was a quarry on which I hold a mortgage, so that we were received with ceremonious hospitality by the Dago owner. The good old Roman set all his men to work hunting specimens, and his sportily Americanised son took us all home in his snappy new roadster—to say nothing of chugging back and fetching the geologist's hammer which Mortonius forgot. That's what I call real Latin courtesy! (*MWM* 155)

Lovecraft even wrote to Morton on 26 December 1928 to remind him of a promise he had made:

> And say—didja ever find out what that *extra heavy* substance was that ya got off the quarry of my vassal, goodman Mariano de Magistris? You'll recall that I promised the excellent fellow to tell him what it was when you found out, & I'd hate to fail in the duties of an indulgent country 'squire. Intelligent curiosity is so rare a virtue in the peasantry, that it ought to be encouraged whenever it does not lead to insurrection. It is one's duty to bring one's honest tenantry closer to the great heart of Nature. (*JFM* 171)

Late in 1931, Lovecraft went once more to the quarry to view some specimen minerals in which Morton was interested. He wrote to his friend on 13 November 1931:

> Well, damn it all, I ben out to see our Latin friend at last, & had a nice social call with him & two of his numberless sons—Ralph, the youth who drove us into town on one occasion & went back for your lost hammer, & Carl, who (though I didn't know it before) is the affable young fellow who runs the steam shovel & has several times spoken to us in the past. Intelligent chaps, on the whole—Carl is the boy who dealt with your friend Hawkins.
>
> Well, as to the situation—there's absolutely nothing in the quarry itself. Just the same as last July—& Ralph says that they haven't been working the side that yields the varied minerals for some time. I judge that the stuff in the shed is of an earlier vintage—it may even have been there during our last visit. (*JFM* 288–89)

In the end, Lovecraft obtained for Morton, a fine example of pyrite and examples of talc and of asbestos and negotiated a reduced price of $12 for the lot (*JFM* 288–92). Lovecraft commented regarding his visit:

> The boys [Ralph and Carlo] seem to be doing most of the active deciding around the quarry these days, & I imagine that Ralph (who, by the way, always makes out my mortgage cheques nowadays) is virtually the head of the business. (*JFM* 290)

Lovecraft reported to Morton on 3 December 1931:

> However—I gotcha rox. Those ingrate serfs wouldn't pack & send 'em . . . said they had no gotta de fahcheelities for such procedure, & that any stuff saved for Gordonius[12] woulda hadda ben kep' aroun' till he come for it . . . . but Signore Carlo (the pleasant steam shovel guy whom we've talked with in prior ignorance of his identity) brung the junk over here in his shiny & sumptuous limousine free of charge. An' oh boy, yuh'd orta see Carlo when he's all dolled up in civilian togs. Hotta dog! Some-a swella macaroni. (*JFM* 291)

By the period 1931–36, the advertisements for the Providence Crushed Stone & Sand Company had a uniform appear-

---

12. Gordon was a rival mineralogist who had visited the Manton quarry, whereas Hawkins (see *supra*) was an agent or friend acting on behalf of Morton.

ance. This example comes from PD 1936 (99):

PROVIDENCE CRUSHED STONE & SAND CO.

*Blue Stone Screenings
for Walks and Driveways*

Trap Rock for Road Construction

Quarry and Plant, 647 MANTON AVENUE - PROVIDENCE, R. I.

TELEPHONE WEst 0781

Please mention this Directory when dealing with Advertisers

One source indicates that the quarry ceased active operation in 1941. However, Ralph De Magistris was still functioning as president of the Providence Crushed Stone & Sand Company as late as 1946. It is possible that the De Magistris family did not sell the property on which the company had operated until 1957, when the mortgage that had been carried on Lovecraft's estate was finally discharged. Mariano's son Ralph De Magistris had died in 1956, leaving a widow and eleven children, so perhaps the mortgage was finally discharged in 1957 so that the quarry property could be sold. Some of the property was later developed for the Hillcrest Apartment complex.

David Haden's Tentaclii blog has an excellent post, "Lovecraft's Quarry" (18 February 2013; www.jurn.org/tentaclii/2013/02/). Haden cites articles in *American Mineralogist* 11 (1926): 334–40, and 13 (1930): 496–98 (the latter article entitled "Minerals at Manton, Rhode Island" by Douglas Stewart, Jr.)[13] that detail the various minerals that had been located in the quarry.

The following map shows the approximate site of the quarry:

---

13. The Tentaclii blog post contains links to these two articles.

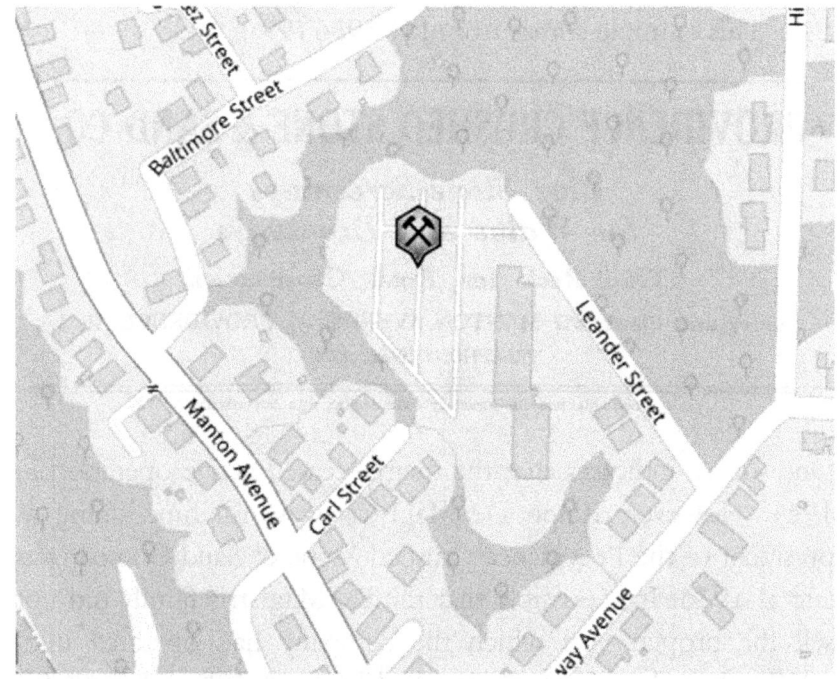

Credit: www.mindat.org/loc-6808.html.[14]

---

14. This site gives the location of the quarry as 41°49'47" North, 71°27'40" West or 41.82973-71.46122 expressed decimally.

The building east of the quarry site is today the Hillcrest Apartments. The 1937 Providence atlas gives some idea of the extent of Mariano De Magistris's holdings:

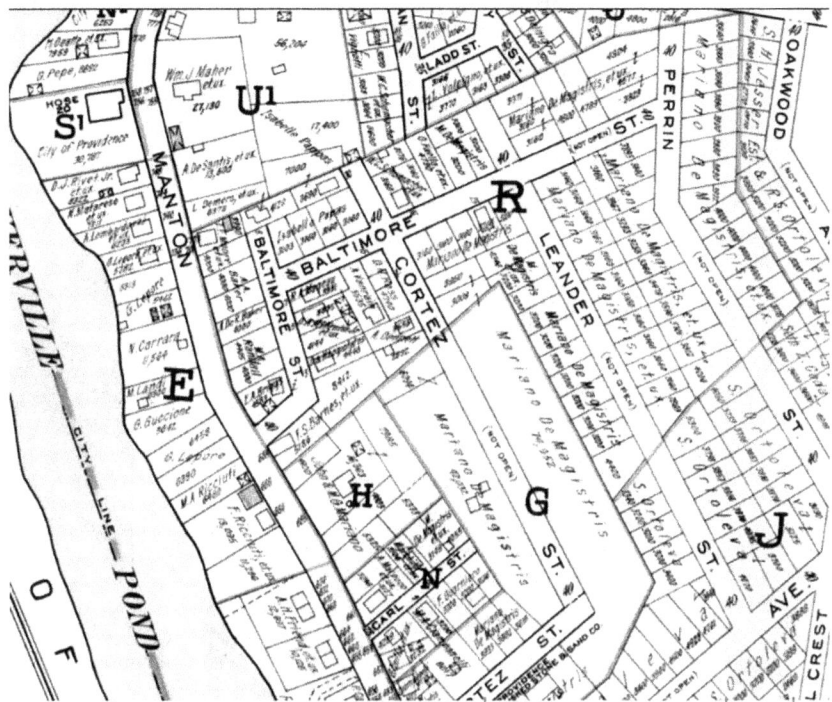

Most of the area outlined was owned by De Magistris—quite a substantial accumulation of real estate. The following detail shows the offices of the Providence Crushed Stone & Sand Company at 647 Manton Avenue—the corner of Manton Avenue and Cortez Street:

An earlier view of the locality comes from the 1918 atlas (plate 34, scan 1b):

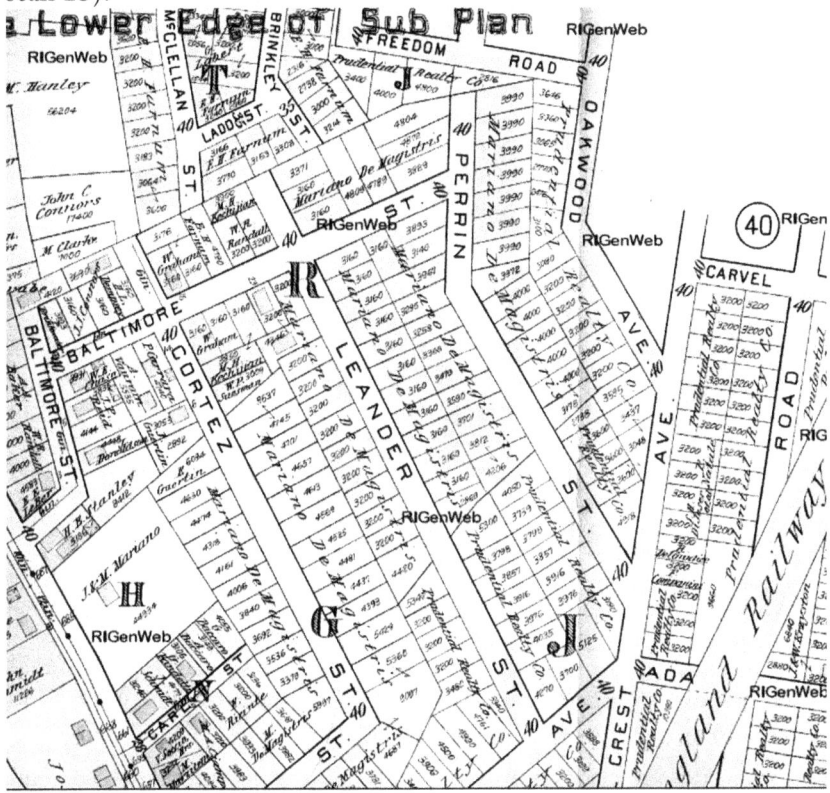

Plate 92 of volume 3 of the 1920–21 edition[15] of the Sanborn Fire map of Providence also shows the site of the "Providence Sand Company" office at the corner of Manton Avenue and Cortez Street:

Manton Avenue began at the end of Atwells Avenue, so the exploration of the Manton section of Providence would have come naturally to contractor and mason Mariano De Magistris, who was probably on the lookout for potential sources for the raw materials needed by his business. Eventually, after his acquisition of the quarry, his primary business became the raw materials themselves. Even today, many a Providence home probably still has stonework or masonry deriving from the Manton (a.k.a. Violet Hill a.k.a. De Magistris) quarry. I wonder if Mariano himself built the ample two-flat at 23 Baltimore Street which accommodated so many generations of his family.

In all, I believe four De Magistris brothers (Giovanni, Mariano, Concezio, and Giacinto) emigrated from Introdacqua,

---

15. The view was essentially unchanged in plate 91 of volume 3 the 1951 edition of the Sanborn Fire map of Providence. I referenced these maps on the Library of Congress website.

L'Aquila, Abruzzo, Italy to Providence in the 1890s. Another De Magistris male, Merino Joseph (1892–1983), followed in 1909. (I believe he may have been a son of Giovanni.) Mariano was unmarried when he arrived in October 1890 or 1891, but he married Carmela Di Meo (1866–1933) on 27 February 1892. Six of a family of ten children born between 1892 and 1909 reached maturity. I think that Mariano was probably the most successful of the brothers. Giovanni (John) worked as a laborer, while Concezio (Charles) and Giacinto (James or George) worked primarily as drivers. Mariano's son Ralph had a family even larger than his father's, and the tradition of large families continued for at least several generations. Not every De Magistris was a blue-collar worker. Giacinto's daughter Inez (Enis) got her degree at Pembroke College (probably about 1931) and taught at Classical High School until her marriage. As for the maternal side of the family, today the Di Meo Construction Company is one of Rhode Island's largest, although its founders are probably only remote relatives.

Mariano De Magistris and his brothers must have hundreds of descendants at the present time. I do not know that Mariano and Carmela even have markers at St. Ann Cemetery, where they were buried in Cranston, R.I. In a working-class family, grave markers were sometimes a luxury that could be foregone. Mariano had apparently mostly retired from the operation of his quarry by the time the 1935 Rhode Island state census was enumerated. Nevertheless, he was still working—as a spinner at a local woolen mill. In a blue-collar immigrant family, everyone had to contribute to the funds needed to meet living expenses. Few could hope to rest their bones unless they survived to their eighties or nineties.

I don't know if the city of Paterson, New Jersey, still maintains its municipal museum, and if so whether many of the stone and mineral samples collected by former curator James F. Morton, Jr. still remain to be seen. Perhaps his interest in these samples enabled his friend Lovecraft to put on the mantle of the landed proprietor for one final time. After all, the last real estate (454 Angell Street) had passed out of the family soon after the death of Lovecraft's grandfather Whipple V. Phillips in 1904. (His Idaho business holdings were soon liquidated as well.) Perhaps the foundation of Mariano De Magistris's two-flat at 23 Baltimore Street in the Manton neighborhood is an example of the kind of masonry that still survives from the operation of the quarry ca. 1905–45.

One hopes that the memory of the courtesy with which mortgagor and mortgagee treated each other—as regards the 1911 mortgage on the Manton or Violet Hill or De Magistris quarry—will not fade entirely. In an era in which Lovecraft is sometimes attacked as a "vicious racist," an opposing reality deserves to be exhibited. One needs to set aside the mock seigneurial joking of Lovecraft's letters to Morton and appreciate the courtesy with which Lovecraft treated his mortgagor and his sons. Researcher R. Alain Everts said the surviving members of the De Magistris family whom he interviewed looked upon Lovecraft as "a god." No deification is needed to assert that Lovecraft always comported himself as a gentleman—both in dealing with his friends and with his Providence neighbors.

The People of 169 Clinton Street

In Memory of Matilda Grey (née King) Burns (1867–1955)

From 31 December 1924 to 17 April 1926, Lovecraft lived in a first-floor room (equipped with washing and dressing alcoves) at 169 Clinton Street in Brooklyn. In his letter to Maurice W. Moe dated 15 June 1925, he admitted that his aunt Lillian, while visiting in New York City and nearby places, had assisted him with the selection of his room. In the same letter, Lovecraft drew a sketch of his room (reproduced in *IAP* 568).[1] Lovecraft's landlady at 169 Clinton Street was Matilda Grey (*née* King) Burns, who lived on the premises with her sons Robert and Warren. Lovecraft's rent was initially $40 per month, increased to $10 per week effective 1 November 1925 (*IAP* 573). According to his wife (who stayed at 169 Clinton Street with Lovecraft for eighty-nine days in 1925), Lovecraft's aunts sent him $15 weekly while he lived there and she supplied any overages (*IAP* 573).

While he lived at 169 Clinton Street, Lovecraft kept a diary (*CE* 5.149–79), mainly as a memory aid for the writing of letters to his aunts. S. T. Joshi provides a very helpful capsule summary of the most notable events of his tenure, including the dates for Sonia's nine visits in 1925 (*IAP* 570). Beginning on 20 January 1925, Lovecraft's friend bookseller George Kirk took up residence in the room directly above his (*IAP* 574). They signaled each other by banging on the radiator pipes (*IAP* 585). Samuel Loveman also considered moving to Lovecraft's building, but ultimately decided on other quarters (*IAP* 574).

---

1. It is not clear from HPL's drawing whether his washing alcove included running water, sink, toilet, or bath. It is possible he had to use shared facilities for some of these needs.

169 Clinton Street, Brooklyn. Credit: Corcoran.com.

Mrs. Burns refused to provide adequate heating for Lovecraft's room, particularly during the coal strike from September 1925 to February 1926, so that Lovecraft was forced to buy an oil heater in October 1925 (*IAP* 577–78). The oil heater came with a stove-top attachment, so that he could also use it for heating the canned foods on which he mostly subsisted. Mrs. Burns also demurred at fixing a light fixture in his dressing alcove that failed in September 1925; its repair had to await a visit from Sonia, who engaged an electrician to make the repair in mid-January 1926 (*IAP* 578). The low point of Lovecraft's tenancy undoubtedly occurred on 24 May 1925, when thieves who had rented the adjoining room broke into his dressing alcove and stole three of his suits, an overcoat, a wicker suitcase belonging to his wife (whose contents were recovered after they were abandoned by the thieves in the adjoining room), and an expensive radio set that he was storing for his friend Samuel Loveman (*IAP* 578). Lovecraft was meticulous about his dress, and the theft was undoubtedly one of the worst psychological blows he endured during his residency in New York.

Of course, Lovecraft's 1925–26 stay in New York was not all misery. He enjoyed the company of the Kalem Club members and entertained them in his room as part of the regular rotation of hosting. He and his fellow club members were not above the occasional flamboyance of young men: as recalled by Rheinhart Kleiner, they loved promenading on Clinton Street in their straw hats with their fancy canes (Hart & Joshi 225). Lovecraft even purchased a metal pail so that he could go out to get hot coffee for Kalem meetings held in his room. On the other hand, the Kalems' social program upon occasion became so time-consuming that Lovecraft sometimes had to ignore knocks at his door and pretend that he was not at home (*IAP* 585). However, he couldn't pretend to be out when mice invaded his room, and he had to buy cheap traps to dispose of the invaders (*IAP* 578). In short, Lovecraft's life had its ups and downs during his stay at 169 Clinton Street.

The residents of 169 Clinton Street enumerated in the 1925 census are summarized in the table on pp. 149–50.[2]

By 1 June 1925, of course, the tenants who had burglarized Lovecraft's room had been gone for a week. Messrs. Araji (#19) and Harma (#20) were probably the Syrians whose strange-to-Western-ears music reached Lovecraft's apartment. However, apart from Lovecraft's landlady Mrs. Burns and her two sons, I have not had much luck tracing the individuals shown in the census schedule. A few observations are appropriate:

1. Residents with alien status may have eventually returned to their native countries.

---

2. 169 Clinton Street was located in Block 3 of Election District 23 in Brooklyn Assembly District 1. The census taker was Minnie L. Hickman.

2. Ages shown as multiples of five are more prevalent than one would expect. Did some of the residents know their ages only approximately? Or did Mrs. Burns provide estimated age information for residents who were absent at the enumeration?

3. The occupation of "engineer" is more prevalent than one would expect. Surely Lovecraft, if asked, would not have described himself as an engineer. I suspect that Mrs. Burns provided made-up occupational information for residents who were absent at the enumeration.

4. The lack of birthplaces more specific than "U.S." for native-born residents makes identification difficult.

Demographically, note that there were no persons classified as Negro or mulatto resident at 169 Clinton Street on 1 June 1925. Out of twenty-five total residents, only five were women. There were only three assumed married couples, the Pausts (#8 and #9), the Dowses (#11 and #12), and the Heddiwicks (#15 and #16). There was only one child, Norman and Madeline Heddiwicks's son Norman Jr. (#17), unless one insists upon counting Mrs. Burns's younger son Warren as a minor at age eighteen. The average age of the residents was young[3]; the oldest resident was sixty-year-old Claus Peterson (#6), while the youngest adult was eighteen-year-old Warren Burns (#3). If we disregard the latter, twenty-year-old Francis Allen (#23) or twenty-three-year-old Charles Ritz (#25) was the youngest adult.

---

3. The average age of all 25 residents was 28.8 years. Excluding Norman Heddiwick [Jr.] (#17), the average age of the remaining 24 residents was 29.9 years. If we exclude Mrs. Burns and her two sons, the average age of all 22 roomers was 28.5 years. Excluding Norman Heddiwick [Jr.] (#17), the average age of the remaining 21 roomers was 29.7 years.

The People of 169 Clinton Street

No	Surname	Given name	Rel	Sex	Age	Where Born	Yrs in U.S. & Citizenship	Occupation
1	Burns	Matilda	Head	F	49	Ireland	32 (husband)[1]	Housewife
2	Burns	Robert	Son	M	25	U.S.	U.S. citizen	Farmer
3	Burns	Warren	Son	M	18	U.S.	U.S. citizen	Student
4	Moore	Rowland	L	M	26	U.S.	U.S. citizen	Boiler maker
5	Halton	Gustave	L	M	40	U.S.	U.S. citizen	Machinist
6	Peterson	Claus	L	M	60	Norway	40 (nat. sup.ct. 1910)	Machinist
7	Price	Walter	L	M	25	England	5 (alien)	Guard
8	Paust	Charles	B	M	25	U.S.	U.S. citizen	Bookkeeper
9	Paust	Margaret	B	F	24	U.S.	U.S. citizen	Housework
10	Kirk	George	B	M	26	U.S.	U.S. citizen	Bookseller
11	Dowse	Marli	L	F	29	U.S.	U.S. citizen	Housework
12	Dowse	Joseph	L	M	29	U.S.	U.S. citizen	File clerk
13	Hoyer	Ernest	L	M	27	U.S.	U.S. citizen	Civil engineer
14	Lovecraft	Howard	L	M	35	U.S.	U.S. citizen	Engineer
15	Heddiwick	Norman	L	M	28	Canada	5 (alien)	File clerk
16	Heddiwick	Madeline	L	F	27	Canada	3 (alien)	Housework
17	Heddiwick	Norman	L	M	5	Canada	3 (alien)	None
18	Messeyek	Alex	L	M	30	U.S.	U.S. citizen	Fireman
19	Araji	James	L	M	30	Syria	15 (nat. sup.ct. 1918)	Embroiderer

Helpers and Neighbors

No	Surname	Given name	Rel	Sex	Age	Where Born	Yrs in U.S. & Citizenship	Occupation
20	Harma	George	L	M	35	Syria	10 (alien)	Machine operator
21	Fischer	Anita	L	F	29	U.S.	U.S. citizen	Engineer
22	Hayden	Peter	L	M	25	U.S.	U.S. citizen	Civil engineer
23	Allen	Francis	L	M	20	U.S.	U.S. citizen	Engineer
24	Ross	John	L	M	30	U.S.	U.S. citizen	Actor
25	Ritz	Charles	L	M	23	U.S.	U.S. citizen	Stock clerk

REL (relationship to head of household)
   Head = head of household
   L = lodger (no meals)
   B = boarder (with meals)

nat. sup.ct. (XXXX) = naturalized in superior court (year XXXX)

[1]. Since her husband Howard M. Burns was a natural-born U.S. citizen, Matilda Grey King would have acquired U.S. citizenship upon her marriage in 1893.

Of twenty-five total residents, eight, including Mrs. Burns herself, were foreign-born. Of these, five were aliens, while three were naturalized, two by the Superior Court and Mrs. Burns herself by marriage to her native-born husband in 1893. There were four engineers, including Howard Lovecraft (!) and Anita Fischer (#21). Perhaps the most unusual occupation recorded (for city dwellers) was farmer for Mrs. Burns's elder son Robert. None of the four married women (Matilda Burns [#1], Margaret Paust [#9], Marli Dowse [#11], and Madeline Heddiwick [#16]) apparently worked outside the home, although Mrs. Burns doubtless worked hard to manage her rooming house. Of the twenty-two non-family residents, only the three boarders, the Pausts and George Kirk, took some or all of their meals with the Burnses; the rest of the residents, the lodgers, fended for themselves for food.

Far more so than applied in the more intimate setting at 10 Barnes Street in Providence (where Lovecraft lived from 1926 to 1933), many of the residents at 169 Clinton Street were probably short-term tenants, and apart from Kirk,[1] Lovecraft probably did not strike up many acquaintances among them. However, he did of necessity have communications with his landlady Mrs. Burns, so we may justifiably seek to learn something more about her.

Fortunately, I have had some success with Mrs. Burns and her sons. Five years before the NY 1925 state census, they were enumerated at 233 51st Street in Manhattan[2] in the 1920 U.S. census:

> Burns, Matilda, head, white female, age 43, widow, born Ireland of Irish-born parents, emigrated 1903, naturalized U.S. citizen, housekeeper (lodging house)

---

1. See Hart for many recollections and photographs of George Kirk.
2. In 2019, 233 West 51st Street in Manhattan is the site of the Times Square Church Annex building, with a McDonald's restaurant on the first floor.

Burns, Robert, son, white male, age 20, single, born NY of NY-born father and Irish-born mother, office clerk

Burns, Warren, son, white male, age 13, single, born NY of NY-born father and Irish-born mother, no occupation

Going back five more years, we find the following household in New York City in the 1915 NY state census:[3]

Burns, Howard, white male, age 47, born U.S., jeweler

Burns, Matilda, white female, age 45, born Ireland, 25 years in U.S., naturalized citizen, housewife

Burns, Robert H., white male, age 16, born U.S., at school

Burns, Arthur W., white male, age 9, born U.S., at school

If we go back another five years, we find the following household at 21 Grand Avenue in Palisades Park, Bergen County NJ[4] in the 1910 U.S. census:

Burns, Howard, head, age 41, married 16 years, born NY of Scottish-born parents, clerk (retail jeweler)

Burns, Matilda, wife, age 38, married 16 years, 2 children borne, 2 living, born Ireland of Irish-born parents, emigrated 1887, retail merchant (ice cream etc.)

Burns, Robert, son, age 10, born NY of NY-born father and Irish-born mother

Burns, Warren, son, age 3, born NY of NY-born father and Irish-born mother

Going back another five years, we find the following household at 41 Passaic in Lodi (Hasbrouck Heights Borough), Bergen County NJ in the 1905 NJ state census:

Burns, Howard (head), born November 1871, age 34, born NY of Irish-born parents, jewelry salesman

---

3. There were also two lodgers in the household.
4. In 2019, this address is the site of a large commercial building.

Burns, Matilda (wife), born December 1873, age 32, born Ireland of Irish-born parents, 16 years in the U.S.

Burns, Robert (son), born November 1899, age 6, born NY of NY-born father and Irish-born mother

Pushing back another five years, we find the following household at 1272 Amsterdam Avenue in Manhattan Ward 23 in the 1900 U.S. census:

Burns, Howard M., head, born November 1868[5], age 31, married 7 years, born NY of Irish-born parents, teamster

Burns, Matilda G., wife, born December 1871, age 28, married 7 years, 1 child borne, 1 living, born Ireland of Irish-born parents, emigrated 1890

Burns, Robert H., son, born November 1899, age 6 months, born NY of NY-born father and Irish-born mother

Shozabura, Mike, lodger, born December 1876, age 23, single, born Japan of Japanese-born parents, emigrated 1898 (alien), student

The usual inconsistencies we expect in successive censuses occur. Howard Burns changed his Irish-born parents (1900 census) to Scottish-born parents (1910 census). Matilda Burns stated her emigration year variously over the years: 1890 (1900 census), 1887 (1910 census), 1903 (1920 census), 1893 (1925 census) and 1889 (1930 census). In actual fact, I believe she was the eighteen-year-old Irish national Matilda King who arrived unaccompanied in New York City aboard the ship *Umbria* on 7 April 1885, having sailed from Queenstown, Ireland.

Fortunately, we can find a New York City marriage record for Mr. and Mrs. Burns. Howard M. Burns, age 25, son of William Burns and Mary J. Miller, married Matilda G. King, age 24,

---

5. Howard Milton Burns was born 1 November 1868 in New York City, the son of William J. Burns, M.D. and Mary J. Miller. He was christened 28 March 1869 at the 42nd Street Presbyterian Church in New York City.

daughter of John King and Hadley Horne, in Manhattan on 14 September 1893 (certificate number 14162). The fact is, however, that Mrs. Burns was not really a widow when the 1920 census was enumerated. Howard M[ilton] Burns died, age 74, in his home at 342 Bergen Street, in Brooklyn on 12 January 1944. He was buried three days later in Bay View Cemetery in Jersey City, N.J. His occupation was stated as clerk and his spouse's name was stated as Ella. He was stated to have been born on 1 November 1869 in New York City. So Mr. and Mrs. Burns had parted company by the time of the 1920 census. It was not uncommon for divorced or separated women to report their status as widowed to the census-taker. Whether Mr. and Mrs. Burns formally divorced, I have not been able to determine.

Matilda Burns did not remain at 169 Clinton Street for very long after Lovecraft's tenancy in 1925–26. By 1928, Matilda, widow of Howard, made her home at 710 South Avenue in Schenectady, N.Y. Her sons Robert H. Burns, a salesman, and Rev. A. Warren Burns, pastor of the People's Christian Church, lived with her (Schenectady NY 1928 directory).

Mrs. Burns did not abandon being a landlady after leaving 169 Clinton Street. She and her son Robert were enumerated with fourteen lodgers at 1310 L Street NW[6] in Washington, D.C., in the 1930 U.S. census:

> Burns, Matilda, head, age 56, widow, born England of English-born parents, emigrated 1889, naturalized U.S. citizen, housekeeper (boarding house)
>
> Burns, Robert, son, age 28, single, born NY of English-born parents, stock clerk (silk manufacturing company)
>
> (lodgers omitted)

---

6. A modern office and apartment building has replaced the Burns rooming house. The current building contains the headquarters of the American Association of University Women.

By 1931, Mrs. Matilda G. Burns again resided in Schenectady, N.Y., at 116 Edward Street; her son Rev. Warren Burns, pastor of the People's Christian Church, resided with her (Schenectady NY 1931 directory). However, when the 1940 U.S. census was enumerated, Mrs. Burns was back with her son Robert Burns at 1310 L Street NW in Washington, D.C., this time with ten lodgers:

> Burns, Robert H., head, age 40, single, born NY, three years of high school, proprietor (rooming house)
>
> Burns, Matilda G., mother, age 72, married, born Irish Free State (Northern Ireland), eight years of primary school, no occupation
>
> (lodgers omitted)

Both Robert Burns and his mother stated that they had resided in the same place as of 1 April 1935. Neither she nor her son Warren Burns was listed in the Schenectady NY 1933 directory, so she had apparently returned to Washington, D.C., by 1933. Although she had no stated occupation in the 1940 U.S. census, I suspect that Mrs. Burns assisted her son in the management of his rooming house to the extent she could.

Matilda G. Burns, age 87, died in Rotterdam, Schenectady County, N.Y., on 1 August 1955 (certificate 54102). She and both her sons are buried in Memory Gardens Cemetery and Memorial Park in Colonie, Albany County, N.Y., where each has a marker. Mrs. Burns's marker states her date of birth as 6 December 1867. Find-A-Grave has a photograph of Mrs. Burns's marker posted by Anne Montague.

Mrs. Burns apparently made at least one return visit to Ireland. Matilda King Burns, age 38, housewife, and Arthur Warren Burns, age 4, arrived aboard the *St. Louis* at Ellis Island on 13 May 1911, having sailed from Southampton, England. While they were in England, they were enumerated in the UK census on 1

April 1911. Matilda Gray Burns, age 36, visitor, married for 17 years, 2 children borne, 2 children living, born Truro, Galway, Ireland, and her son Arthur Warren Burns, age 4, visitor, born New York City, U.S. citizen, were enumerated in the household of John Charles Norton and Daisy Sara Norton in Balsall Heath, Worcestershire. Today Balsall Heath is an inner-city, working-class neighborhood within Birmingham, West Midlands.

Alas, all the residents enumerated at 169 Clinton Street on 1 June 1925 are deceased, so we have to rely on the recollections of the Kalems (particularly as assembled by Mara Kirk Hart) for Lovecraft's New York years. However, landlady Matilda Grey (*née* King) Burns played a part in that experience, as evidenced by Lovecraft's own correspondence. The hows and whys of Lovecraft's return to Providence in April 1926 are beyond the scope of this paper, but his longing for his native city is painfully evident from his surviving correspondence and the recollections of his wife and of his friends. We will never have the opportunity to ask Matilda Burns about her experiences with her resident "engineer" Howard Lovecraft. She might have had recollections as colorful as Lovecraft's own of her.[7]

Works Cited

Hart, Mara Kirk. So Many Lovely Days: The Greenwich Village Years. Duluth, MN: Kirk Press, 2013.

———, and S. T. Joshi, ed. Lovecraft's New York Circle: The Kalem Club, 1924–1927. New York: Hippocampus Press, 2006.

---

7. Writing to Frank Belknap Long on 6 July 1927, Lovecraft described his former landlady as "that enigmatical ogress of yesterday—the tart & inimitable Mrs. Burns!" (*SP* 389). Writing to Long earlier, on 21 August 1926, he had described Florence Reynolds (1861/62–1962), the manager at 10 Barnes Street as "Honest Miss Reynolds, the local Sibyl, (for I cannot libel such a gentle, gracious old creature by the use of the harsh term landlady [oh, shades of dear Madame Burns!!!])" (*SP* 323).

The following photographs taken at Memory Gardens Cemetery and Memorial Park in Colonie, Albany County NY and Burns family photographs are used with the written permission of Jeni (#47733487) at Find-A-Grave.

The People of 10 Barnes Street

In Memory of Florence Louise Reynolds (1861/62–1962)

Abbreviations

US XXXX means United States census for the year XXXX. UK XXXX means United Kingdom census for the year XXXX. RI XXXX means Rhode Island census for the year XXXX. PD XXXX means Providence RI directory (surname order) for the year XXXX. PHD XXXX means Providence RI house directory (street address order) for the year XXXX. EPD XXXX means East Providence RI directory for the year XXXX. USPS abbreviations are used for states.

Introduction

When Lovecraft returned to Providence from Brooklyn in April 1926, there was a home waiting for him: his elder aunt Lillian Clark had obtained rooms for her nephew and herself at 10 Barnes Street. Ten Barnes was half of the duplex numbered 10–12 Barnes, originally erected in the early 1880s. Lovecraft had an entry-level room with kitchenette alcove, while his aunt had a room one floor above. Lovecraft's own drawing of his quarters at 10 Barnes Street is reproduced in *IAP* 635. Lillian Clark died in July 1932, but Lovecraft would remain at 10 Barnes Street until he and Annie Gamwell united their households at 66 College Street in May 1933.

Alas, the Providence House Directories only recorded the name of Lovecraft's landlady at 10 Barnes: Florence F. Reynolds. But in the US 1930 census schedule we have a full picture of the then residents of 10 Barnes on the 1 April 1930 enumeration date:

Florence S. Reynolds, head, age 53, single, born Australia of English-born parents, housekeeper (rooming house), emigrated 1887, alien,[1] rent $100.

Amy H. Reid, roomer, age 69, single, born RI of NY-born parents, sales girl (publishing company).

Howard P. Lovecraft, roomer, age 39, divorced, born RI of NY-born father and RI-born mother, writer-poetry.

Tryphena B. Hodgdon, roomer, age 57, widow, born MA of MA-born parents, secretary to physician.

Rebecca A. Stafford, roomer, age 48, single, born RI of RI-born parents, clerk (insurance company).

Nellie R. Bates, roomer, age 72, widow, born MA of MA-born father and NH-born mother, no occupation.

Lillian D. Clark, roomer, age 73, widow, born RI of RI-born parents, no occupation.

Let's see what genealogical sources can reveal about Lovecraft's 1930 neighbors (excluding his aunt Mrs. Clark).

Florence Louise Reynolds. Born 1861/62 Australia (based on RI 1875 [see below]), d. 8 May 1962 (Barrington RI). Florence F.[2] Reynolds was listed as the householder at 10 Barnes as early as PD 1922 and as late as PD 1939. She was not the owner of the property, but managed it for the owner. A young Flor-

---

1. There is a file for Florence Reynolds, born 7 November 1862, in the index to alien case files.

2. Florence was not always consistent in the use of her middle initial. Generally she stated her middle initial as "L." through 1916; however, in RI 1915 she was enumerated as Florence L. F. Reynolds. In US 1930 she was enumerated as Florence S. Reynolds; however, PD 1922–39 listed her as Florence F. Reynolds at 10 Barnes Street. In PD 1941–44, in her sister Minnie A. (Reynolds) Clapp's home at 38 Upton Avenue, she was listed as Florence L. Reynolds. Her death certificate (for which her sister Minnie was the informant) stated her name as Florence Louise Reynolds.

ence Reynolds, age 9, scholar, born Australia, was enumerated in her parents' household in Lady Wood, Birmingham, Warwickshire, England, in UK 1871.

As a young girl, she was a member of the family enumerated at 14 Dwight Street in Providence Ward 9 in RI 1875: Joseph Reynolds, head, age 38, born England, jeweler; Eliza Reynolds, wife, age 35, born England, housekeeper; Florence Reynolds, daughter, age 13, born Australia; Rosa Reynolds, daughter, age 6, born England; Minnie Reynolds, daughter, age 1, born England; John Angilly, cousin-in-law, age 52, born England, German silver polisher; Charles Angilly, boarder, age 16, born England, German silver polisher.

In RI 1885, Florence L. Reynolds, age 23, born England, dressmaker, was enumerated in a family of five persons[3] in Providence RI Ward 8 (district 74 family 271). PHD 1895–96 listed Florence L. Reynolds as a dressmaker at 34 Gallup Street, the home of her father Joseph Reynolds. In US 1900, Florence was enumerated in her parents' household at 34 Gallup Street in Providence, R.I. She and her parents all stated their emigration year as 1872, while her sister Minnie stated hers as 1880. Florence stated her month and year of birth as March 1870, and her occupation as milliner.

PD 1900–08 listed Florence L. Reynolds as a milliner at 142 Ocean.[4] In US 1910, she was enumerated at 829 Elmwood Avenue in Providence Ward 6 as a member of this household: Eliza A. Reynolds (head), age 75, widow, 3 children borne, 3 living, born England of English-born parents, emigrated 1875; Florence L. Reynolds (daughter), age 30, single, born Australia of

---

3. Probably consisting of Florence's parents, herself and her two sisters Rosa and Minnie.
4. PD 1901 listed her as boarding at 34 Gallup Street. PD 1906 listed her as boarding at 829 Elmwood Avenue.

English-born parents, milliner (at home), emigrated 1885; Minnie A. Reynolds (daughter), age 23, single, born England of English-born parents, milliner (at home), emigrated 1890. In RI 1915 the same family was enumerated at 831 Elmwood Avenue in Providence Ward 6: Eliza A. Reynolds (head), age 73, born England of English-born parents; Florence L. F. Reynolds, age 42, born Australia of English-born parents, millinery store; Minnie A. Reynolds (daughter), age 37, born England of English-born parents, millinery store.[5]

PD 1910–12 listed Florence L. Reynolds and her sister Minnie A. Reynolds in partnership as milliners F. L. & M. A. Reynolds, with business and home at 829 Elmwood Avenue. In PD 1914 and PD 1916, the sisters had gone into partnership with Eva C. Weightman (b. 1892/93 MA), the daughter of Arthur P. and Eliza (Burton) Weightman, as milliners Reynolds & Weightman, with offices at 57 Eddy Street, room 407. The sisters still resided at 829 Elmwood Avenue, while Eva (1915) resided with her parents at 71 Lexington Avenue. PD 1918 listed F. L. Reynolds, 829 Elmwood Avenue, in its list of milliners. PD 1918 listed Florence L. Reynolds as the householder at 829 Elmwood Avenue and Minnie A. Reynolds as a boarder at the same address. The sisters evidently gave up their partnership with Eva Weightman and their lease of room 407 at 57 Eddy Street after the marriage of Minnie Reynolds in 1918.

US 1920 enumerated Florence L. Reynolds, age 48, single, as head of household at 100 Waterman Street, Providence, R.I. She claimed to have been born in Australia of English-born parents, to have emigrated in 1881, and to have become a naturalized U.S. citizen in 1896. She claimed no occupation but was

---

5. The family shared their home at 831 Elmwood Avenue with the household of Edward Ken Reynolds Jr., his wife Rosa Reynolds (sister of Florence and Minnie), and their daughter Martha M. B. Reynolds.

evidently a busy woman, since she had ten boarders in her household. Perhaps taking care of the roomers at 10 Barnes Street offered lighter duties when she assumed that position by 1922. PHD 1919 had listed 100 Waterman Street as vacant. PD 1920 and 1921 listed Miss Florence L. Reynolds with home at 100 Waterman Street.[6]

In PD 1941, 1942, and 1944, Florence L. Reynolds was listed as a resident of 38 Upton Avenue, which was the home of her sister Minnie A. (Reynolds) Clapp and her husband Frederick Otis Clapp. In 1947/48, Florence L. Reynolds removed with her brother-in-law Frederick Otis Clapp and her sister Minnie A. (Reynolds) Clapp from 38 Upton Avenue in Providence to 70 Nayatt Road in Barrington. She died there on 8 May 1962, after fourteen years of residence in Barrington. Her sister was the informant for her death certificate. Minnie stated Florence's place of birth as Australia, but didn't know her sister's date of birth; she estimated her sister's age as "98?" years. Florence died of acute cardiac failure (onset one week) and cardio-vascular disease (onset two years). She was buried in Swan Point Cemetery in Providence on 11 May 1962.

We can clearly see "age contraction" occurring for Florence Reynolds as we pass from RI 1875 to US 1910 and RI 1915. If she was the individual recorded in RI 1875, she was probably a recent arrival from England with her parents.

Amy H. Reid. Amy H. Reid was born in Providence, R.I., in 1859/60, the daughter of Andrew and Ann (———) Reid. She remained single throughout her life. She was enumerated in the following household in Providence Ward 9 in US 1870: Andrew Reid, age 67, gardener, born NY, $200 personal estate; Ann I. Reid, age 52, housekeeper, born NY; Alice A. Reid, age 32, mil-

---

6. 100 Waterman Street, on the north side of the street two doors west of Thayer Street, is still (2019) standing.

liner, born NY; Eliza L. Reid, age 27, at home, born NY; Agnes M. Reid, age 23, milliner, born NY; Henry A. Reid, age 14, at home, born RI; Amy H. Reid, age 11, at school, born RI. This household was again recorded in Providence Ward 9 in RI 1875: Andrew Reid (head), age 72, born NY, gardener; Ann Reid (wife), age 56, born NY, housekeeper; Eleanor J. Reid (daughter), age 33, born NY, harness loom; Agnes M. Reid (daughter), age 26, born NY, harness loom; Euphemia Reid (daughter), age 23, born Providence, teacher; Henry Reid (son), age 18, born Providence; Amy H. Reid (daughter), age 16, born Providence, scholar. US 1880 recorded the following household at 39 Colfax in Providence: Andrew Reid (head), age 79, at home, born NY of US-born parents; Anna J. Reid (wife), age 63, housekeeper, born NY of NY-born parents; Agnes M. Reid (daughter), age 30, harness loom, born NJ of NY-born parents; Andrew H. Reid (son), age 25, at home, born RI of NY-born parents; and Amy H. Reid (daughter), age 29, at home, born RI of NY-born parents.

In PD 1901–09, Amy H. Reid was a stenographer working at 136 S. Water Street. In 1906–08, she boarded in Edgewood; in 1909, she boarded at 188 Meeting Street. PD 1910 recorded that Amy H. Reid had removed to Boston, MA. By the time US 1920 was enumerated, Amy had returned to Providence: age 50, single, born RI of RI-born parents, jewelry bench hand, she was enumerated in the 240 Camp Street home of dressmaker Sarah C. L. Swett. Her information for RI 1925 was unchanged, except that her occupation was recorded as [business] partner of Ms. Swett. PD 1924 and 1928 also recorded Amy H. Reid at 240 Camp Street. PD 1931 listed Amy E. Reid, saleswoman, residing at 10 Barnes Street. US 1940 enumerated Amy Reid, age 80, single, born RI, traveling saleslady (chemical manufacturer), as a lodger in the household of Lou Davis at 216 Brown Street in Providence RI. She had resided at the same address as of 1

April 1935. PD 1941 and 1944 recorded Amy H. Reid residing at 187 Wayland Avenue. Amy died, age 86, in the State Hospital in Cranston, R.I., on 7 November 1946.

Tryphena Betsey Hodgdon. Tryphena was born in Wrentham, Mass., on 18 January 1873, the daughter of Granville Morse and Catherine E. Shepardson. She married 1894/95 David A. Hodgdon (1869–1922), the son of David S. and Mary P. (———) Hodgdon. She and her husband were recorded in her parents' household at 228 South Street in Wrentham in US 1900: Granville Morse (head), born August 1842, married 37 years, born MA of MA-born father and ME-born mother, coal dealer; Catherine E. Morse (wife), born October 1843, married 37 years, 6 children borne, 5 living, born MA of MA-born parents; Elmer Morse (son), born August 1866 MA; Frances C. Morse (daughter), born November 1870 MA; Tryphena B. Hodgdon (daughter), born January 1873, married 5 years, 0 children borne, born MA; David A. Hodgdon (son-in-law), born August 1869, married 5 years, born RI of MA-born father and French-born mother, brakeman (railroad).

US 1920 enumerated the following household at 6 Cargill in Providence Ward 9: David A. Hodgdon (head), age 50, born RI of ME-born father and French-born mother, trainman (steam railroad); Tryphena Hodgdon (wife), age 46, born MA of MA-born parents. Tryphena B. Hodgdon was listed as David A. Hodgdon's widow at 6 Cargill in PD 1924. PD 1928, PD 1930 and PD 1931 listed Tryphena Hodgdon, clerk, residing at 10 Barnes Street.[7] The Attleboro MA 1937 directory listed Tryphena Hodgdon, widow of David, with home at 64 High Street in North Attleboro MA. PD 1939–53 recorded Tryphena B.

---

7. PD 1930 also listed Mrs. Betty Hodgdon, assistant at 290 Westminster room 610, residing at 10 Barnes Street. I suspect this is a duplicate listing for Tryphena Hodgdon.

Hodgdon, widow of David, working as a companion, residing at 55 Vassar Street. US 1940 enumerated Tryphena B. Hodgdon, companion, age 67, widow, born MA, in the household of Annie F. Peckham, age 78, single, born RI, at 55 Vassar Avenue in Providence RI. Miss Peckham had resided at the same address on 1 April 1935; Tryphena Hodgdon had resided in North Attleboro MA on the same date. The RI State Archives searched 1946–68 for a death record for Tryphena Hodgdon but did not find one. Perhaps she died in MA, where she had lived in 1873–1900 and again in 1935–37.

Rebecca Amelia Stafford. Rebecca was born in Rhode Island on 26 June 1881, the daughter of Charles Lippitt Stafford (1842–1919) and Ada Alice Andrews (1847–1908). She died in Rhode Island in May 1969.

Rebecca was enumerated in her parents' household at 2 Humboldt Avenue in Providence Ward 2 in US 1900: Charles Stafford (head), born June 1842, married 24 years, born RI of RI-born parents, druggist; Ada A. Stafford (wife), born December 1847, married 24 years, 7 children borne, 7 living, born RI of MA-born father and PA-born mother; Alice H. Stafford[8] (daughter), born October 1869, born RI of RI-born parents; Helen A. Stafford[9] (daughter), born November 1874 RI of RI-born parents; Ada H. Stafford (daughter), born August 1876 RI of RI-born parents, student; Elizabeth R. Stafford (daughter), born May 1878 RI of RI-born parents, teacher; Rebecca A. Stafford (daughter), born June 1881 RI of RI-born parents, at school; Charlotte L. Stafford (daughter), born May 1884 RI of RI-born parents, at school; Charles L. Stafford Jr. (son), born January 1886 RI of RI-born parents, at school.

---

8. Surname Wayland struck out.
9. Surname Wayland struck out.

RI 1935 recorded Rebecca A. Stafford as a resident of 10 Barnes Street in Providence. She was single and her usual employment was as an insurance map clerk at 36 Canal Street; she was not employed in 1935 and had been idle for fifteen months. US 1940 recorded Rebecca A. Stafford as householder at 69 Barnes Street. She had no occupation, and had resided in the same place on 1 April 1935. She was 58 years old and single. PD 1942–45 listed Miss Stafford at 69 Barnes Street. PD 1958–64 listed Miss Stafford at 115 Butler Avenue; PD 1964 noted that she was retired.

Nellie R[ockwood] Bates. Nellie Rockwood was born in Bellingham, Mass., on 2 August 1857, the daughter of a Bellingham-born father and a Piermont NH-born mother. Francis A. Bates, age 25, miller, married Nellie Rockwood, age 23, at home, in Bellingham on 8 September 1880. It was the groom's second marriage, the bride's first. The groom was the son of Francis D. and Hannah E. (——) Bates. The bride was the daughter of Martin and Lydia W. (——) Rockwood. Both bride and groom had been born in Bellingham and resided there at the time of their marriage. US 1900 enumerated the following household at 88 Highland Avenue in Somerville MA Ward 3: Francis A. Bates (head), born December 1855 MA of MA-born parents, parcel delivery; Nellie R. Bates (wife), born August 1857 MA of MA-born father and NH-born mother; Harrie M. Bates (son), born March 1883 MA, dry goods salesman. US 1910 enumerated the following household in Pembroke MA: Francis A. Bates (head), age 55, in first marriage for 30 years, born MA of MA-born parents, farm manager (working out); Nellie R. Bates (wife), age 53, in first marriage for 30 years, 1 child borne, 1 living, born MA of NH-born father and MA-born mother.

The 1916 Rockland MA directory listed Francis E. Bates (wife Nellie R.), caretaker, house 19 Dunbar. US 1920 enumerated the following household at 19 Dunbar in Abington MA: Francis E. Bates (head), age 65, born MA of MA-born parents, caretaker (private estate); Nellie R. Bates (wife), age 62, born MA of MA-born father and NH-born mother, no occupation; plus two boarders. RI 1925 enumerated Nellie R. Bates, age 68, housekeeper, born MA, in the household of Roland Haymond, age 49, born MA, at 50 Boylston Avenue in Providence Ward 2. PD 1925 listed Mrs. Nellie R. Bates at the same address. PD 1928 listed Nellie R. Bates as a housekeeper, residing at 371 Broad Street. PD 1930 listed Nellie R. Bates residing at 10 Barnes. A woman named Nellie R. Bates died in Medford MA in 1934 (MA death index volume 85 page 158).

Mrs. Corrader (?). In his letter to Annie Gamwell dated 5 August 1928, Lovecraft mentioned that "a Christian Science Healer[10] named Mrs. Corrader or something like that" had rented an attic and a downstairs room at 10 Barnes Street. He continued: "Being unable to sleep in the room with anyone else on account of nervousness, the poor creature is obliged to sleep on a cot in the hall near L D C's[11] door, surrounded only by a screen" (*LFF* 726). I have failed to trace Mrs. Corrader. However, I did manage to trace one other 10 Barnes Street resident mentioned in Lovecraft's correspondence.

Writing to Frank Belknap Long on 6 July 1927, Lovecraft mentioned that one resident of 10 Barnes Street, "aged Miss Fowler on the 2nd floor" was "a retired art-museum curator" (*SP* 389). I believe I can identify her as:

Sybil Ada Fowler. Miss Fowler was born in 1844 in Newport, R.I., the daughter of Thomas Fowler (1805–1846) and Harriet

---

10. Perhaps Mrs. Corrader became acquainted with Miss Reynolds through mutual membership in the First Church of Christ, Scientist at 71 Prospect Street.
11. HPL's aunt Lillian D. Clark, who lived on the second floor at 10 Barnes Street.

Bliss (1807–1875). Her mother was the daughter of Jeremiah and Mary (Little) Bliss. Thomas's and Harriet's Newport marriage was reported in the *Columbian Chronicle* for 12 July 1837. Sybil's father was a member of the Society of Friends and is buried in the Friends Cemetery in Jamestown, Newport County RI. Sybil had an older sister Harriet Bliss Fowler (1837–1891). In US 1850, Sybil A. Fowler, age 6, and her sister Harriet B. Fowler, age 10, were enumerated in the Newport home of their widowed mother Harriet Fowler, age 42. All the household members had been born in R.I. Sybil and Harriet were attending school. US 1860 enumerated Harriet Fowler, age 52, $2000 real property, $1000 personal property, as head of household in Providence RI Ward 6. Also in her household were Harriet B. Fowler, age 20, clerk, and Sybil A. Fowler, age 16, no occupation. All the members of the household claimed RI birth. RI 1865 enumerated the household of Harriet Fowler, age 52, Harriet B. Fowler, age 24, and Sybil A. Fowler, age 20, in Providence. All the household members claimed birth in Newport. PD 1878 and PD 1879 included S. Ada Fowler, 12 Dawson Street, in its list of music teachers. In US 1880, Harriet B. Fowler, age 35, was enumerated as head of household at 12 Dawson Street in Providence. Her sister Adda S. Fowler [*sic*], age 30, was also enumerated in Harriet's household. Both sisters claimed RI birth, and both stated their occupation as housekeeper. RI 1885 enumerated Harriet B. Fowler, age 40, single, housewife, as head of household in Providence Ward 7. Her sister S. Ada Fowler, age 36, single, also resided in the household and was employed as an assistant. Both sisters had been born in Newport. Harriet Fowler died in January 1891, age 51.

PHD 1896 and 1897 listed Miss Sybil A. Fowler, artist, as a boarder in the home of Lewis P. Allen, clerk, at 8 Angell Place. US 1900 enumerated Sybil Fowler, age 40, single, artist, as a boarder in the home of Emeline Greene at 8 DeFoe Place in

Providence. Miss Fowler claimed January 1860[12] birth in RI of RI-born parents. PD 1904 listed Sybil A. Fowler as a boarder at 68 Lloyd Avenue, where she remained for many years. PD 1906 listed her as a museum attendant for the Rhode Island School of Design (RISD). US 1910 enumerated Sybil A. Fowler, age 51, single, art museum curator, born RI of RI-born parents, in the household of Ruth A. Harkill at 68 Lloyd Avenue, Providence RI Ward 1. PD 1914, 1918, and 1922 listed Sybil A. Fowler as an attendant at RISD, boarding at 68 Lloyd Avenue. PD 1924 listed Sybil A. Fowler as a resident of 68 Lloyd Avenue. PD 1919, 1923, 1926, and 1927 included Miss Sybil A. Fowler in their listings of members of the Providence Art Club. On 22 April 1925, RI 1925 enumerated Sybil A. Fowler, age 71, born RI, as a lodger in the home of May S. Smith at 78 Congdon Street. Perhaps Miss Fowler resided at 10 Barnes Street in 1926–28.

Sybil A. Fowler died in 1928, and was buried with her sister Harriet in Swan Point Cemetery in Providence.

The only other 10 Barnes Street resident I could identify for Lovecraft's residency there (April 1926–May 1933) was:

Mrs. Myrtie E[llen] Page. Myrtie E. Page, age 19, daughter of Charles Page and Almira Hunt, married on 25 November 1889 (Brownington VT) Frank A. Cloukie, age 24, son of Joseph C. Cloukie and Sophia King. The VT-born bride was a resident of Brownington at the time of her marriage. Canadian-born laborer Frank A. Cloukie was a resident of Westmore VT. It was a first marriage for both the bride and the groom. William N. Roberts, pastor of the local Methodist Episcopal Church, officiated. Frank A. Cloukie died of typhoid, age 42 years 4 months, in Worcester VT on 12 August 1908. Myrtie married (2) [date unknown] —— Fanyeau. Age 50, she married (3) June

---

12. Miss Fowler was understating her age by sixteen years in US 1900.

30, 1924 (Waterville VT) Elias Cheney Stygles,[13] age 49, son of Alphonse Stygles and Cornelia Foster. Her third husband died of a cerebral hemorrhage on 12 October 1928, in Waterville VT.

PD 1918 listed Mrs. Myrtie E. Page, nurse, boarding at 265 President Avenue. PD 1931–32 and 1934 listed Mrs. Myrtie E. Page, residing at 10 Barnes. RI 1935 enumerated Mertie Page, widow, born 14 August 1875, residing at 14 Barnes Street. She had no occupation listed. US 1940 enumerated Myrtie E. Page, age 66, widow, born VT, county agricultural agent, in the household of Lenora Scruggs, age 60, widow, born VT, private duty nurse, on Maple Street in Haverhill NH. Mrs. Scruggs had resided at the same address on 1 April 1935; Mrs. Page had resided in Providence. PD 1945 listed Mrs. Page residing at 69 Barnes Street. PD 1946 listed her as a nurse boarding at 173 Congdon Street; PD 1947–52 listed her as a nurse with house at 173 Congdon Street. PD 1953 listed her without occupation with house at 173 Congdon Street. I am not sure whether she was the Myrtie Page (1884[14]–1954), child of Gains and Eunice (Hase[15]), who was cremated at Swan Point Cemetery in Providence.

Closing Reflections

Lovecraft the hermit of 10 Barnes?

It is customary to regard Lovecraft as fairly cloistered at 10 Barnes. B. K. Hart's widow Philomena complained that Lovecraft had avoided occasions for meeting her husband B. K. Hart, the literary editor of the *Providence Journal*. The fact that Lovecraft's marriage to Sonia Greene was still hanging fire in 1926–29 may

---

13. However, note that the FamilySearch ID LVTF-HSK for Elias Cheney Stygles states that he married Sept. 25, 1897 (Waterville VT) Myrtie May Burns (1880–1973).
14. Note discrepancy with 14 August 1875 as recorded in RI 1935.
15. Possible mistranscription of "Page"?

have inhibited his sociability during that period, although in 1926 he did befriend Brown University special student Wilfred B. Talman, whom he had met earlier in Brooklyn in 1925. The summer of 1927 was probably the era of the most visitors for Lovecraft at 10 Barnes Street: Reynolds found a "poet's garret" for Donald Wandrei on the third floor for $3.50 per week, and she surrendered two of her own rooms for the use of Frank Belknap Long and his parents.[16] In 1932, she found a room for Lovecraft's visitor Carl F. Strauch. Reynolds seems to have been accommodating to her roomer, who as a male was very much in the minority at 10 Barnes. We even know such a trivium as her telephone number (DExter 9617), which she allowed Lovecraft to use when coordinating the logistics of friends' visits.[17]

Wilfred Talman even recalled having tea there with Lovecraft and his wife at 10 Barnes (*AAV* 114).[18] Harry Kern Brobst was left with a less favorable impression of Lovecraft's room at 10 Barnes when he visited in 1931–33 (*AAV* 312–13): he encountered Lovecraft's dusty topcoat hanging in the common hallway, found his room stuffy and closed-off, and his bed linen "dirty." On several occasions when he arrived unannounced, Mrs. Clark (who lived on the floor above) appeared on the landing and informed him that her nephew was out. Lovecraft offered to introduce Brobst to his aunt, but said that she could not receive

---

16. James F. Morton, who visited at the same time, preferred to stay downtown at the Crown Hotel.
17. HPL cites this number in his letter to Donald Wandrei dated 2 June 1927. This fact is also cited in *IAP* 685.
18. As S. T. Joshi points out in his annotation, Sonia Lovecraft never lived at 10 Barnes Street, but she did visit her husband in Providence from time to time in 1926–28. Whether she stayed in hotels or rented a room at 10 Barnes is not recorded. Since HPL's room contained only a couch, he would presumably have had to sleep in his Morris chair had Sonia stayed overnight in his room, unless the couch unfolded into a bed. HPL did have such an unfolding couch-bed in his room at 169 Clinton Street in 1925–26.

visitors because of illness. In fact, Lovecraft never did introduce Brobst to Mrs. Clark.

The demographics of 10 Barnes—how did Lovecraft fit in?

When US 1930 was enumerated, Lovecraft was the youngest inhabitant of 10 Barnes. Rebecca Stafford, at age 48, was the next youngest inhabitant after Lovecraft. Given his nocturnal habits and drawn shades, the women of 10 Barnes probably regarded their resident poet as somewhat eccentric. Nevertheless, he was not totally helpless in household matters, and the women, including Florence Reynolds, were probably glad to have him around. There was probably a maintenance man on call to handle heavier duties such as the furnace[19] and the plumbing. The women, or at least some of them, were probably aware of Lovecraft's unsettled marital status. He described himself on the 1930 census schedule as divorced, and probably grudgingly acknowledged his status to any of the women who inquired.

Note that 10 Barnes Street was a rooming house, rather than a boarding house, so common facilities, other than bathrooms,[20] would probably have been minimal and no meals would have been offered.[21] Lovecraft did most of his shopping downtown

---

19. According to the plan he drew (*IAP* 635), HPL had a floor heating vent in his room, so a forced hot air heating system was apparently in place at 10 Barnes. His room also contained a fireplace, but I assume that it was not functional.

20. HPL wrote to Frank Belknap Long on 6 February 1927: "An excellent bathroom exists on the second floor—reached by a very easy flight of stairs & kept in faultless condition" (*SP* 389). The floor plan has no indication of any toilet in Lovecraft's room.

21. According to HPL, there was no water in the individual rooms at 10 Barnes. He wrote to Frank Belknap Long on 6 February 1927: "There is no running water in the rooms, but an excellent washbowl and mirror will be found in an alcove on the same floor—and one has only to light the gas-heater in the kitchen to get hot water in five minutes from the faucet" (*SP* 389).

(particularly in the small grocery on the northeast corner of Thomas and North Main Streets),[22] rather than venturing over to Thayer Street. From the state of Lovecraft's bed linen as described by Brobst, it appears evident that Lovecraft did not subscribe for any laundry service.[23] In fairness to Lovecraft, part of his reluctance to receive visitors at 10 Barnes may have been related to the fact that he had no curtain or screen to separate his bed (or couch as the plan identifies it) from the rest of his quarters.[24]

In the last analysis, apart from the considerations his landlady Florence Reynolds extended to him, did the women of 10 Barnes mean anything to Lovecraft? They were not quite the academic crowd that he encountered at The Arsdale (53–55 Waterman), across the back garden from his final home at 66 College Street.[25]

---

22. He liked to patronize the delicatessen counters at downtown groceries to purchase single-serving treats (e.g., chop suey, spaghetti and meatballs) to supplement his predominant diet of canned goods. He did buy small amounts of bread and cheese; according to Brobst, cheese was the only food he observed in HPL's room at 10 Barnes. HPL would also eat out from time to time. During the height of the visiting season during the summer of 1927, he often took his guests to Jacques Lunch at 9 Canal Street (Central Hotel building), an inexpensive diner to which Talman had introduced him in 1926.

23. Perhaps there was a sink with water tap in the basement where he could wash his socks and underclothing. He would have taken his suit coats and pants to a dry cleaner for cleaning as necessary. He may have taken his shirts to Delilah Townsend at 6 Olney Street for laundering.

24. HPL did try to paint a favorable portrait of 10 Barnes Street to his 1927 visitors. He wrote to Frank Belknap Long (6 July 1927): "In quiet and social tone nothing could be superior." In the same letter he said of the surroundings: "They [the rooms offered to the Long family] front on a quiet bye-street—good old Barnes—and reveal exquisite glimpses of fresh village scenery: an old, decaying mansion with wooded yard in picturesque wildness, a trim little yellow cottage, and a well-kept Georgian garden with white fence and urn-topped posts" (*SP* 389). The "old, decaying mansion" may be a reference to the Thomas Lloyd Halsey house at 140 Prospect Street.

25. The Arsdale was a boarding house, rather than a rooming house, and

One hopes, certainly, that Lovecraft and the women of 10 Barnes extended ordinary courtesies to one another. Perhaps they even had occasion to discuss that perennial subject the weather.

The women, with the exception of Reynolds, were mostly of New England descent, and perhaps they might have discussed common surnames in their ancestry with Lovecraft or his aunt Mrs. Clark. Both Reynolds, born in Australia of English-born parents, and Lovecraft had Devonshire ancestry, and one hopes they had occasion to discuss their common heritage. Lovecraft wrote to Frank Belknap Long on 6 July 1927:

> Miss Reynolds herself is from England[26]—solid, precise, fastidiously conscientious yeoman stock—a faded, gentle-mannered soul whose chief interest is Christian Science and whose quaint, innately well-bred ways cause her to be greatly liked and admitted to equal conversation by all her tenants. Only an infrequent dropped "'h" reveals her as born to less than armorial dignity—and I must say that even this plebeianism from one so amiable and instinctively refined is vastly more acceptable than the choicest Mayfair accent of that enigmatical ogress of yesterday—the tart and inimitable Mrs. Burns![27] I may add that Reynolds's sisters[28] have all married into good old Providence families, so that her position amongst gentlefolk is really on the firmest possible basis. (*SP* 389)

Mrs. Gamwell customarily took her midday meal there. HPL himself ate there on major holidays such as Thanksgiving.

26. In fact, Florence Reynolds had been born in Australia in 1861/62 of English-born parents. The family had returned to England by the time Florence's sister Rosa Reynolds was born in London in 1868/69.

27. Matilda Burns (1867–1955) (née King) was Lovecraft's landlady at 169 Clinton Street in Brooklyn in 1925–26.

28. In fact, Reynolds's sister Rosa Reynolds married her first cousin Edward Ken Reynolds, Jr., also born in England, and died in 1915. Reynolds's other sister Minnie A. Reynolds married Frederick Otis Clapp in 1918 and lived until 1966. Perhaps HPL had occasion to meet her during his residency at 10 Barnes Street in 1926–33.

One can never tell when a neighbor may have something significant to say about a person of interest—witness Clara Hess's comments to Winfield Townley Scott (*AAV* 165–67). Whether we might have learned much about Lovecraft from the women of 10 Barnes will forever remain unknown. I think they were all gone from 10 Barnes by the time Scott was researching Lovecraft in 1944–48. One might wish that Scott had at least traced Florence Reynolds, who survived to be nearly a century old.

Lillian D. Clark—the most important fellow tenant

Of course, the most important fellow tenant at 10 Barnes for Lovecraft was his aunt Lillian Clark. When he was in town, Lovecraft usually spent an hour each day reading to, and conversing with, Lillian. By 1928–32, Mrs. Clark was badly crippled by arthritis and often had to have assistance with her daily activities.[29] Lovecraft wrote to Donald Wandrei on 2 June 1927 of the "sedate Victorian retreat" where he and his aunt maintained their "modest & limited households" (*DW* 117–18). Because Lovecraft and his aunt each had only a single room at 10 Barnes Street, many of the family furnishings had to be stored. Some of these furnishings were finally retrieved from storage when Lovecraft and his younger aunt Mrs. Gamwell united their households in the relatively commodious second-floor suite at 66 College Street in 1933. Lovecraft still had opportunity to interact with "neighbors" at 66 College Street, since Mrs. Gamwell took her midday meals at The Arsdale boarding house across the

---

29. While she lived at 115 Waterman, Mrs. Clark still had periodic assistance from Delilah Townsend (1870?–1944), who had been a servant at 454 Angell Street. I do not know whether Mrs. Townsend continued to assist Mrs. Clark at 10 Barnes Street. Lovecraft wrote to James F. Morton on 30 July 1929: "My aunt is better than at the time of my former bulletin; but has to have the landlady help her dress, & can't get downstairs" (*JFM* 174).

back garden. There he met friends such as fellow cat fanciers Marian Bonner and Evelyn Staples. He had particular occasion to interact with these neighbors during Mrs. Gamwell's recovery from a mastectomy in 1936.

The aunts who had formerly been so protective of their nephew in fact became the protected ones during Lovecraft's residency with them at 10 Barnes Street (1926–33) and 66 College Street (1933–37). In many ways, their presence helped to make this final decade the capstone of Lovecraft's life. They were not only their nephew's charge to protect, but they also provided important services such as forwarding of mail during his frequent travels. The correspondence they preserved testifies to the loving care their nephew bestowed upon them. The people of 10 Barnes Street and of The Arsdale (53–55 Waterman Street) could probably have told us much about Lovecraft and his relationship with his aunts. As history transpired, only Marian Bonner (*AAV* 432–33) left any memoir of Lovecraft.[30] We can nevertheless try to imagine what some of the other neighbors might have had to say.

Acknowledgments

I am grateful to David E. Schultz for references to the letters of H. P. Lovecraft that mention Florence Reynolds, particularly those to Frank Belknap Long. I am grateful to the Rhode Island State Archives for help with vital records. However, I remain solely responsible for all opinions and errors.

---

30 A Providence visitor, Dorothy C. Walter, left a memoir, "Three Hours with H. P. Lovecraft" (*AAV* 367–78). It is one of only a handful of memoirs of HPL written by persons not affiliated with either the amateur journalism or the science fiction/horror fields.

OTHERS

OTHERS

Lovecraft and the Irish

> In the early historic period the peoples of Britain & Ireland were very much alike—& very much like the Gauls of the Continent. Ireland probably surpassed Britain in settled folkways & arts, but the condition was hardly what one would call an actual civilization. It probably paralleled the advanced barbarian-cultures of Gaul & Spain—which of course included settled town-dwelling & considerable artistic craftsmanship.
>
> —H. P. Lovecraft to Elizabeth Toldridge, mid-March 1930 (*ET* 140)

When it came to debates over history and culture, H. P. Lovecraft and Robert E. Howard were often on opposite sides. While Lovecraft admired the Romans and their empire, Howard forcefully took the side of their barbarian opponents. While Lovecraft considered the Teutons (i.e., Anglo-Saxons) the supreme race of humanity, Howard took the side of the Celts. Lovecraft wrote to his correspondent F. Lee Baldwin on 16 February 1935 that Howard was "so fond of his Celtic heritage that he has Gaelicised his middle name Ervin into EIARBIHN—as the fanatics of Ireland nowadays Gaelicise theirs" (*FLB* 128).

The Irish literary figure most admired by Lovecraft was undoubtedly Lord Dunsany (1878–1957), whom he saw lecture in Boston in 1919 (*IAP* 335–37). Lovecraft liked best Dunsany's early fantasies and was lukewarm toward his more nuanced later work. Lovecraft placed his discussion of Dunsany under the chapter heading "Modern Masters" in his treatise "Supernatural Horror in Literature" and remarked upon Dunsany's "Celtic wistfulness" (*SHL* 90). Although he divided his time between Dunsany Castle in County Meath and Dunstall Priory in Kent, Dunsany was wholly aligned with England in opposition to the Irish rebellion of 1916.

Earlier Irish literary figures in the domain of the spectral influenced Lovecraft less significantly. Irish-born Bram Stoker (1847–1912), who used Irish folklore to advantage in his work, moved to London upon his marriage in 1878. Joseph Sheridan Le Fanu (1814–1873), by way of contrast, spent his entire life in Dublin. Irish novelist Regina Maria Roche (*née* Dalton) (1764–1845) wrote many Gothic novels over her long career. Stoker (*SHL* 74), Le Fanu (*SHL* 48), and Roche (*SHL* 42) receive only brief mentions in "Supernatural Horror in Literature." However, even apart from literary influences, Ireland and persons of Irish descent played a significant role in Lovecraft's own life.

Lovecraft was not without a component of Irish blood: his five times great-grandfather Thomas Casey, who died about 1719 in Newport, R.I., was an emigrant from Ireland.[1] Thomas Casey's grandson John Casey (1723–1794)[2] of Kingstown, R.I., had for a brother the noted silversmith Samuel Casey, who was freed by his neighbors after being sentenced to death for counterfeiting in 1770 and was believed to have escaped to Canada. Lovecraft loved to regale his correspondents with the story of Samuel Casey.[3] Lovecraft's great-grandmother Roby Rathbun (1797–1848) was the daughter of John Rathbun (1750–1810) and John Casey's daughter Sarah Casey (1755–1813).

---

1. For the descent of immigrant Thomas Casey, see Thomas Lincoln Casey, "Early Families of Casey in Rhode Island," *Magazine of New England History* 3, No. 2 (April 1893), reprinted by Higginson Books.
2. John Casey's wife was long identified as Mercy Dyer, and through her HPL claimed descent from the Quaker martyr Mary (Barrett) Dyer (d. 1660). However, more recent research indicates that John Casey's wife was born Mercy Babcock and only assumed the surname Dyer after her mother took Richard Dyer as her second husband (Faig 24).
3. See for example HPL's letter to Wilfred B. Talman dated 19 March 1929 (*WBT* 108–10).

After Lovecraft's maternal grandfather Whipple V. Phillips (1833–1904)—the son of Jeremiah Phillips (1800–1848) and Roby Rathbun (1797–1848)—established himself at 454 Angell Street[4] on the East Side of Providence about 1881, Irishwomen customarily provided domestic service in his household. By the time the U.S. census was enumerated on 1 June 1900, the servant staff at 454 Angell Street had been reduced to one person—Maggie Corcoran, age twenty-three, single, born April 1877 in Ireland to Irish-born parents, who emigrated in 1895. In fact, the female servants in the household were customarily called "Maggie," regardless of their actual given names.

One of Rhode Island's most illustrious Irish-born citizens was a near neighbor of the Phillips family. Michael Joseph Banigan (more commonly known as Joseph Banigan in later life) was born 17 June 1839 in County Monaghan, Ireland, to Bernard (1799–1867) and Alice (1811[5]–1889) Banigan. After leaving Ireland, he and his family spent two years in Dundee, Scotland, before arriving in Providence in 1847. He received only one year of formal schooling and as early as 1856 was working at the New England Screw Company in Providence. In 1858, Bernard Banigan, laborer, resided at 8 Winslow Place in Providence.[6] His sons Michael, a jeweler, and Patrick, a tailor, boarded at the same address. The 1860 U.S. census captured Bernard Banigan

---

4. Originally numbered 194 Angell Street before the renumbering of the street in 1896. The house, demolished in 1960, stood on the northwest corner of Angell Street and Elmgrove Avenue.
5. Year of birth also given as 1813. She died in Providence on 15 October 1889.
6. Bernard continued to reside at 8 Winslow Place until his death on 21 December 1867. He was the son of Patrick and Alice (———) Banigan. His widow Alice continued to reside there until she removed to 50 Lester Street in 1874 and to 59 Dean Street in 1875. Her son Patrick continued to reside with her until he removed to 189 Angell Street in 1882. By 1903, he had removed to 244 Angell Street.

and his family in the Sixth Ward of Providence: Bernard, age 59, laborer, born Ireland; Alice [wife], age 45, born Ireland; Patrick [son],[7] age 23, tailor; Michael [son], age 20, born Ireland, jeweler; Margaret [daughter],[8] age 14, born Ireland; Mary A. [daughter],[9] age 4, born Rhode Island.

Joseph early became interested in the rubber industry. By the time the 1865 Rhode Island census was taken, Joseph Banigan had his own household in Smithfield: Joseph, age 25, born Scotland, rubber worker; Margaret [wife], age 21, born England, housekeeper; Mary A. [daughter], age 3, born Massachusetts; John J. [son], age 2, born Massachusetts; William B. [son], age 8 months, born Massachusetts. By 1866, Joseph and his partners Lyman A. and Simeon S. Cook had formed the Woonsocket Rubber Company, which grew into an enterprise of worldwide significance. Joseph lived in Woonsocket from 1867 to 1873, but by 1874 transferred his residence to the East Side of Providence, where he lived at 276 Angell Street in 1874–75 and at 214 Angell Street thereafter.

The Rhode Island 1875 census recorded the Banigan household at 276 Angell Street in Providence: Joseph [head], age 37, born Ireland, rubber manufacturer; Maria [wife], age 33, born Ireland, housekeeper; Mary A. [daughter], age 13, born Massachusetts, at Catholic school; John J. [son], age 11, born Massachusetts, at Catholic school; William B. [son], age 9, born

---

7. Patrick T. Banigan (1829–1909) spent most of his life working as a merchant tailor on Westminster Street in Providence. He married Catherine J. Brophy (1850–1923) and had sons Joseph Henry Banigan (1879–1970) and John Bernard Banigan (1880–1943). His son John was associated with him in business as a merchant tailor.
8. Margaret Theresa Banigan married James Finnigan on 17 January 1869 in Providence. She died 30 July 1875 in Providence.
9. Mary Ann Banigan was born in Providence on 5 February 1857. She died on 12 April 1939.

Cumberland, Rhode Island, at Catholic school; Alice [daughter], age 7, born Woonsocket, Rhode Island, at Catholic school. The 1880 U.S. census recorded the Banigan household at 214 Angell Street (renumbered as 468 Angell Street in 1896) in Providence: Joseph [head], age 40, owner (felt mill), born Ireland of Irish-born parents; Maria [wife], age 38, born Ireland of Irish-born parents; Mamie [daughter], age 18, born Connecticut, at school; Johnnie [son], age 16, born Connecticut, at school; Willie [son], age 15, born Rhode Island, at school; Allie [daughter], age 14, born Rhode Island, at school; Maggie [brother's daughter], age 15, born Scotland of Irish-born parents, at school. There were also a coachman and a domestic servant in the household.

Photograph of Joseph Banigan (1839–1898)

Joseph Banigan was eventually bought out by the United States Rubber Company. As a wealthy man, he was well known as a philanthropist. Pope Leo XIII created him a Knight of St. Gregory the Great. In 1897, he built a magnificent mansion at 510 Angell Street. However, he was not to occupy this home for long, as he died on 28 July 1898, age 59, of a gall bladder ailment—just nine days after Winfield Scott Lovecraft (1853–1898) died at Butler Hospital. The mansion at 510 Angell Street became the home of Joseph's daughter Mary A. Banigan (Mrs. William B. McElroy). It

Posthumous painting (1901) of Joseph Banigan owned by Brown University.

remained in the family until it was sold and torn down to facilitate the construction of Wayland Manor, which opened in 1927. Joseph Banigan and many of his close family members were originally entombed in the Banigan Chapel constructed on the grounds of St. Francis Cemetery in Pawtucket, R.I. The chapel was torn down when the expenses connected with its maintenance became too great, and the Banigans are now memorialized by medallions in the basement of the cemetery administration building.

In any case, Lovecraft was early admitted to the precincts of the Banigan home at 468 Angell Street, where he became the playmate of John Joseph and Mary Catherine Banigan's sons Joseph, John Joseph, and Richard Davis Banigan.

Joseph Banigan was born on 20 June 1888 in Blackstone [Millville], Massachusetts. He removed to Canada on 10 September 1911, and on 22 April 1912 (Toronto, Canada) he married Olive Juanita Loudon (b. 18 March 1886 Picton, Ontario), the daughter of John Samuel Loudon (banker) and Sarah Wilson. At the time of his marriage, Joseph Banigan stated his occupation as social worker. When he registered for the draft on 8 June 1917, he stated his legal residence as 176 Medway Street, Providence. However, he was residing in Toronto, Canada, with his wife and two children and employed as an architect by the firm of Banigan, Mathews & Johnson. He and his wife Olive arrived at La Guardia airport for a visit to Danielson, Connecticut, on 14 April 1944. In 1957, he was an advertising manager (with wife Marguerite) residing at 59 Chestnut Hill Parkway in York West, Ontario. He died in Canada in 1962. He and his first wife Olive had children (both born in Toronto): Elizabeth Banigan (b. 17 September 1913) and Joseph Banigan Jr. (b. 18 November 1915).

John Joseph Banigan [Jr.] was born on 10 July 1894 in Providence.

Grandson John J. Banigan,
1916 passport application.

He resided in his mother's household at 248 Waterman Street in Providence when the 1910 U.S. census was taken. When he registered for the draft on 5 June 1917, he was a single man residing at 176 Medway Street in Providence, employed as secretary by the M.B. Tool Company in Danielson, Connecticut. He married (1) Eleanor Criddle (1899–1926) and (2) Julia A. Carroll (1894–1968). The 1924 Providence directory listed him at 349 Lloyd Avenue; the 1930 and 1931 directories, at 21 Harwich Road. He died on 3 October 1967 and was survived by daughters Jean Eleanor Banigan Parker (1920–1973), Kathryn J. Vassett (1921–1995), and Phyllis L. Hawkins (1925–2013), and a son, John Joseph Banigan (1926–2007).

Richard Davis Banigan was born on 29 May 1890 in Blackstone [Millville], Massachusetts. He was a member of Brown University's class of 1916. He resided with his widowed mother at 468 Angell Street in Providence through at least 1916. When he registered for the draft on 5 June 1917, he was a single man residing at 176 Medway Street in Providence and was employed as treasurer by the M.B. Tool Company in Danielson, Connecticut. He served as a sergeant in Motor Truck Company 473 (Motor Supply Train 418). He departed Newport News, Virginia, on the *Aeolus* on 14 August 1918 and departed Brest, France, on the *Mt. Vernon* on 28 June 1919, arriving in Hoboken, New Jersey, on 5 July 1919. On 1 October 1919 (Manhattan, New York City, New York) he married Eileen E. O'Connor (1892–1949). The 1930 and 1940 U.S. censuses enumerated Richard and his wife Eileen in Killingly (Danielson), Connecticut. Richard was listed as a filling station manager in the 1930 census and as president of a petroleum company in the 1940 census. When he registered for the draft in World War II, he resided on Peckham Lane in Danielson, Connecticut, and was employed by the Danielson Oil Company, 7 Railroad Street, Danielson, Connecticut. He named his wife of the same residence address as the person who would always know his address. The 1942–47 Pawtucket, Rhode Island, directories listed him as president of the Atwood Crawford Company, residing at Danielson, Connecticut. In

1950, he married Mary G. L. —— in Lawrence, Massachusetts [60:1]. Richard Davis Banigan died on 12 May 1973.

Lovecraft told the story of his relationship with the Banigans in his letter to Robert E. Howard dated 4 October 1930:

> Another Celtic sidelight of my youth was still nearer home—my next-door neighbours and best playmates being three brothers whose relation to the Irish stream might be said to be your own, *reversed*—that is, they were descended from a line of Irishmen given to marrying Rhode Island Yankees, so that although they were about 80% Anglo-Saxon, they considered themselves heirs to the Irish tradition through descent in the male line and the possession of the name of Banigan. Their family always made a point to travel to Ireland as often as possible, and were great collectors of Celtic antiquities. Their grandfather [Joseph Banigan] had a veritable museum of prehistoric Irish artifacts—indeed, I wish I knew what has become of that collection now that the family has left Providence and the brothers are all dispersed! Observing my admiration for these reliques of unknown yesterdays, they gave me two little greenish figures which they held to be of vast antiquity, but concerning which they admitted very little was known. Some seem to be metallic, whilst others are clearly carved of some light sort of stone. Their average length is only an inch and a half, and they are all overlaid with a greenish patina. They are grotesque human figures, sometimes in conventional poses and with curious costume and headdresses. Their vast age is held to be indicated by the prodigious depth at which they are found in ancient peat-bogs. My two—one stone and one metal—have always appealed prodigiously to my imagination, and have formed high spots of my own assortment of curiosities. I think I will try to sketch them here, and see if your Celtic researches can throw any light on them. My friend Bernard Dwyer—pure Irish and 3 generations from the old sod—cannot explain them, but it is very possible that actual archaeologists have long known and described such things. Their outlines and features, unfortunately, are exceedingly chipped and worn down. But here they are—exact size and all. What are they? Were they ancient and buried and forgotten when Partholan first sighted Iërne's strange green shore? Did some Atlantean colonist, remem-

bering strange secrets from hoary Poseidonis, fashion them in the light of primordial dawns? It's a wonder that I haven't asked museum authorities about them long ago—but perhaps I dread being disillusioned and told that they are either fakes or something relatively recent! Sooner or later I shall probably get one or two tales out of them—for they certainly possess the most fascinating possibilities. (*MF* 74–75)[10]

In fact, Lovecraft's mother and aunts had known the Banigans, particularly Joseph's daughters Mary and Alice, years before Lovecraft was born.[11] They were next-door neighbors—the Phillipses at 454 Angell Street and the Banigans just to the east across Elmgrove Avenue at 468 Angell Street (addresses reflect 1896 renumbering). Both Banigan daughters attended Elmhurst Academy on Smith Street—Mary in 1874–80 and Alice in 1878–84 (Faig 79). The poet-to-be Louise Imogen Guiney (1861–1920) attended Elmhurst Academy in 1873–79 and visited frequently thereafter. She probably met Sarah Susan Phillips on one of her visits to the Banigan household at 468 Angell Street.

In the succeeding years, the Banigan grandsons dispersed, and Lovecraft lost track of them. (He knew that Richard had served in the armed forces in World War I.[12]) He wrote to Alfred Galpin of his acquaintance with the various Banigan grandsons:

---

10. The two figures were traced too faintly in the Arkham House Transcripts to be reproduced in *MF*. HPL's original letters to Howard were lost.
11. "My mother and aunts knew the daughters of Joseph Banigan from childhood, and found them really worthy in every respect" (HPL to the Gallomo, 30 September 1919; *ML* 66).
12. See his letter to Rheinhart Kleiner dated 5 June 1918 (*RK* 116). HPL described the visit of Cardinal Mercier in his letter to Kleiner dated 27 September 1919 (*RK* 142). One of his aunts (most likely Annie E. P. Gamwell) attended the honorary degree conferral at Brown and the reception at the home of Mrs. William B. McElroy; HPL himself did not.

Grandson Robert B. McElroy, 1909 passport application

Granddaughter Margaret Tyree Banigan (1894–1988).

> The grandchildren were my earliest playmates, though it made me shudder in my British soul to know "Dicky Banigan," "Robert McElroy,"[13] "Edmund Sullivan,"[14] etc. However, there is some consolation in the fact that Dick, Joe, and John Banigan, who lived nearest me (next house to #454 Angell) were only a quarter Irish. Their father had followed the example of his own father and married into an old American family.[15] Still, I wished they could have been solidly Saxon! (*ML* 66–67)

The home of Mrs. William B. McElroy at 510 Angell Street was the focus of attention in late September 1919 when it served as the headquarters for Cardinal Mercier, who was in town to receive an honorary degree from Brown University. Lovecraft described the occasion in his letter to the Gallomo dated 30 September 1919:

---

13. Robert Bernard McElroy (1886–1953), son of William B. McElroy (1857–1914) and Mary A. Banigan (1861–1923).
14. Edmund James Gibbons Sullivan (1893–1936), son of Dr. James Edward Sullivan (1849–1920) and Alice Margaret Banigan (1866–1909).
15. In fact, John J. Banigan's wife Mary Catherine Davis was the daughter of Irish-born parents.

This neighbourhood is quite honoured today, His Eminence Cardinal Mercier of Belgium being entertained in the McElroy mansion only four houses west of Castle Theobald [598 Angell Street] on Angell St. My aunt is now there at the reception being given in his honour. The extensive grounds are all fenced off to deter curious crowds, and awnings cover the long drives whereby the mansion is reached from the street. . . . The McElroy house is the only local stronghold of Hibernianism. It was built by the late Joseph Banigan, sometimes called "The Rubber King," who was Mrs. McElroy's father. He was a poor Irish peasant who succeeded in business and lived to found a family whose innate good qualities gave them a definite social standing hereabout. He married an American lady, and gave his children the best education obtainable, so that they are rather influential in the community. . . . The Banigan or McElroy Mansion, where Mercier is now receiving the homage of local society, is one of the "show places" of the neighbourhood, and excited Klei's vast admiration when he was here. It is a Gothic manor house of brick and stone, such as its peasant builder may have seen and admired at a distance in his boyhood in Ould Oireland. The grounds are extensive and beautifully kept, with hedges, trees, and stables of pleasing architecture. It lies almost exactly half way betwixt the house where I was born [454 Angell Street] and that which I inhabit [598 Angell Street]. Altogether, I fancy the Irish have helped rather than harmed the locality! (*ML* 66–67)

The domestic servants at **454 Angell Street** were not the only working-class Irish Lovecraft met early in his life. In April 1914, Edward F. Daas recruited him for the United Amateur Press Association, and by November of the same year Edward H. Cole introduced him to the newly formed Providence Amateur Press Club,[16] whose leaders were Victor L. Basinet (1889–1956), of French-Canadian ancestry, and John T. Dunn (1889–1983), of

---

16. For the Providence Amateur Press Club, see Kenneth W. Faig, Jr., *The Providence Amateur Press Club: 1914–1916* (Glenview, IL: Moshassuck Press, 2008). An enhanced electronic edition of this text was later published by David Haden.

Irish ancestry. Of the club members, Peter Joseph McManus (1888–1971) had actually been born in Ireland. Other club members with probable Irish ancestry included Frederick Aloysius Byland (1894–1967), Edmund Leo Shehan (1891–1972), and William Aloysius Henry (1884–1950). The club was originally formed primarily from evening high school students in Providence. Lovecraft was unlike most of the other club members in that he was not holding down a "day job"—a circumstance that was the origin of some resentment among the other members.

Banigan Rubber Co., Woonsocket RI.

The stiff, formal Lovecraft inevitably generated some laughter as well, and Sarah "Sadie" Henry (1879–1957), the elder sister of member William A. Henry, even called the Lovecraft residence to ask for a date. Club member John T. Dunn recalled that Lovecraft told Miss Henry that he would have to ask his mother for permission.[17] After producing two issues of the *Providence Amateur* the club had largely lapsed into inactivity by 1916. Dunn, who worked as a plumber, ardently supported the Irish rebels against British rule in 1916. Along with his refusal to register for the draft—for which he served two years in prison—Dunn's support of the Irish rebels spelled the end of his relationship with Love-

---

17. Dunn's recollections of this incident can be found in L. Sprague de Camp, "Young Man Lovecraft" (*AAV* 172–74).

craft.[18] After his release from prison, Dunn eventually entered a Maryland seminary and was ordained a Catholic priest in 1930. He served most of his long career as a hospital chaplain in Ohio.

Lovecraft's connection with the amateur journalism hobby persisted after the failure of the Providence Amateur Press Club. He served as president of the United Amateur Press Association in 1917–18 and as interim president of the National Amateur Press Association in 1922–23. He was later a member of the National's Bureau of Critics in 1931–35, serving as chairman in 1933–35. He had served one term as a National Executive Judge in 1923–24, but served another term—a taxing one on account of disputes dividing the association—in 1935–36. He more or less refrained from most amateur activity—other than through the mails—after his return to Providence from New York City in 1926 until his attendance at the National's Boston convention in 1930. The years 1914–23 were undoubtedly his busiest as an amateur journalist. In 1924–25 Lovecraft and his wife presided over the sad decline of the so-called Hoffman-Daas faction of the United, which expired a year later in 1926.

Lovecraft's Hub Club visits in 1919–23 probably represented the peak of his social activity in the hobby. He attended Hub Club meetings in Boston with some regularity during this period. At the meeting held to celebrate St. Patrick's Day on 10 March 1921 (one week in advance of the actual holiday), he read his Irish-set story "The Moon-Bog" and was applauded by his fellow club members.[19] Significantly, Lovecraft set his story in County Meath, which is also home to Dunsany Castle. The protagonist Denys Barry plans to drain the peat-bog adjoining his recently acquired

---

18. HPL's surviving letters to John T. Dunn, edited by S. T. Joshi, David E. Schultz and John H. Stanley, were published in *Books at Brown* 38–39 (1991–92): 157–223; also in *AG*.

19. For HPL's reading of "The Moon-Bog," see *IAP* 314–15 and 384–85.

ancestral residence. While the amulets or figurines the Banigans had given him were reportedly recovered deep below peat-bogs, there is no direct reference to amulets or figurines in "The Moon-Bog." The story did not see publication until June 1926 in *Weird Tales*. The Hub Club included a fair share of persons of Irish descent, of whom the most devoted Hibernophile was probably J[oseph] Bernard Lynch (1879–1952), born in Boston of Irish-born parents and composer of "On a Starry Irish Night" (1936). Other club members teased member Laura Anna "Laurie" Sawyer (*née* Moody) (b. 1865) over her refusal to enter a Protestant church.

Banigan Mortuary Chapel, St. Francis Cemetery, Pawtucket RI. Demolished.

The last of the Banigan grandsons died in 1973, and Joseph Banigan's mansion at 510 Angell Street in Providence fell to the wrecker's ball to allow the construction of Wayland Manor, opened in 1927. The houses at 9 Orchard Avenue (home of Joseph Banigan before the completion of 510 Angell Street) and 254 Wayland Avenue (home of his daughter Alice Margaret Banigan and her husband Dr. James Edward Sullivan) remain as reminders of the Banigan clan. Lovecraft's own boyhood home at

454 Angell Street was demolished in 1960, but his later residences at 598 Angell Street, 10 Barnes Street, and 66 College Street (moved to 65 Prospect Street) remain. The site of the Banigan home at 468 Angell Street is now occupied by a Starbucks.

Lovecraft's equivocating over the Anglo-Saxon component of the Banigan's heritage is difficult to read in more tolerant times. That he did admire the Banigans' allegiance to the best of their Irish cultural traditions is to his credit. Lovecraft was not an easy fit with the working-class majority of the Providence Amateur Press Club and he had a special conflict with John T. Dunn, who supported the 1916 Irish rebels and resisted the draft. By the time of his association with the Hub Club in 1919–23, he could more readily navigate social, cultural, and economic differences. That the club reacted with approval to the reading of his only Irish-set story "The Moon-Bog" is heartening. All told, Lovecraft's favorable opinion of ancient Irish culture, as expressed in his letter to Elizabeth Toldridge quoted above, redounds to his credit. A master of the supernatural could hardly deny all merit to a culture which had produced legends like the fairy folk and the banshee.

Works Cited

Bayles, Richard M. *History of Providence County, Rhode Island.* New York: W. W. Preston & Co., 1891. 2 vols.

Faig, Kenneth W., Jr. *The Unknown Lovecraft.* New York: Hippocampus Press, 2009.

Lovecraft, H. P. *The Annotated Supernatural Horror in Literature.* Ed. S. T. Joshi. 2nd ed. New York: Hippocampus Press, 2012. [Abbreviated in the text as *SHL*.]

Molloy, Scott. *Irish Titan, Irish Toilers: Joseph Banigan and Nineteenth-Century New England Labor.* Durham, NH: University of New Hampshire Press, 2008.

Edwin Baird: The Man Who Discovered Lovecraft

For David Goudsward

Introduction

Calling Edwin McClearon Baird, the first editor of *Weird Tales* in 1923–24, the man who discovered Lovecraft might be perceived by some readers as an exaggeration. That Baird accepted *en bloc* five stories originally submitted as single-spaced typescripts by Lovecraft in 1923, on the condition that the author resubmit them in double-spaced format,[1] was probably the critical factor in opening for the author the venue that served as his principal market during the rest of his lifetime. However, others might say that Edward F. Daas (1879–1962), who recruited

---
1. For an account of this episode, *IAP* 451–53.

Lovecraft for the United Amateur Press Association (Hoffman-Daas faction) after the author's letter controversy in *Argosy* magazine in 1913–14, was really the man who discovered Lovecraft. Others might contend that W. Paul Cook (1880–1948), who published Lovecraft's first weird fiction in his amateur magazines, was really the man who discovered Lovecraft. Others might award the honor to August Derleth (1909–1971), Lovecraft's young correspondent who single-handedly secured the preservation of the author's works in hardcover. Others might cite S. T. Joshi, who has edited critical editions of all Lovecraft's works (some in collaboration with David E. Schultz) and written the standard biography of Lovecraft and bibliography of his works. All these potential contenders notwithstanding, it is surely true that Baird played a critical role in the development of Lovecraft's career as a professional writer.

Despite all the attention that has been devoted to Lovecraft, Baird has remained relatively obscure. The few facts known of him can be narrated relatively concisely.

Family Background

Edwin McClearon Baird was born in Chattanooga, Tennessee, on 28 June 1886, the son of William Campbell Baird (1850–1922) and his wife Mary (Kaylor) Baird (1855–1899). His mother's family is difficult to trace back farther than her father Daniel Kaylor (1825/26–1898), who married Canadian-born Sarah McBride and emigrated from New York to Tennessee. Baird's father William Campbell Baird was the son of TN-born James Perry Baird (1822–1908) and his wife Parmelia R. (——) Baird (1831/32–1880+). James Perry Baird was in turn the son of NC-born Edwin M. Baird (1797–1883) and his TN-born wife Jane (Clampitt) Baird (1802–1878), who married on 20 July 1820. Baird was apparently named for his great-grandfather. Edwin eventually established his homestead at Totty's Bend in Hickman County TN.

An Ancestry family tree provides some further ancestors for Baird's great-grandfather. He was the son of Samuel McClearon Baird (1761–1807) and his wife Dorcas Campbell (1770–1876). Samuel and his family emigrated from Buncombe County NC to TN. Samuel was in turn the son of John Baird II (1737–1808) and his wife Hannah McCleary (1741–1804). John was born in Chambersburg, Franklin County PA and died in Clover, York County SC. Perhaps Edwin Baird's middle name derived from his great-great-great-grandmother Hannah McCleary. John Baird II was in turn the son of John Baird (1709–1784) and his wife Frances Scott (1713–1789). The first John Baird was born in Hamilton, Franklin County PA and died in Salisbury, Mecklenburg County NC. Further than this the Ancestry family tree does not extend.

A FamilySearch tree extends Baird's paternal ancestry back several more generations: William Baird (b. 1677) of Franklin County PA and John Baird (b. 1640, Blandford, Hampden County MA).[2] The Baird or Beard family derived ultimately from Scotland. Savage's *A Genealogical Dictionary of the First Settlers of New England* lists a number of early New England settlers under the Beard surname. For example, shoemaker Thomas Beard arrived in Salem on the *Mayflower* in 1629.

Early Life through Marriage

Baird's elder brother William Campbell Baird, Jr. was born in St. Louis in April 1884, but the family had returned to Chattanooga

---

2. However, according to Wikipedia, Blandford, in Hampden County MA, was first settled in 1735, primarily by Scots-Irish settlers. The town was not incorporated until 1741. So a 17th-century Baird born in Blandford stretches credibility.

in time for Edwin's birth in June 1886. They later lived in Tullahoma, Coffee County TN, where Baird's father probably farmed. Baird and his younger brothers Warren Edgarton Baird and Howard Whitfield Baird were baptized at St. Barnabas Episcopal Church in Tullahoma on Christmas Day 1893. Baird's father was baptized in the same church on 30 April 1895, his sister Mary Williams Baird and his nephew Walter Whitfield Hickerson on 26 January 1896. Baird's mother Mary (Kaylor) Baird died in 1899 and was buried in Chattanooga Confederate Cemetery.

The 1900 U.S. census found the widowed William C. Baird, his children, and his widowed father James Perry Baird in Nashville. William C. Baird was then working as a police inspector. Sons William C. Jr., Edwin, and Warren were all in school. By 1910, William C. Baird had removed to Chicago, where he worked as a plumbing salesman. William's son Edwin and William's younger brother James Perry Baird, Jr. (1868–1913) were also in William's household in that year. The occupation of twenty-three-year-old Edwin Baird was recorded as "magazines drugs." Whether this meant that he operated a store where these commodities were sold or that he was an agent for these commodities remains undetermined.

On 20 November 1911, Baird married Mildred (Connelly) Ward (1886–1948) of Chicago.[3] The 1930 U.S. census records that she was then age forty, having been born in WI of NY-born

---

3. This statement derives from Baird's sketches in the 1926 and 1936 editions of *Who's Who in Chicago*. I have not been able to find the marriage in Cook County IL marriage records; perhaps the couple was married elsewhere, despite Mildred's then residence in Chicago. Mildred's 1948 death record gives her father's surname as Connelly. (The death certificate does not provide first names for Mildred's parents, but does state that her parents were born in New York State, her father in New York City.) Perhaps Ward was her surname from a prior marriage. The author has failed to identify parents for Wisconsin-born Mildred (Connelly) Ward or to find her in the 1900 or 1910 U.S. censuses.

parents.[4] When he registered for the draft on 12 September 1918, Baird was working for the Liberty Loan Commission of the Federal Reserve at 105 W. Monroe Street in Chicago. He misstated his date of birth by one year as 28 June 1885, and provided the name of his wife as Mildred Connoly [*sic*] Baird. He was then living at 1721 Boomer Place in Evanston IL. In fact, the Evanston city directories for 1914, 1920, and 1922 all recorded Baird and his wife at this address. The 1915 Chicago city directory recorded Edwin Baird as a manager at 3233 N. Clark St., residing in Evanston.

Editorial and Literary Career

Baird published a novel, *The City of Purple Dreams*, set in Chicago, with F. G. Browne & Co. of Chicago in 1913.[5] The novel is dedicated to "Mildred, Jessie and Mary," Baird's wife, elder half-sister, and younger sister, respectively. A second novel, *The Heart of Virginia Keep*, followed from Ward, Lock & Co. of London in 1918.[6] A third novel, *Fay*, followed from E. J. Clode of New York in 1923. A final novel, *Will o' the Wisp*, was serialized in *Flapper's Experience* magazine in 1925–26. These four

---

4. Mildred understated her age by three years in the 1930 U.S. census, as did her husband. In the 1940 U.S. census, Edwin Baird stated his age correctly as 53 years while his wife Mildred understated her age by three years as 50 years.

5. The New York Public Library copy of the novel can be read online without charge at Hathi Trust Digital Library: babel.hathitrust.org/cgi/pt?id=nyp.33433074801220;view=1up;seq=7. There is also a paper reprint by Scholar Select Editions. Baird did not allow his literary properties to lie fallow. *The City of Purple Dreams* was serialized in the *Carbondale* [IL] *Daily Free Press* in 1919–20. Baird's first novel was also adapted twice for the screen, the first time in 1918.

6. *The Heart of Virginia Keep* was first published in *Argosy* for April 1915. It was the first novel by Baird to be adapted for the screen, in 1916. It was also serialized in the *Bloomington* [IL] *Pantagraph* (and probably other newspapers) in 1921.

novels, together with the treatise *How to Write Detective Stories* (1932), were listed in Baird's biographical sketch in the 1936 edition of *Who's Who in Chicago*.[7] A detective novelette by Baird entitled *Signed "Z,"* comprising about fifty pages, was edited as an e-book for Prairie Farm Press by Kateri Maloney in 2015.

The City of Purple Dreams—named for its Chicago setting—is notable as the first of Baird's four published novels. Baird, his father, his uncle, and several siblings had come to the great Midwestern metropolis in the first decade of the twentieth century. Baird's first novel reflects the powerful impression Chicago—where he was to spend the rest of his life—made on him. He was recently married and living with his wife in Evanston when the novel was published. Baird worked various jobs before beginning his editorial career in 1923, but his primary employment during his early years in Chicago was as a newspaper reporter. His chief focus as a reporter was crime and criminals, but his first novel makes it evident that he became intimately familiar with the city's business and social affairs as well.

Baird's protagonist, Hugh Daniel Fitzrandolph, of an old Maryland family, is introduced to readers while living the hobo life. In a penniless state, he encounters a large Socialist demonstration and follows it to Smulski's Hall on the West Side. Outside he encounters the dark-haired radical Esther Strom, who induces him to try his hand at addressing the crowd inside the hall. With no special knowledge, Fitzrandolph's eloquence nevertheless carries the day, and he makes a resolution to try to make something greater of his life. He encounters Kathleen Otis, the daughter of Board of Trade magnate Symington Otis, but be-

---

7. Another publication, *The Colossus of the Press: A Brief Journey through the World's Greatest Printing Plant* (Chicago: W. F. Hall Printing Co., 1926?) is listed on Worldcat, as well as *Vagabonden* (translated by M. K. Nørgaard), published in Denmark, in 1920. The last is a translation of *The City of Purple Dreams*.

comes a fugitive after threatening Symington. Esther provides refuge for a while, but a jealous boyfriend eventually drives Fitzrandolph away. Deprived of the company of either Kathleen or Esther, Fitzrandolph resolves to make his mark in the business sphere. After working for a couple of shysters, Fitzrandolph uses winnings at poker to begin a career trading in futures contracts in the wheat pit at the Board of Trade, where the elder Otis reigns supreme. Eventually, Fitzrandolph manages to corner the market in wheat futures and drives his mortal enemy, the elder Otis, to ruin. Otis rejects Fitzrandolph's bid for his daughter's hand and is left with only a small remnant of his once vast fortune.

Meanwhile, Esther Strom returns from Russia and chides Fitzrandolph for his neglect. When she announces her intention to go to Washington to assassinate the president, Fitzrandolph reports her to the Secret Service, and when apprehended at the railroad terminal in Washington, Esther commits suicide with prussic acid. The chastened Fitzrandolph decides to make an independent bid for the Chicago mayoralty, but loses to the dominant Democratic candidate, despite the expenditure of a considerable portion of his fortune. Symington Otis goes into exile in Europe and dies on the boat headed back to America. His wife and his daughter have to abandon their once extravagant lifestyle and live in such places as Oconomowoc, Wisconsin—the birthplace of Baird's own wife Mildred—and Rhode Island. After his defeat in a mayoral election, Fitzrandolph decides to devote the remainder of his life to philanthropy by establishing residences for the deserving poor named in honor of Esther Strom in major cities across the United States. Finally, Fitzrandolph wins back the affections of Kathleen and resolves to keep part of his fortune for their life together.

The novel's vivid depiction of Chicago's neighborhoods and business and social institutions helps to save *The City of Purple*

Dreams from classification as a mere page-turner. It is clear that the author walked the same streets in which he depicts the lives of his characters. He himself lived in an apartment on the same Lake Shore Drive where Symington Otis had his mansion. Baird met and courted his own wife Mildred in the same city where his protagonist Fitzrandolph met Esther Strom and Kathleen Otis. Altogether, *The City of Purple Dreams* was an auspicious beginning for Baird as a novelist. However, the book did not rise to become a bestseller, and thus it probably became clear that Baird was destined to continue to earn his livelihood as a newspaper reporter.

The Heart of Virginia Keep followed in *Argosy* in 1915 and was published in book form in England by Ward, Lock in 1918. The main action of *Virginia Keep* follows the fortunes of St. Louis banker Alfred Keep, who is tried and convicted for manslaughter in the killing of two men in a tavern altercation twenty-five years earlier. Keep, just elected president of a St. Louis bank, disappears from his St. Louis home on the evening of his election, after a youth leaves a crudely written message for him. Keep is apprehended in Canada, tried, and convicted. His daughter Virginia stands by her father and breaks her engagement to prosecutor Grant Mattock when he insists upon fulfilling his duty in prosecuting her father.

By way of contrast, Keep's second wife Priscilla, of a genteel Lexington, Kentucky, family, departs and divorces her husband. Virginia goes so far as to offer monetary inducements to the daughter of the slain tavern proprietor to drop the prosecution, which only benefits the prosecution when her father comes to trial. Meanwhile, she finds an ally in the eccentric Arnold Dempster Trude, masquerading as a humble reporter at the newspaper he actually owns. When Virginia has to sell the family home, Trude obtains employment for her as a society columnist at his newspaper at a salary of $100 per week, despite her lack of experience. Finally, it develops that a gang of three, including a reprobate brother McAllister Keep, had been blackmailing Alfred Keep over the long-ago slayings. Virginia actually ventures into the lair of the blackmailers, disguised as a boy, and receives the confession of McAllister Keep on his deathbed. Fleeing from the other blackmailers, she bumps into Trude, who is seeking a messenger boy to convey to her the just-received news that her father has been paroled.

The plot of *Virginia Keep* could surely have benefitted from some further development and clarification. Perhaps the most notable aspect of the novel is its portrayal of romantic love. For the time, some fairly intense scenes of lovemaking between Virginia and Trude are depicted, especially kissing in a hammock in the backyard. The allure of the somewhat boyish Virginia, with her full head of lush, black hair offset by her pale complexion, and her daring V-neck costumes, is vividly described by the author. Whether she allows more than kisses to her lover Trude is left to the reader's imagination—probably not, given the mores of the time. Feminists will probably approve of the novel's frank depiction of a woman's sexual passion.

Just before her perilous encounter with her father's blackmailers, Virginia and Trude quarrel over his impersonation of a humble reporter. Feminists will doubtless be less comfortable with her final plea to her lover for forgiveness after their collision in the street. The novel ends with the sentence: "He drew her closer"—so the reader must imagine the subsequent lives of Virginia and Arnold and of Virginia's father. If there is any consistent note in *Virginia Keep,* apart from the author's usual predilection for melodrama, it is Baird's perception of the paramount value of romantic love in human affairs. His admiration of the beautiful heroine Virginia Keep is apparent, as is his detestation of the obese, effeminate debauchee Roy Fraser, who also seeks the hand of the heroine. Baird's depiction of Lizbeth, Virginia's attendant since her Kentucky days, is one of unquestioning loyalty and affection for her mistress, not without the tempering of wisdom, but may still prove unsatisfactory for modern readers seeking to detect any tincture of racism in the words of an admittedly Southern writer.

The sale of *Virginia Keep* for film adaptation (first sold in 1916) probably encouraged Baird to continue to devote some of his time to novel-writing. His third novel to attain hardcovers, *Fay*, appeared in a 316-page edition from Edward J. Clode in New York City in 1923. The novel is dedicated "To M.," doubtless indicating Baird's wife Mildred. The novel begins with Arlo Bowen returning to his hometown of Tallahatchee, Tennessee (probably modeled on Baird's own hometown of Chattanooga), after a long absence. He is greeted by mother and father, sister Edith, brother Nevil, and Fay, a red-haired, rather homely foster child given a home by his parents. Arlo returns at the height of the small-town summer season and is soon involved in multiple flirtations.

After Arlo saves Jean Sturgis from a cad whom he had encountered during his time as a journalist, the two become engaged. But Jean resists any public announcement of their engagement, in the belief that one or both may become enamored of someone else. Her prophecy proves accurate as respects herself. In the meantime, Arlo finds his feelings for his foster sister Fay deepening. She has a beautiful voice and is often called upon to perform at local social occasions. One acquaintance with experience of professional singing maintains that Fay might become a star with the proper training. Eventually, Arlo quarrels with his alcoholic father and returns to Chicago, where he resumes his work as a journalist. However, his mother falls ill and dies and Arlo returns to Tallahatchee.

Arlo abandons his literary ambitions to work in his father's failing grocery business, but soon finds more congenial employment at the local newspaper owned by Col. Littlefield. After Fay rejects a younger suitor, she and Arlo agree to become engaged. Col. Littlefield dies sitting in his study when he reads of the state's adoption of Prohibition. It turns out that the colonel has left $25,000 to Fay to develop her musical talents. Fay agrees to go to Paris to study music, and she ultimately rises to the height of the musical profession as an opera star. Arlo witnesses the failed marriage of his sister Edith to an undesirable spouse, and at the same time rejects an adulterous gambit from the erstwhile Jean Sturgis. Fay's operatic success leaves her with virtually no time to devote to her fiancé Arlo, and he begins to sink into the same alcohol-fueled despondency that bedeviled his father. Learning of his situation, Fay decides to abandon her career to return to Tallahatchee to make common household with Arlo.

Fay is filled with plans gone awry and depictions of human faithlessness. Col. Littlefield's son at first promises his father's property on Peachtree Street to provide space for a settlement house envisioned by Arlo and Fay, but withdraws his promise when Fay rejects his own suit for her hand. The fluctuating affections of the members of the young social set in Tallahatchee are also vividly depicted. Arlo is not immune to the charms of the opposite sex, but he is ultimately rewarded by Fay's faithfulness. *Fay* has less *Sturm und Drang* than *The City of Purple Dreams* and *The Heart of Virginia Keep*, but nevertheless presents a lively story in a somewhat quieter setting than Chicago or St. Louis. Baird's love for the physical beauty and the gracious living of his native South are apparent from his narration. *Fay* was the last of Baird's novel-length works to attain book publication.[8] While of very

---

8. In his column "Books and Bookmen" in the *Chicago Tribune* for 18 May 1924, Gene Mackey noted *Fay* among four recent books by Chicago authors. Mackey called Baird's work "a novel of the southern mountains."

modest stature as a work of literature, it boasts both a beautiful setting and a lively narration of the foibles of romantic affection. Reading the novel makes one wish that he knew more of the author's own courtship of his wife Mildred.

Baird's final known novel-length work, *Will o' the Wisp,* was serialized in *Flapper's Experience* in 1925–26. An advertisement announcing the appearance of the novel in the magazine described it thus:

> The scene is laid in Chicago—the time is now—a horrid Mephistophelian countenance with pointed ears, green eyes, and saturnine grimace peers into the window of a millionaire's limousine—and from then on the most startling tale since *Dr. Jekyll and Mr. Hyde* takes hold of the imagination and grips the soul until the reader feels that he too is in the clutches of this insatiable force.[9]

There is no known book publication for *Will o' the Wisp*. Perhaps Baird's editorial duties in 1923–35 prohibited his devoting more time to novel-writing. Baird was generally aggressive in seeking second publication for his novels: both *The City of Purple Dreams* (1913) and *The Heart of Virginia Keep* (1918) appeared in newspaper serialization following book publication. Both of these novels were also adapted for motion pictures.[10] Perhaps his failure to sell *Will o' the Wisp* for book publication or newspaper serialization discouraged the author from writing more novels. Baird was a busy creator of shorter fiction beginning as early as 1910; however, his short fiction also trails off after 1925. The

---

In R.H.L.'s [Richard Henry Little] column "A Line o' Type or Two" in the same newspaper for 8 February 1924, correspondent P.A.H. praised *Fay* and stated it was well worth its $2 price. The column "A Line o' Type or Two" was originally written by Bert Leston Taylor (1864–1921). Gyan Books of Delhi, India, has issued an ebook reprint of *Fay*.
9. I am indebted to David Goudsward for this information.
10. I am not aware of newspaper serializations or film adaptations of Baird's later novel *Fay* (1923).

appendix lists known appearances of Baird's fiction in periodicals. Perhaps the shift of *Real Detective* to all nonfiction content in 1931 also motivated its editor to shift his own writing to factual crime and detection articles.

In 1923, J. C. Henneberger retained Baird as the first editor of *Weird Tales*. The publication of the work of H. P. Lovecraft was doubtless the hallmark of Baird's career at the magazine. By no later than August 1924, Farnsworth Wright (1888–1940) had replaced Baird as editor. However, Baird remained as editor and vice president of *Real Detective Tales*[11] through 1933, when he assumed the position of editor and publisher of *Real America* magazine,[12] owned by Real America, Inc.[13] Baird's sketch in the 1926 and 1936 editions of *Who's Who in Chicago* indicated that he had contributed to newspapers and magazines since 1906 and had been a feature writer for the *Chicago Daily Journal* and the

---

11. A gallery of covers of *Real Detective Tales* from 1922 to 1934 can be found at: www.philsp.com/mags/real_detective_tales.html. The magazine commenced publication as *Detective Tales* in September 1922, but the title changed to *Real Detective Tales & Mystery Stories* as of June 1924. A final title change to *Real Detective* occurred in May 1931, when the magazine's content changed to primarily nonfiction. The December 1934 number is the final one pictured in the gallery; the cessation date for the periodical is not certain.

12. The Wisconsin Historical Society holds four numbers of *Real America* and lists the full run of the magazine as extending from Vol. 1, No. 1 (February 1933) through Vol. 6, No. 6 (March 1936). It was a monthly magazine and each volume apparently contained six monthly numbers. I am indebted to David Goudsward for this information. The December 1933 number of *Real America* ("The Outspoken Magazine") shows Mount Morris IL as the place of domicile of Real America, Inc. The executive and editorial offices were located at 1050 N. LaSalle St. in Chicago. Officers included J. M. Lansinger, president; Edwin Baird, vice-president; Velma S. May, secretary; and Hugh Stafford, circulation manager. Harley L. Ward of 360 N. Michigan Ave. in Chicago was advertising manager.

13. Baird corresponded with many literary and public figures as part of his editorial duties. A file of his correspondence with Theodore Dreiser forms folder 5018 of the Theodore Dreiser Papers at the Van Pelt Library of the University of Pennsylvania in Philadelphia.

Chicago Evening American. Both sketches identified his religion as Episcopalian. In both years he resided at 1120 Lake Shore Drive in Chicago. His offices were at 1050 N. LaSalle Street in 1926 and at 666 Lake Shore Drive in 1936. By 1940, he was residing at 1214–1220 N. State Street.

The letters of Chinese-American journalist Flora Belle Jan (1906–1950) provide an anecdote (presumably dating from the mid- to late-twenties) concerning the acceptance of one of Miss Jan's stories by Edwin Baird at *Real Detective Tales:*

> I had gone to the country house of Zelda Ferguson in Reynolds, Indiana, for a few days, and during my last two days there, I felt uncomfortable. I came home and spent a miserable two weeks trying to get over it. The minute that I felt I was getting over it I hurried to the school and made the final copy of the suicide story. Then I went to see Harry Stephen Keeler, the mystery novelist. He read it and liked it, said it sounded authentic, and should go big with Edwin Baird, the editor of *Real Detective*. On the strength of his encouragement, I retyped it and took it down to Mr. Baird. He talked with me a few minutes, said he'd take it home to read. In the meantime we walked out of the office. He was meeting his wife at a movie and asked me to go along. I did. She was the oldest, dowdiest thing you ever saw! She looked like his mother instead of his wife. Well, he read it that night and called me up the next morning and said it was all right and asked for more pictures. I went down the next day and had some pictures taken, to be used with the article, and directed the photographer to go to the Evans home and the cemetery. He got those pictures all right, so that helps my story. Two days after Mr. Baird gave me a check for $75. That makes 1½ cents a word, the total being 5000. I am going to see him tomorrow to see the pictures. He made some extra prints for me, he said, and would drive me home afterwards.[14]

The rather uncomplimentary portrait of Mildred Baird (then probably in her early forties) probably reflects a young woman's

---

14. Fleur Yan and Saralyn Daly, eds., *Unbound Spirits: Letters of Flora Belle Jan* (Urbana: University of Illinois Press, 2009), 88–89.

point of view. The anecdote does show that Baird was ready to pay ready cash for publishable material, when he discovered it.

Last Years

Baird lost his position as editor and publisher of *Real America* by the end of 1935. His job loss may have been related to a criminal libel action brought by the Lake County state's attorney on behalf of Mayor William Merrian Edwards (1888–1936) of Zion IL. The libel action was based on an article by Miss Lucille Hecht entitled "Voila Voliva"[15] published in the July 1935 issue of *Real America*, while Baird was still serving as editor and publisher. On 29 January 1936, Baird was arrested in his home at 1120 N. Lake Shore Drive on a warrant sworn by Edwards. After being held for eight hours in jail, Baird was released on $1,000 bond by Justice of the Peace Harry Hoyt in Waukegan. His case was set for trial on 6 February 1936.

The *Chicago Tribune* for 27 March 1936 reported on legal developments in the case, which Edwards brought despite a correction and apology subsequently published by the magazine. At the 25 March 1936 hearing, Baird testified that the reference to Edwards was "a regrettable error, caused when an associate editor deleted part of the original article."[16] Baird's attorney maintained that the libel action could only be brought in Chicago, where the magazine was printed. In addition, Edwards filed a

---

15. The article quoted Wilbur Glenn Voliva (1870–1942), overseer of the Christian Catholic Church of Zion and a political enemy of Mayor Edwards.
16. The *Ironwood* [MI] *Daily Globe* for 29 January 1936 reported: "Baird blamed a typographical error for the inference to which Mayor Edwards objected. He said the error incorrectly joined two sentences, one referring to Mayor Edwards and the other to the alleged amorous escapades of another man, who was not named and that later the magazine printed a correction and explanation."

civil suit seeking $50,000 damages from Baird, Real America, Inc., and Hecht. The *Tribune* reported that Justice of the Peace Hoyt would rule on the various motions on 2 April 1936. *Real America* magazine itself apparently expired in March 1936, before the legal proceedings could be concluded. Zion Mayor William Merrian Edwards himself died on 6 July 1936, so the proceedings may have become moot.

Regardless of the outcome of the legal proceedings, the loss of his position and the expense of the legal proceedings were doubtless a severe blow to Baird. Baird didn't soon forget his imprisonment at the behest of Mayor Williams. In "Murder Is My Business" (*Inside Detective,* January 1945), he wrote:

> The fact is I was once singled out as the victim for one of the oldest confidence games, the Spanish Prisoner racket,[17] and I was arrested and thrown in jail by the mayor of Zion, Ill., (where they believe the earth is flat) because his honor believed I had libeled him.

When he registered for the draft in 1942, Baird and his wife were residing in the Admiral Hotel at 909 Foster Avenue (corner of Foster Avenue and Marine Drive) in Chicago.[18] Perhaps they had had to reduce the expenses incurred at their former residences at 1120 Lake Shore Drive (1926, 1930, 1936) and 1214–1220 N. State Street (1940). Or perhaps one or both were ailing and required the additional services available at the hotel. Baird was no longer listed in *Who's Who in Chicago* in the 1945 and 1950 editions. He seems to have concentrated most of his attention on crime writing in his later years. In his "Among the Authors" column in the *Chicago Tribune* for 31 December 1944, Frederic Babcock (1896–1979) reported that Baird's arti-

---

17. In this racket, a variation of the "pigeon drop," the con man convinces the mark that he must raise funds to free a wealthy imprisoned man.
18. The Admiral Hotel was demolished in 2007 to construct the Admiral at the Lake retirement community.

cle "Murder Is My Business," covering famous Chicago murders, was appearing in *Inside Detective* for January 1945.[19] Babcock described Baird as a former police reporter and editor of *Real Detective Tales*.

Writing in "Murder Is My Business," Baird recalled his association with Ben Hecht (1894–1964) and others with whom he had worked in reporting crime in Chicago. He recalled of the scene where much of his work transpired:

> Most of these murder cases centered in the old Cook County Criminal Courts building on North Dearborn Street, a gloomy, dungeon-like brick and stone structure. And the gloomiest chamber in it was the press room.
>
> Its unswept floor was littered with cigarette stubs and empty whisky bottles; the unwashed window was flyspecked and broken, and the grimy walls covered with typical drawings and scurrilous verse. In one corner stood a bettered old desk and typewriter, the property of the City Press reporter.

His purview extended to the federal courts as well, from which he remembered Judge Kenesaw Mountain Landis (1866–1944):

> I especially remember Judge Kenesaw Mountain Landis, whose federal court I often covered. Once you saw the judge you couldn't forget him. With his mane of flowing white hair and leonine face, he looked like an oil portrait by one of the old masters, and when he went into action he was like a whirlwind.

---

19. Because of advance-dating practices, this magazine was probably already on the newsstands when Babcock's column was published.

He not only presided as judge in his court. He was jury, prosecuting attorney, and lawyer for the defense. He ran the whole show alone. The others just stood aside and watched. And he usually put on a good show whenever a newspaper-man showed up, for he was never averse to publicity. In fact, he loved it.

Baird recalled the occasion when Frank H. Thompson, arms supplier for the Chicago mob, showed up late at his apartment on Lake Shore Drive. On another occasion, in February 1929, a visitor to his editorial offices was expressing skepticism regarding the level of gun violence in Chicago, when his assistant burst into his office to announce that the St. Valentine's massacre had just transpired a few minutes' walk away on North Clark Street. Of the cold-blooded killer Carl Wanderer (1895–1921), Baird wrote: "The hangman never did a better job." Baird admired the skill of attorney Clarence Darrow (1857–1938), who saved the killers Leopold and Loeb from the death penalty.[20] Of his own crime reporting, Baird wrote: "There was plenty of dirt in those days, and I went in for exposing everything I could find out. Our pages dripped with horror and righteous wrath."

Inside Detective ran four different photographs of Baird with "Murder Is My Business," which was featured on the front cover. A trio of photographs of Baird wearing a hat was captioned: "A dapper fellow, Mr. Baird. And a reader as well as a writer of the best in fact-detective stories. He knows the field from experience." Another photograph depicted a cigarette-smoking Baird with loosened tie in his office (probably in his home at the Admiral Hotel) and was captioned: "Flanked by a typewriter at either side, the author delves into the crime history of Chicago."

In a letter published in the *Chicago Tribune* for 17 February 1946, Baird praised the newspaper's *Magazine of Books*. He stat-

---

20. Baird included a photograph that Darrow had inscribed to him on 27 May 1935, in "Murder Is My Business."

ed: "The work I'm doing now brings me in contact with the police, the coroner, secret service agents, the state's attorney, and such, but not with writers. So I hardly know what the other guys are doing." Of course, Baird had his own literary connections from days of yore, and he assured the *Tribune* that he was not seeking a position on its literary magazine. He did have many connections in the law enforcement and legal communities from his work as a police reporter and a detective magazine editor. On 26 October 1929, he and Dr. Ben L. Reitman (1879–1942) lectured on criminology to a group of fifty Northwestern University and University of Chicago students at the Press Club at 71 E. Monroe Street, reported in the *Chicago Tribune* for 27 October 1929. "Black Thursday" had hit the financial markets only two days before their lectures, on 24 October 1929.

A flavor of Baird's crime writing can be found in his editorial "Why Is a Criminal?" in *Real Detective Tales & Mystery Stories* for June–July 1927.[21] Concerning the poor remuneration achieved by most criminals, Baird wrote in part:

> In my newspaper days I met many criminals of different sorts, from the petty sneak thief to the big bank robber, and I can recall none who made crime pay, or who could not have done better in any honest employment. But your criminal, it seems, prefers one crooked dollar to two that are honest. I remember the case of a counterfeiter who specialized in lead nickels. Court examination disclosed that it cost him seven cents for every nickel he manufactured—and all he got for making them was a stretch in the federal penitentiary.
>
> Even the more successful of our enterprising criminals—again excepting a few prosperous bootleggers—are playing a losing game. His "easy money" goes much easier than it comes. The dope peddler, the lawyer, the grafting politician—when these and others get through with him he has nothing left. Nothing to show for all

---

21. This number of the magazine can be found online at: comicbookplus.com/?dlid=36860.

the time, thought, shrewdness and cunning he has spent in a hazardous occupation.

Thus, observing it solely from a pecuniary viewpoint—disregarding all moral considerations—crime does not pay, and never has and never will.

Why, then, is any man a criminal?

The question remains unanswered.

Baird generally took a dim view of criminals. Of the murderers whom he met in his years as a crime reporter, he wrote in "Murder Is My Business": "I never knew one who showed any remorse for his crimes." In the same article he wrote of the criminals he had met:

> For more than 30 years now I've seen them come and go in Chicago—a motley procession of murders, mobsters, hopheads, thugs, con men, thieves—knaves of high and low degree. They were crooks who made headlines from coast to coast, and two-bit killers who rated only a paragraph on the back page of the bulldog edition. But each was memorable in his own way.

Baird suffered a major blow when Mildred (Connelly) Ward Baird, his spouse of more than thirty-six years, died in Chicago on 23 June 1948. Mrs. Baird died at 6:55 P.M. in Columbus Hospital, 2548 Lake View Avenue, where she had been admitted on 6 June. The immediate cause of her death was a cerebral hemorrhage, which she suffered about five hours before her passing. She had suffered from auricular fibrillation for seven years preceding her death. The couple was still residing in the Admiral Hotel at 909 Foster Avenue when Mildred died. Mildred's remains were cremated at the crematory at Graceland Cemetery in Chicago on 26 June. Her ashes were strewn by the chapel pines in the cemetery on 12 July 12 at the direction of Drake & Sons Funeral Home.

In 1953, Baird put his art collection up for auction at Sheridan Art Galleries, 4820 Sheridan Road, on 18–20 August. Advertisements placed by the gallery in the *Chicago Tribune* for 13 and 16 August 1953 announced: "BY ORDER OF / EDWIN BAIRD, NOTED / CHICAGO COLLECTOR / Fine Art Removed from His / Admiral Hotel Apt." Works to be auctioned included etchings by Rembrandt, Van Dyck, Dürer, and Whistler, along with antique engravings by John Smith and F. Bartolizzi. Apparently the consignor was breaking up the household at the apartment he formerly shared with his wife at the Admiral Hotel. By this time Mildred Baird had been dead for more than five years.

Baird was a widower residing at 5107 [N.] Kenmore Avenue in Chicago at the time of his death on 27 September 1954. His occupation was stated as writer. For the final month of his life, from 29 August 1954 until his death, he was under the care of Don P. Sando, M.D., at Cook County Hospital. The cause of his death was Laennec's cirrhosis of the liver, usually indicative of alcoholism in an older adult. His remains were cremated in the crematory at Graceland Cemetery in Chicago on 1 October 1954.

Appendix

	Chronological Listing of Fiction by Edwin Baird[22]
bg	biographical information
n	novel
na	novella
nv	novelette
sl	serial segment
ss	short story
tc	true crime
ts	true story
vi	vignette

---

22. Information from "The Fiction Mags Index," edited by William G. Contento and Phil Stephenson-Payne, except as noted by [*] at end of listing. See www.philsp.com/homeville/fmi/0start.htm.

"Four Telegrams" (ss), *All-Story Magazine* (January 1910)
"The Black Sheet" (ss), *Scrap Book* (December 1910)
"The Hungry Man" (ss), *All-Story Magazine* (January 1911)
"The Butterfly Circuit" (ss), *All-Story Magazine* (February 1911)
"Heads, I Win—" (ss), *Munsey's Magazine* (February 1911)
"Blind Man's Buff" (ss), *All-Story Magazine* (March 1911)
"Double-Shuffle" (ss), *All-Story Magazine* (April 1911)
"The $100 Cash" (ss), *Cavalier* (June 1911)
"The Golden Hoodoo" (ss), *All-Story* (June 1911)
"Survival of the Fattest" (ss), *All-Story* (July 1911)
"The Ohio Jay" (ss), *All-Story* (August 1911)
"Tying the Terrors" (ss), *Scrap Book* (October 1911)
"Real Stuff" (sl), *All-Story* (December 1911–May 1912)
"How Nelson Markle Became Hemingway Breen" (ss), *Blue Book Magazine* (February 1912)
"The Hippogrif" (ss), *All-Story* (September 1912)
"Golden Grain" (ss), *All-Story* (April 1913)
"Liars and Lovers" (ss), *Smart Set* (June 1914)
"Three Ways Out" (ss), *Black Cat* (July 1914)
"The Heart of Virginia Keep" (n), *Argosy* (April 1915)
"The Greatest Thing in the World" (ss), *Smart Set* (November 1915)
"Blackie" (ss), *Munsey's Magazine* (October 1916)
"Fists and Pacifists" (ss), *All-Story Weekly* (26 January 1918)
"A Handful of Straw" (ss), *Detective Story Magazine* (22 April 1919)
"Only Sons" (ss), *People's Favorite Magazine* (10 May 1919)
"But We Didn't, Mr. Baird" (bg), *Chicago Ledger* (15 November 1919)
"The Golden Vagabond" (sl), *Chicago Ledger* (commenced 15 November 1919)
"Z" (na), *Detective Story Magazine* (27 August 1921)
"The Man in the Dark" (na), *Ace-High Magazine* (January 1922)

"The Red Shell" (nv), *Wayside Tales* (April 1922)
"Pass the Bacon" (ss), *Ace-High Magazine* (June 1922)
"The Revolver" (nv), *Mystery Magazine* (15 August 1922)
"An Inside Job" (ss), *Ace-High Magazine* (January 1923)
"The Web-Footed Monster" (nv), *Action Stories* (January 1923)
"Vanishing Shadows" (ss), *Action Stories* (February 1923)
"The Shadow of Yesterday" (ss), *Detective Magazine* (20 July 1923)
"This Way Out" (vi), *Black Mask* (1 August 1923)
"The Billion-Dollar Robbery" (ss), *Black Mask* (1 September 1923)
"Keep It Dark" (vi), *Black Mask* (15 October 1923)
"Even This Can Happen" (ss), *10 Story Book* (January 1924)
"Cordelia's Ghost" (ss) [with Mildred Baird], *Fawcett's Triple-X Magazine* (July 1924)
"The Frame-Up" (ss), *Detective Magazine* (15 August 1924)
"Why Be Wise?" (ss), *10 Story Book* (August 1924)
"The Amazing Case of Fargo Dorn" (sl), *Fawcett's Triple-X Magazine* (October 1924–January 1925)
"An Eye for an Eye" (nv), *Detective Magazine* (7 November 1924)
"What Every Young Man Should Know" (ss), *10 Story Book* (November 1924)
"Watch Your Step!" (ss), *10 Story Book* (December 1924)
"Will o' the Wisp" (n), *Flapper's Experience* (November (?) 1925–? 1926) [*]
"If She Meets Another Man" (ss), *Macfadden Fiction Lovers Magazine* (February 1925)
"Clue of the Golden Horse" (tc) [as "E. McLeary Baird"], *True Detective Mysteries* (March 1939)
"Murder Is My Business" (bg/tc), *Inside Detective* (January 1945) [*]
"The Fantastic Mr. Wupper" (ts) [as "E. McCleary Baird"], *Master Detective* (September 1950)

Lovecraft's 1937 Diary

Perhaps the most widely circulated news story relating to H. P. Lovecraft relates to the diary he had commenced to keep for 1937. S. T. Joshi tells the story succinctly in *IAP* (1009):

> On the evening of March 15 the *Providence Evening Bulletin* ran an obituary, full of errors large and small; but it made mention of the "clinical notes" Lovecraft kept of his condition while in the hospital—notes that "ended only when he could no longer hold a pencil." This feature was picked up by the wire services, and an obituary entitled "Writer Charts Fatal Malady" appeared in the *New York Times* on March 16. Frank Long, Lovecraft's best friend, learnt of his death from reading this obituary.

The fate of Lovecraft's 1937 diary is not known. We do know that Robert H. Barlow apparently had it in his possession on 31 March 1937, when he wrote a lengthy letter to August Derleth from the YMCA's William Sloane House in New York City. This letter is currently among the Derleth Papers at the Wisconsin Historical Society in Madison. Starting on the third page of his referenced letter, Barlow copied out for Derleth "items from Howard Lovecrafts' [*sic*] 1937 diary," including (i) a "remembrancer" section of personal data and birthdays, (ii) an alphabetical list of friends/correspondents ("addresses"), and (iii) "entries in HPs 1937 diary," the famous "death diary," with transcribed entries dated between 1 January and 11 March. Barlow transcribed complete entries only for 1 and 2 January and 9, 10, and 11 March; for other dates, he provided "condensations." From the reference to "page covering [January] 17–23" among the condensed entries, we may surmise that the diary purchased by Lovecraft contained one page per week. Since 1937 commenced on Friday, 1 January, Lovecraft probably had extra room for his entries for the first two days of the year before the regular weekly sequence commenced on Sunday, 3 January. In addition to the principal diary section, commercial diary books of this kind typically also contained sections for addresses, personal data, and birthdays.

Lovecraft does not appear to have been a diary-keeper by custom. The most significant exception is the diary he kept for January 1925–January 1926, which was first published in *Collected Essays* 5.149–79. This diary corresponded to the first thirteen months of the period that he spent at 169 Clinton Street in Brooklyn, after his wife Sonia departed to take a job in the Midwest. Writers have speculated that Lovecraft maintained this diary in order to facilitate the day-by-day accounts of his life in New York City which he sent primarily to his aunt Lillian D. Clark during this period. Then in 1932–33 Lovecraft purchased another notebook that he used primarily for notes on weird fiction. "Weird Story Plots" and "Notes on Weird Fiction" from this notebook were published in *Collected Essays* 2.153–69 and 169–75 respectively. The "remembrancer" section of this diary was published in *Collected Essays* 5.264. Sometime during the fall of 1936, sensing that his health was deteriorating, he penned his "Instructions in Case of Decease," which survives in the form of a transcription that Annie E. P. Gamwell made for Robert H. Barlow (published in *Collected Essays* 5.237–40). It is likely that he also purchased a commercial diary for 1937 during this period, with the intention of better organizing his records. The "addresses" section of the 1937 diary, for example, contains significantly more names than are found in "Instructions in Case of Decease."

The only names listed in "Instructions in Case of Decease" that do not appear in the "addresses" section of the 1937 diary are T. Kemp Boardley, Jr., James Ferdinand Morton, Charles W.

"Tryout" Smith, and Elizabeth Toldridge. The 90 names included in the "addresses" section of the 1937 diary include 36 names included in "Instructions in Case of Decease" and 54 names not found in that document. Excluding Annie E. Phillips Gamwell, just 40 names appear in "Instructions." Of course, the document concerned the actual disposition of Lovecraft's effects and therefore probably contained only his closest and most important friends. In addition, Lovecraft made one disposition of all his amateur journalism papers, to Edwin Hadley Smith for the Library of Amateur Journalism (then at the Franklin Institute in Philadelphia), so he may not have seen any need to include any but his closest friends in the amateur journalism hobby. Note that while James Ferdinand Morton and Charles W. ("Tryout") Smith are not included in the "addresses" section of the 1937 diary, they are included in the very short listing of birthdays in the 1937 diary. To some extent, the "addresses" section of the 1937 diary, while considerably more extended than that of "Instructions in Case of Decease," appears to contain a significant number of names whose principal connection with Lovecraft was either relatively minor or significantly removed in time. It is possible that Lovecraft compiled the "addresses" section shortly after Christmas 1936 and included a number of relatively minor associates from whom he had received Christmas greetings. It is important to remember that we have only Barlow's transcriptions of the 1937 diary in his letter of 31 March 1937 to August W. Derleth; it is possible that he made errors in the transcriptions.

We may speculate concerning the fate of the original 1937 diary. It seems likely—although it is not absolutely certain—that Barlow had it with him when he wrote to August Derleth from New York City on 31 March 1937.[1] (The alternative is that he

---

1. Christopher M. O'Brien related to me accounts that some members of the Kalem Club in New York City resented Barlow's display of the 1937

made a transcription of the diary contents while he was still in Providence and relied upon that transcription when writing to Derleth from New York City.) Whether he retained the diary or returned it to Annie Gamwell after extracting data from it is not known. For either Barlow or Gamwell, the diary would certainly have been a treasured keepsake—although potentially a painful one. It is possible that one of them eventually elected to destroy the diary because of its personal, painful character.

Barlow sent virtually all his Lovecraft material to Brown University, some of it passing first through August Derleth in Sauk City. The major exceptions were the manuscript of "The Shadow out of Time," which he gave to his student June Evelyn Ripley (1915–1994), and his own letters from Lovecraft, which his literary executor George T. Smisor sent to Brown University following his death in 1951. (The manuscript of "The Shadow out of Time" reached Brown University years later, the gift of the children of June Evelyn Ripley.) If retained by Annie Gamwell, it is possible that the 1937 diary was missed by bookseller H. Douglass Dana when he went through the contents of Lovecraft's library following the death of Mrs. Gamwell in 1941. If retained by Barlow, it is possible that Smisor missed the 1937 diary in going through Barlow's literary effects. Of course, it is also possible that either Mrs. Gamwell or Barlow may have given the 1937 diary to another person before their deaths. If the 1937 diary were to be recovered today, I speculate that a bookseller might ask $50,000 or more for it because of its poignant personal contents. Only major letter groups or major holograph fiction manuscripts would be likely to be priced higher.

---

diary during his stay there following HPL's death. If these accounts are to be credited, Barlow apparently had the 1937 diary with him in New York City following HPL's death.

Regardless of the fate of the original 1937 diary, we are fortunate to have the Barlow transcriptions that survive in his letter to August Derleth. R. Alain Everts first published the "death diary" transcriptions in *The Death of a Gentleman* (1987).[2] S. T. Joshi included Barlow's "death diary" transcriptions in *Collected Essays* 5 (2006). The "addresses" section of the 1937 diary is first published in the Appendix of this essay. The addresses in particular contain a number of individuals elsewhere unmentioned, or little noticed, in the vast secondary literature concerning Lovecraft. I have added a few annotations on some of the more obscure individuals in the notes for the appendix. For example, I was surprised to find not two, but four, Providence residents in the addresses:

[12] Harry Brobst, Hayward Apts., 61 Beacon Ave.
[23] C. M. Eddy, Jr., 1 Providence St.
[25] Thomas S. Evans, 145 Medway St.
[86] Frederick A. Wesley, 6 Hammond St.

Harry Brobst (1909–2010) was probably the last of Lovecraft's surviving close personal friends. Brobst knew Lovecraft while working as a nurse and attending school in Providence in the 1930s. Clifford Martin Eddy, Jr. (1896–1967) and his wife, Muriel (Gammons) Eddy, knew Lovecraft from an earlier period, and Clifford collaborated with Lovecraft on several projects, including work for the magician Harry Houdini. The names of Thomas S. Evans and Frederick A. Wesley were, however, completely unknown to me when I first encountered them in the 1937

---

2. The "death diary" transcriptions appear on pp. 25–28 of Everts's work. He reproduced the final entries from 9, 10, and 11 March in facsimile from Barlow's letter of 31 March 1937 on p. 22 and also published the contents of the "remembrancer" (personal data) and the "birthdays" sections of the 1937 diary on p. 17.

diary. David E. Schultz subsequently informed me (email dated 14 September 2011) that Thomas S. Evans receives three mentions in the surviving Lovecraft correspondence, while Frederick A. Wesley receives none. Lovecraft wrote to Frank Belknap Long on "Sun's Day April 1931":

> This epistle is a two-day job, broken by one of my very rare excursions into the outside world. The amiable if not excessively profound Thomas S. Evans—he of the dramatick and playwriting predilections—called me up and urged me to accompany him to a concert of the newly organised Providence Concert Band in historick Infantry Hall (now remodell'd on the interior, tho' still possesst of that nauseous Victorian belfry), and having no striking objection, I acquiesced. (*SP* 749)

After he had departed for his southern journey of that year, Lovecraft wrote to Lillian D. Clark on 5 May 1931: "This outfit which I put on for the Infantry Hall concert with Evans is going to see St. Augustine yet—though it may not last till next Christmas" (*LFF* 883). He wrote again to Mrs. Clark on 30 May 1931: "Interested to hear that Evans called up. I wasn't sure about how we left the telephoning business, and that accursed typing job erased nearly everything else from my memory. I have dropped Evans one or two cards from along my route" (*LFF* 903). Evans was still on a 1934 "List of Correspondents to Whom Postcards Have Been Sent" (*CE* 5.267).

Thomas Stuart Evans was born in Providence on 1 February 1885, the son of (Ashton[3]) English-born engineer Thomas Evans (1841–1927) and his Pawtucket-born wife Martha Alice (Pollett) Evans (1844–1921). The elder Thomas Evans, the son of Ephraim Evans and Hannah (Jenkins) Evans, had emigrated in 1863 and become a naturalized citizen in 1875. His wife Martha Alice Pollett was the daughter of William Pollett (1820–

---

3. Probably Ashton-under-Lyne in Greater Manchester.

1888) and Susan (Scott) Pollett (1811?–1888). The elder Thomas's and his wife Martha's daughter Anna Louise Evans (1868–1949), who like her brother Thomas never married, was born in Providence on 17 February 1868. There is a 22 February 1881 Rhode Island death record for Winslow J. Evans, age 18, with kin Thomas S. and Anna L. Evans. I do not know whether Winslow was a full-sibling, half-sibling, or other relation of Thomas S. and Anna L. Evans.

When Thomas and Martha (Pollett) Evans and their children were enumerated at 94 Almy Street in the 1900 census, Thomas was working as a steam engineer and his daughter Anna as a bookkeeper, while son Thomas S. was still in school. In 1910, Thomas S. Evans, age 22, was living at 410–412 West 23rd Street in New York City, pursuing his career as a theatrical actor. By 1920, however, son Thomas S. was back in his father's home, then at 405 Lloyd Avenue in Providence. The elder Thomas Evans was continuing to work as a mechanical engineer, while no occupations were listed for either daughter Anna or son Thomas. Martha (Pollett) Evans died in Providence on 22 May 1921, only two days before Lovecraft's mother died on 24 May 1921.

By 1923, the widowed Thomas, still working as a consulting engineer at 75 Westminster St. (room 15), was living at 145 Medway Street, which remained the family home until the death of daughter Anna L. Evans on 30 April 1949. The senior Thomas Evans, age 86, died at home of a cerebral hemorrhage on 17 June 1927. Son Thomas and daughter Anna continued on in the family home at 145 Medway Street. In the 1930 city directory, Thomas S. Evans still listed his occupation as actor. When Evans died on 8 November 1940, five days after suffering a heart attack, he was a self-employed cosmetician working from his home at 145 Medway Street. The death certificate noted that he had been employed in this occupation for ten years.[4] He and his sister Anna L. Evans were both buried by Horace B. Knowles' Sons, in the family lot at Pocasset Cemetery.

Thomas S. Evans's interest in the theater would certainly have provided the basis for a friendship with Lovecraft. How they originally became acquainted is not known to me. Evans was more than five years older than Lovecraft, so it does not seem likely that they were schoolboy acquaintances. They lost their mothers within two days of each other, so one wonders if they might have become acquainted at the Horace B. Knowles' Sons funeral parlor, patronized by both families. Is it possible that Evans's knowledge of theatrical makeup qualified him for employment by one or more Providence undertakers as a cosmetician? Of course, we also know from Sonia Lovecraft's memoir that her husband suffered from ingrown facial hairs—whether this might have provided an occasion for Lovecraft to meet a cosmetician remains unknown. A detailed check of Providence directories 1885–1937 might reveal whether Lovecraft and Evans were at any time close neighbors. Otherwise, it does not seem particularly likely that we will gain more knowledge of the friendship of H. P. Lovecraft and Thomas S. Evans in the future.

The friendship of H. P. Lovecraft and Frederick Allen Wesley will probably remain an even tougher puzzle to resolve. Frederick Allen Wesley was born in Providence on 14 October 1885 and died in the same city of colon cancer on 20 April 1948. His death certificate shows his parents as Warren B. Wesley and Martha A. (——) Wesley, both born in Plymouth, Massachusetts. However, the 1900 census shows Fred A. Wesley, son,

---

4. A 1935 Rhode Island state census punch card uncovered by Chris Perridas on FamilySearch recorded Evans's usual occupation as actor (independent) and his present occupation as chemist (research). It also recorded that he was employed for twelve months in 1935.

born October 1888 in Rhode Island, living in the 42 Hudson Street household of his father Martin A. Wesley, born December 1853 in Connecticut, of Connecticut-born parents and his mother Martha A. Wesley, born March 1861 in Rhode Island of a Massachusetts-born father and a Rhode Island–born mother. Martin Wesley was then working as a shoe store manager. He and Martha had been married for fifteen years and Fred was their only child. Perhaps Martha's Massachusetts-born father represents the family link with Plymouth.

By 1910, Fred A. Wesley and his wife Corinne A. Wesley had their own home at 330 Plainfield Street. Fred was working as a streetcar conductor. Their son Frederick R. Wesley, born 6 January 1910, was also living in the household. The 1910 census confirms the Connecticut birth of Fred Wesley's father. Fred's wife Corinne was the daughter of a Philippines-born father and a New York–born mother. When he registered for the draft in 1917, Fred was working as a steamfitter's helper for Smith Gibbs Company at 11 South Main Street in Providence. He and his wife resided at 161 Newell Avenue in Pawtucket. A second son, Robert H. Wesley, had been born to Fred and Corinne on 29 November 1913. The 1930 census recorded Frederick A. Wesley residing at 6 Hammond Street in Providence and working as a furnace steamfitter. He was then divorced from his former wife Corinne, who married John (Gorm) A. Giguere in Providence on 20 April 1926.

On 26 August 1930, Frederick A. Wesley married Edna C. Allen in Providence. When he registered for the draft in 1942, he was working for Brown & Sharpe and residing with his second wife Edna at 243 Adelaide Avenue in Providence. In the 1944 city directory, Frederick continued to work as a helper at Brown & Sharpe and resided at 222 Thurbers Avenue. He worked as a machinist's helper at Brown & Sharpe for seven and a half years and only stopped working in January 1948, a few weeks before his death on 20 April 1948. He was still a resident of 222 Thurbers Avenue at the time of his death, although he spent the last five days of his life at Price Nursing Home. On 23 April 1948, he was buried at Grace Church Cemetery. His widow Edna was 52 years old at the time of her husband's death. His second son Robert H. Wesley died in August 1961 in Rhode Island, aged only 47. His first son Frederick R. Wesley died in February 1981 in Scituate, Massachusetts, aged 71.

Like Thomas S. Evans, Frederick Allen Wesley seems too much older than Lovecraft to have been a likely schoolboy acquaintance. We know that Lovecraft vastly appreciated the steam heat furnished by Brown's John Hay Library when he lived at the adjoining 66 College Street. Whether Wesley or his employer might have been under contract with Brown to provide maintenance for the heating system we do not know. Certainly, such a circumstance could have provided an opportunity for Lovecraft and Wesley to meet. What would have formed their common ground is more difficult to speculate. Lovecraft was willing to admit acquaintances from all walks of life and seems to have been friendly even with the Negress Delilah Townsend (1870?–1944), who provided housekeeping services for Lillian D. Clark. As far as we know, Lovecraft's butcher, baker, and candlestick-maker do not occupy places of honor in the "addresses" section of his 1937 diary.

One possibility that may merit consideration is that Lovecraft's acquaintance with Evans and Wesley may have been related. The senior Thomas Evans's occupation was recorded as steam engineer in the 1900 U.S. census and Frederick Allen Wesley was working as a steamfitter by the time he registered for the draft in 1917. From the recollections of Brown University professor Robert Kenny, confirmed by Harry Brobst, we know that Lovecraft held a job as a ticket seller at a downtown Providence movie theater in the late 1920s (*IAP* 821). It seems likely that Lovecraft was under some pressure from his uncle Edwin E. Phillips (1864–1918)—and from his mother and his aunts after Edwin's death—to secure gainful employment in order to supplement the family finances. I wonder if Lovecraft might have worked at some time in the downtown Providence office of Thomas Evans Senior, thereby making the acquaintances of his son Thomas Stuart Evans and of steamfitter Frederick Allen Wesley. Thomas Evans Senior was a contemporary of Lovecraft's uncle Dr. Franklin Chase Clark (1847–1915), who might possibly have helped his nephew secure a position.

If Lovecraft's relationships with Thomas S. Evans and Frederick A. Wesley are linked, two lesser possibilities are that (1) they participated with him in the Men's Club of Providence's First Universalist Church in 1908–12 or (2) they participated with him in the Providence Amateur Press Club in 1914–16. Evans was living in New York City in 1910, and neither Evans nor Wesley is mentioned in the surviving issues of the *Providence Amateur*. While it seems unlikely that we will ever know more about the relationships of Evans and of Wesley with Lovecraft than the little we know today, their presence in his life, as documented in the 1937 diary, seems worth noting for what we can make of it. See Haden (179–80) for more information on Wesley.

I hope that the "addresses" section of Lovecraft's 1937 diary will continue to yield useful information concerning his friends and relationships. I have attempted to shed some light on some of the more obscure individuals in the notes, but even where individuals can be identified from the census or by other means, the connection with Lovecraft sometimes remains unknown. Perhaps it is not beyond hope that the 1937 diary itself will one day be recovered. We can be grateful that the young Robert H.

Barlow took the time to transcribe most of the 1937 diary contents for August Derleth from his New York City YMCA room on 31 March 1937. Barlow's intention in transcribing the "addresses" section of the diary was doubtless to provide Derleth with as many leads as possible for the already-projected collection of Lovecraft's letters, finally realized in five volumes from Arkham House in 1965–76. We can surmise that Barlow transcribed or summarized the diary entries from January 1 through March 11 because they so movingly recorded the final illness of his friend.

I wish to acknowledge the assistance of Marcos Legaria, Christopher M. O'Brien, Chris Perridas, David E. Schultz, and the Rhode Island State Archives. However, I remain solely responsible for all opinions and any errors contained in this paper. Readers should refer to S. T. Joshi and David E. Schultz's *An H. P. Lovecraft Encyclopedia* (2001) as a primary reference for most of the names included in Lovecraft's 1937 diary. My objective in the notes for this paper is to provide supplementary information about lesser-known associates of Lovecraft, such as his Providence friends Thomas S. Evans and Frederick A. Wesley discussed in the body of the paper. Evans [25] and Wesley [86] have in common with Curtis F. Myers [53], Horatio L. Smith [71], and C. L. Stuart [78] the fact that I can identify them with fair certainty, but have not been able to establish the basis of their relationships with Lovecraft. Establishing the connection of any of these five individuals with Lovecraft would constitute exciting progress.

With ongoing conversion of vital records and other information to electronic form, it seems probable that future generations will know far more about Lovecraft and his associates than we know today. I hope that the readers of the future will forgive my errors; if I have succeeded in shining a little light into some obscure corners, I will rest content. The vital statistics appearing in this paper and its notes are not fully cited, but most (including all U.S. census, draft registration, and Social Security Administration Death Master File references) can be readily validated using Ancestry.com. The Rhode Island State Archives provided me with death records establishing many of the facts about Thomas S. Evans [25], Frederick A. Wesley [86], and their families; the Archives also provided a death record for Evelyn M. Staples. The acronym SSDI stands for the Social Security Administration Death Master File. The acronym SSN stands for Social Security Number, cited only by state of issuance.

Appendix

ITEMS FROM LOVECRAFT'S 1937 DIARY
TRANSCRIPTION BY ROBERT H. BARLOW
(Robert H. Barlow to August W. Derleth, 31 March 1937,
Wisconsin Historical Society)

Editorial Notes:
1. Annotations by Barlow appear in italics.
2. Correspondent numbers in brackets added by me.
3. Correspondent numbers followed by an asterisk indicate an individual not included in "Instructions in Case of Decease."

Height 5 foot 11[5]
Weight 145
Sleeve length 34
Gloves 7¼
Collar 14½
Hat 7
Shoes 8½

---

5. These data can be compared with the data published as "Remembrancer" in *CE* 5.264, which derives from a separate notebook used mainly by HPL for "Weird Story Plots" and "Notes on Weird Fiction."

Birthdays

SL 1-14-1887[6]
MS 4-26-18[7]
FBL 4-27-02[8]
EAE 10-4-67[9]
JFM 10-18-70[10]
CWS 10-24-52[11]

Addresses

[1*] Fred Anger 2700 Webster St Berkeley Calif
[2*] Victor E. Bacon[12] 1965 A Bund Ave St Louis Mo (*amateur journalist prob. not in touch recently*)
[3*] J. O. Baily[13] Box 414 Chapel Hill, N.C. (*might have good letters in conn. with science-fiction thesis*)
[4*] F. Lee Baldwin, Gen. Deliv. Grangeville, Idaho
[5] (Barlow)

---

6. Samuel Loveman (1887–1976).
7. Margaret Sylvester (1918–2010). Christopher M. O'Brien discovered an SSDI record for Margaret (Sylvester) Ronan (SSN issued NY before 1951), born 25 April 1918 (only one day different from the date of birth shown in HPL's diary), died 14 December 2010, Hudson, Summit County, OH.
8. Frank Belknap Long (1901–1994). Long's record in SSDI indicates that he was born 27 April 1901, not 1902.
9. Ernest Arthur Edkins (1867–1946).
10. James Ferdinand Morton (1870–1941).
11. Charles W. ("Tryout") Smith (1852–1948).
12. Victor E. Bacon (1905–1997) was HPL's recruit for the Hoffman-Daas branch of the United Amateur Press Association and served as its final Official Editor in 1925–26. Bacon was also President of the National Amateur Press Association in 1930–31. His own amateur journal was *Bacon's Essays*.
13. James Osler Bailey (1903–1979), author of *Pilgrims through Space and Time* (1947), an early treatise on science fiction that discusses HPL.

[6*] Bell[14]—15 Pine Ave., Old Orchard, Ne. % E Dixon, Box 292 (*sic*)
[7] Mrs. D. W. Bishop 5001 Sunset Dr. KC Mo
[8*] Jim Blish 69 Halsted St E. Orange NJ
[9] Robt. Bloch, 620 E. Knapp St, Milwaukee Wis
[10*] J E C Blossom,[15] 117 Church St., Rutland Vt
[11*] Hyman Bradofsky, 315 W Second St, Pomona Calif. (*amateur journalist, not likely to have remarkable material*)
[12] Harry Brobst,[16] Hayward Apts, 61 Beacon Ave, Prov RI

---

14. I did not find the surnames Bell and Dixon in membership lists of the National Amateur Press Association or the United Amateur Press Association in the 1930s. (HPL's "Hoffman–Daas" faction was extinct by this time, but the "Erford–Noel" faction based in Seattle continued and in fact experienced several subsequent splits.) No place named Old Orchard appears in NE gazetteers. Johnson County, NE, has a small community named Crab Orchard (population 49 in the 2000 census); it is possible that Barlow mistranscribed "Crab" as "Old," given the similar shapes of the initial and final letters. However, Internet maps show no Pine Avenue in Crab Orchard. HPL did have relatives bearing the Dixon surname, since Whipple V. Phillips's sister Abbie Emeline Phillips (1839–1873) had married Henry D. Dixon (1835–1905) in Sterling CT on 26 October 1859. The Dixons had four sons, three of whom, Wilfred H. (b. 1861), Walter S. (b. 1865), and Alva J. (b. 1867), were living with their families in CT when the 1920 U.S. census was taken. One son, Whipple Van Buren Phillips Dixon, born 31 July 1870, died 29 February 1872, as a result of a scalding accident. Haden 182-183 corrects my erroneous identification. Edith Bell (1914–2002) lived in Maine, not Nebraska.

15. Josephine E. Crane Blossom was born 17 July 1861, Mayatta KS, and died 4 January 1952, Rutland VT. In the 1900 U.S. census, she was recorded in Shrewsbury, Rutland County, VT in the household of her husband William R. Blossom, born April 1854 VT of VT-born parents, a physician. They had then been married twenty-one years and Josephine was the mother of seven children, of whom five were then living, all of them in the paternal household: Elsie C. (b. August 1885 VT), Ethel C. (b. March 1889 VT), Fay E. (b. August 1890 KS), Franklin O. (b. August 1890 KS), and Wilhelmina J. (b. August 1896 VT). Josephine Blossom was active as a poet in amateur journalism.

16. Harry Kern Brobst (1909–2010) was probably the last survivor of HPL's personal friends. A memoir of Brobst by Christopher M. O'Brien

[13*] Paul J Campbell,[17] 5720 Westmoreland Pl, E St Louis Ill
[14*] E H Cole, 53 Freeman St, Wollaston Mass
[15] W. Paul Cook 1305 Missouri Ave, E St Louis Ill.
[16*] William Crawford, 122 Water St, Everett Penn
[17*] Edw F. Daas, 1723 W Cherry St, Milwaukee Wis (*introduced HP to amateur journalism, 1914, Out of touch later*).
[18*] W. L. Davies,[18] Westville, N.H
[19] Adolphe de Castro, 1732 S. Catalina St, Los Angles Cal
[20] Willis Conover, Jr. 27 High Street, Cambridge, Md
[21] August W. Derleth.

---

was published in the *Lovecraft Annual* 4 (2010).
17. Paul Jonas Campbell was born 8 November 1884 in Georgetown IL. He married fellow amateur journalist Eleanor J. Barnhart as his second wife in Chicago on 4 October 1918. A longtime stalwart of the United Amateur Press Association, he died 16 August 1945 in East Saint Louis IL. His memoir of his career in the amateur journalism hobby, "Adventures in Amateur Journalism" (originally published in *Courage* for December 1941–January 1942), was republished in the *Fossil* for January 2006 (www.thefossils.org). Two of Campbell's best-known amateur magazines were the *Scotchman* and the *Liberal*.
18. Barlow has mistranscribed M. L. Davies (i.e., Myrta (Little) Davies). Myrta Alice Little was born 15 January 1888 NH, the daughter of Albert Little (b. June 1852 NH) and Abbie J. Little (b. June 1860 NH). In the 1900 U.S. census, she was recorded in Hampstead, Rockingham County, NH, along with her younger sister Edith M. (b. January 1893 NH) and her parents in the home of her paternal grandfather Tristram H. Little (b. December 1816 NH), a widowed farmer. The household was the same in 1920 U.S. census except that grandfather Tristram was deceased and sister Edith was working as a stenographer. Myrta Alice Little was involved in the amateur journalism hobby and HPL visited her and her mother in their NH home in 1921 and 1922. On 5 May 1923, Myrta Little married Arthur R. Davies. In the 1930 U.S. census, Arthur R. Davies, age 60, born England of English-born parents, a teacher, was recorded with his wife Myrta L., age 42, writer, and their son Robert L. Davies, age 6, born NH, in their home on East Road in Hampstead, Rockingham County, NH. SSDI shows that Myrta Davies (SSN issued NH 1956–58) died in West Ossipee, Carroll County, NH, in December 1967. I acknowledge the assistance of Chris Perridas on Myrta Alice (Little) Davies.

[22] Bernard Austin Dwyer, Box 43, West Shokan NY or CCC Camp SP-8 Co. 26, Peekskill NY
[23*] C. M. Eddy, Jr. 1 Providence St., Prov. RI
[24] E A Edkins,[19] 925 Lincoln Ave, Highland Pk, Ill. (San Sebastian Hotel, Coral Gables Fla in winter)
[25*] Thomas S. Evans, 145 Medway St Providence
[26*] Harold S. Farnese, 4001 S. Harvard Blvd, Los Angles. (*This man, dean of a calif. music inst., wanted H P to co-operate in a weird opera—never done—and set two of his sonnets to music, holding the only copies. I suggest transcriptions be obtained*)
[27] Virgil Finlay 302 Rand St, Rochester NY
[28] Harry O. Fischer, 3515 W. Kentucky St, Apt 15, Louisville, Ky.
[29*] Geo. FitzPatrick,[20] Box 3413 R, G.P.O. Sydney, NSW, Australia
[30*] Nils H. Frome, Bx 3, Fraser Mills, B.C. Canada
[31*] Alfred Galpin, 723 E. College Ave, Appleton Wis. (*likely to have a long series of 1920–25 philosophical letters*)

---

19. Ernest Arthur Edkins was born 4 October 1867 in Aston, Warwickshire, England, and died 3 July 1946 in Coral Gables FL. He and his parents emigrated to Canada in 1867 and to the United States in 1869. He had a career in the amateur journalism hobby stretching from 1883 until his death. Late in life he collaborated with HPL in publishing *Causerie* and with Timothy Burr Thrift in publishing the *Aonian*. The April 2006 issue of the *Fossil* (www.thefossils.org) was devoted to his life and work.

20. George Fitzpatrick, born c. 1885 Parramatta, Australia, arrived in San Francisco from Sydney, Australia, on 10 September 1934. George Fitzpatrick, born c. 1887, arrived in Sydney from London, England, on 22 November 1889. George D. Fitzpatrick was born in Sydney in 1891. George L. Fitzpatrick was born in 1899 in Sydney. George Fitzpatrick married Jessie J. Browne in Sydney in 1920. Whether any of these can be identified with HPL's George FitzPatrick remains unknown. It seems likely that George FitzPatrick is the unidentified "Fitz P" in the 1934 "List of Correspondents to Whom Postcards Have Been Sent" (*CE* 5.267). Haden (180–81) identifies George FitzPatrick.

[32*] Arthur Harris,[21] "Caynton," Llanrhas(?) [*sic*] Road, LLANDUDNO Wales
[33] Woodburn Harris,[22] Route 1, Vergennes, Vt. *should have many pink discussions*
[34*] Hazel Heald, 249 School St. Somerville, Mass. or 15 Carter St Newtonville, Mass
[35*] Chas. D. Hornig 121 Jefferson Ave, Eliz. N.J.
[36*] Dr. I. M. Howard L.B. 313, Cross Plains Texas
[37*] George W. Kirk, Chelsea Bk. Shop, 58 W 8, NYC
[38] Rheinhart Kleiner, 116 Harman St Brooklyn

---

21. Arthur Harris (who lived at Llanrhos Road) was a Welsh amateur journalist. He published *Interesting Items* as a monthly over many decades, beginning with a handwritten journal as early as 1904. He discovered organized amateur journalism in 1912. Harris died 15 March 1966, at age 73. His large amateur journalism collection, estimated at 15,000 items in 1962, passed to Eric Webb, then to Almon Horton, then to Roy Heaven (see Willametta Keffer, "After Many an Irish Moon," *Fossil*, January 1981). His letters from HPL were acquired by Gerry de la Ree in 1970s and are now held by the Lovecraft Collection at Brown University.
22. Woodburn Prescott Harris was born on 17 July 1888 in Mendon VT, and died on 20 June 1988 in Bristol VT. In the 1900 U.S. census, he was living with his parents Sidney and Alice Harris and five siblings on a farm in Panton, Addison County, VT. In the 1910 U.S. census, Woodburn P. Harris was still living with his parents, now in Middlebury, Addison County, VT; the occupation of his father was now given as Methodist Episcopal clergyman. Woodburn Harris had no occupation in the 1910 U.S. census. However, he had found employment as a teacher in Epping, Rockingham County, NH, when he registered there for the draft on 5 June 1917. In the 1920 U.S. census, he and his 23-year-old English-born wife Pauline E. Harris were living in Littleton, Middlesex County, MA, where Harris was employed as high school principal. However, by the time of the 1930 U.S. census, Harris had returned to Panton, Addison County, VT, where he operated a farm. His 32-year-old English-born wife (now listed as Ethel) and his 44-year-old sister Jennie (who worked as a stenographer in an insurance office) were also in his household in 1930. Harris was a widower by the time he died at age 99 in 1988, less than one month from the century mark. Refer to *An H. P. Lovecraft Encyclopedia* for additional information regarding Woodburn Harris.

[39] H C Koenig 540 E 80th NYC
[40] Eugene B. Kuntz Bx 736 Clovis NM.
[41] Henry Kuttner 145 S. Canon Dr. #3, Beverly Hills Calif.
[42] Arthur Leeds Hotel Rutledge, 161 Lexington Ave. NYC
[43] Fritz Leiber Jr. 459 N. Oakhurst Dr. Beverly Hills
[44] FBL 230 W 97 NYC
[45] Samuel Loveman, Rm. 1705 105 5th Ave NYC
[46] Wm. Lumley.[23] 742 Wm. St, Buffalo, NY.
[47*] J. Bernard Lynch,[24] 17 Hemenway St, Boston

---

23. William Sylvester Lumley, then resident in Buffalo NY and working as a porter, claimed a date of birth of 20 March 1880 when he registered for the draft on 12 September 1918. In the 1900 U.S. census, he was enumerated in the home of his parents, Edward Lumley (b. August 1844) and Belle M. Lumley (b. January 1857) on West Farms Road in Bronx NY. William (b. March 1881), a sister Marie (b. June 1898) and a brother Benjamin (b. March 1896) also lived in the Lumley household in that year. Edward Lumley was working as a roofer. The family of Edward and Belle M. Lumley was located in the same place when the 1910 U.S. census was enumerated; by then Edward was working in real estate and his son William S. Lumley's occupation was listed as writer and artist (magazine work). In the 1930 U.S. census, William Lumley, a 50-year-old single white male employed as a watchman, born NY of a NY-born father and a PA-born mother, was rooming in the Buffalo NY home of Lewis and Lena Groner. Today Lumley is best known for his story "The Diary of Alonzo Typer," which was revised by HPL. Refer to *An H. P. Lovecraft Encyclopedia* for additional information regarding William Lumley.

24. Longtime Boston-area amateur journalist, organizer of the famous 4 July 1923 "roundup" that included a Boston Harbor cruise. Joseph Bernard Lynch was born 27 March 1879 in Boston, the son of Irish immigrants Thomas and Catherine Lynch. He lived in the parental home at 17 Peabody Street when the 1900, 1910, and 1920 U.S. censuses were taken, with occupations listed as author, advertising manager, and insurance agent, respectively. In the 1930 U.S. census, with occupation reverted to author, he was living with his MO-born wife Florence M. Lynch, a hairdresser in a beauty parlor, on Cortes Street in Boston. The Lynches had then been married six years. Lynch was the author of one published collection of stories, *Props: Tales of the Pawnshop and Other Stories* (Boston: Meador Publishing Co., 1932), collectible today because some of the stories have mystery elements. He was also involved with a trade journal for

[48*] A. Merritt 235 E 45 NYC
[49] Moe,[25] 1810 W Wisconsin Ave, Milwaukee
[50*] Robert E Moe, 334 Ridgefield Ave, Bridgeport, Conn
[51] C. L. Moore, 2547 Brookside Ave., S. Dr. Indianapolis Ind
[52] Richard E. Morse 40 Princeton Ave Princeton NJ
[53*] Curtis F. Myers,[26] 70 Clifton Ave, Clifton NJ
[54*] Frederic J. Pabody,[27] 1367 E 6th St, Cleveland O

---

hairdressers. As a composer of music, he published "On a Starry Irish Night" (H N Publishing Co., 1936) and "Boston Is My Home Sweet Home" (Meredith Music Co., 1946).

25. Maurice Winter Moe (1882–1940). Robert E. Moe [50] was one of his sons.

26. Curtis F. Myers, born 15 August 1897, son of John Myers, registered for the draft in Brooklyn NY on 24 August 1918. In the 1910 U.S. census, John D. Myers, age 40, a widowed boatman, was recorded on Orrington Avenue in Brooklyn NY with his daughter Eva E., age 18, twin sons Harold A. and Herbert B., age 16, and son Curtis F., age 12; everyone in the household was born NY of NY-born parents. In the 1920 U.S. census of Brooklyn NY, John D. Myers, age 55, a marine broker, was recorded at 44 Waldorf Court with daughter Eva E., age 28, unemployed, and son Curtis, age 22, secretary for a chiropractor. (In this census, John Myers was recorded as married, with parents born in Germany.) In the 1930 census, Curtis F. Myers, age 32, born NY of NY-born parents, was living with his wife Leolia L., aged 36, born NJ of Alsace-Lorraine-born parents, at 32 Harrison Place in Clifton, Passaic County, NJ. Curtis was then working as a machinist in a woolen mill. The couple had been married for seven years in 1930, but there were no children in their household in that year. Christopher M. O'Brien found a 15 August 1897 Brooklyn NY birth certificate (#12898) for Curtis F. Myers as well as an SSDI listing for Curtis Myers (SSN issued NY before 1951), born 15 August 1897, died July 1985, St. Augustine FL. Haden 183 has more information concerning Curtis F. Myers.

27. Frederic J. Pabody (b. 23 March 1910, Hamilton, Butler County, OH; d. 18 December 1993, West Lake, Cuyahoga County, OH) wrote to HPL after noting the character Professor Frank H. Pabodie of the Miskatonic University Antarctic Expedition in *At the Mountains of Madness*. In the 1930 U.S. census, he was recorded at 1237 Ramona Avenue in Lakewood, Cuyahoga County, OH, in the home of his father Earl Pabody, a 47-year-old insurance company agent, born in PA of OH-born parents, and his wife

[55*] Chas A A Parker.[28] 114 Riverside Ave, Medford Mass.
[56*] Emil Petaja, Bx 85 Milltown Montana
[57*] Dean P. Phillips,[29] 1676 E 117, Cleveland O
[58*] Jennie K. Plaisier[30] 1321 Albion Ave. Chicago

Jessie (Daggett) Pabody, age 45, born NY of OH-born parents, along with a brother Charles, age 17, and a sister Mary, age 14, both born OH. The Pabody family had been at 412 14th Avenue in Columbus OH in 1920 and at 414 Park Avenue in Hamilton, Butler County, OH, in 1910.

28. Charles A. A. Parker (1878–1965) was a longtime Boston-area amateur journalist. His best-known journals were the *Literary Gem* (1900–11), *L'Alouette* (1921–34?), and *Bavardage* (1935–44). Parker printed the ultimate issue (July 1923) and probably the penultimate issue (March 1923) of HPL's amateur journal, the *Conservative* (see *IAP* 179). His private press did subsidy publishing in the 1920s and the 1930s. He published two subsidy poetry anthologies, *Threads in Tapestry* (1934) and *Threads in Tapestry* (1935) (both subtitled *An Anthology of Verse*), with Rachel Hall and Marcia A. Taylor as coeditors. He served as president of the National Amateur Press Association in 1942–43. The January 2011 issue of the *Fossil* (www.thefossils.org) contained material by and about Parker.

29. In the 1920 U.S. census, Dean Phillips, age 5, born OH, was living in the household of his parents Edwin and Flora A. Phillips at 10615 Everton Avenue in Cleveland OH. Edwin Phillips, age 38, born OH, was a dentist with his own office. His wife, Flora A., age 40, was NE-born. Dean had a sister Margaret, age 11, born OH, and a brother Edwin, age 8, also born OH. It is possible that this Dean Phillips is the same Dean P. Phillips, born 15 December 1914 OH, whose 17 December 1998 death at Auburn, Placer County, CA, is recorded in SSDI. Dean Phillips is mentioned as a friend of Samuel Loveman in HPL's correspondence files with Barlow, Bloch, and Rimel (information courtesy David E. Schultz). Dean Phillips is probably the unidentified "Phillips" of the 1934 "List of Correspondents to Whom Postcards Have Been Sent" (*CE* 5.267).

30. Jennie Irene Plaisier was born Jennie Irene Maloney in IL in February 1884, the daughter of Timothy Maloney (b. November 1840 Ireland) and Mary Maloney (b. December 1846 Ireland). The family was recorded at 84 East Clifton Avenue in Chicago when the 1900 U.S. census was enumerated. Jennie and two sisters and two brothers were then residing in the parental home; her mother Mary had had eleven children, of whom eight were then living. Jennie was still in the parental home at 2107 Clifton Avenue in Chicago when the 1910 U.S. census was enumerated; she was then working as a stenographer in a law office. Jennie became involved in

[59] E. H. Price, R. 2 Bx 100 U5, Redwood City, Calif
[60*] Seabury Quinn, 34 Jefferson Ave, Brooklyn NY
[61*] Anne T. Renshaw, 1739 Conn Ave NW, Washington DC
[62] Duane W. Rimel 1009 Chestnut Clarkston Wash
[63*] J. M. Samples,[31] 742 Walnut, Macon Ga

---

the amateur journalism hobby during the first decade of the 20th century and met her husband Frank Austin Kendall in the hobby. Kendall was elected president of the National Amateur Press Association for the 1913–14 term but died in November 1913 and was succeeded by his widow. Jennie married John Plaisier in Cook County, IL, on 7 January 1920. In the 1930 U.S. census, they were recorded in Chicago at 7123 Merrill Avenue: John, age 53, born Holland of Holland-born parents, was a public school teacher, and his wife Jennie, age 47, was working as secretary to an attorney. Also in their home in that year was Jennie's daughter Betty J. Kendall, age 17, born MO of a NE-born father and an IL-born mother. Jennie Kendall Plaisier remained active in the amateur journalism hobby for many more years. During the tumultuous 1935–36 official year, Jennie served with HPL and Vincent B. Haggerty as executive judges of the National Amateur Press Association. They had during the year to resolve several contentious disputes raised by Edwin Hadley Smith. Jennie's daughter Betty J. Kendall Heitz (1912–2011) became a successful copywriter and was a frequent contributor of poems to the *Chicago Tribune*'s "Line O'Type or Two" column.

31. John Milton Samples published the *Silver Clarion* for the UAPA in 1918–20. It was one of the publications most frequently mentioned in HPL's reviews in the *United Amateur* and also featured contributions by HPL. At the time he was publishing the *Silver Clarion*, Samples was living in Macon GA (still his address in 1937) and taking courses at Mercer University. (HPL's UAPA faction concentrated much of its recruitment efforts among high school and university students.) John M. Samples was the eldest of seven sons of William M. Samples (b. April 1865 GA) and Mollie A. Samples (b. April 1869 GA), and was living with his parents and his brothers in Fairplay District, Douglas County, GA, when the 1900 U.S. census was enumerated. His father William M. Samples was a farmer. When the 1910 U.S. census was enumerated, John M. Samples was boarding in the Fairplay District, Carroll County, GA, and working as a teacher in a literary school. He self-published a collection of his poetry, *Visions in Verse*, from Carrollton GA in 1912. (WorldCat records only one copy, at the University of Virginia.) When he registered for the draft on 5 June 1917, Samples was residing in Macon GA and working as a rural let-

[64*] J. Schwartz 255 E 188 NYC
[65] R F Searight 19946 Derby Ave Detroit
[66] E F Sechrist, Bx 191 Papeete, Tahiti
[67] J. V. Shea, Jr. 4779 Liberty Ave, Pittsburgh
[68*] W. Shepherd, Oakman Ala
[69] C A Smith, #385 Auburn Calif
[70] E. H. Smith,[32] 235 Emerson st, [sic] NW, Wash D.C. (*amateur journalist, said once he did not keep letters*)
[71*] Horatio L. Smith,[33] 36 Dodd St, Montclair NJ

---

ter carrier and already married. He gave his date of birth as 9 January 1887 and his place of birth as Carroll County, GA. When the 1920 U.S. census was enumerated, Samples and his 30-year-old SC-born wife Mamie (Knight) Samples were recorded in Macon, Bibb County, GA, with their 2-year-old daughter Layce Ruth Samples. Samples was still working for the post office when the 1920 U.S. census was enumerated. His wife can probably be identified with Mamie F. Knight, born October 1889 SC, living with her parents Joseph C. Knight (b. June 1846 SC), her mother Nancy L. Knight (b. July 1848 SC), and her niece Ruth E. Knight (b. February 1898 GA) in Appling County, GA, when the 1900 U.S. census was enumerated. I have not succeeded in finding John Milton Samples in the 1930 U.S. census. Mamie Samples, age 55, born SC, normal school graduate, no occupation, was recorded at 1204 14th Street in Precinct 24 of Manatee County, FL, when the 1945 FL census was enumerated. Living with her was B. Samples, age 22, born GA, high school graduate, Salvation Army employee. I am indebted to Christopher M. O'Brien for assistance on John Milton Samples.

32. Edwin Hadley Smith (1869–1944) was a longtime amateur journalist. His bound collection of amateur journals was purchased by Charles C. Heuman for The Fossils in 1916 and formed the basis of the Library of Amateur Journalism Collection owned by the University of Wisconsin (Madison) Special Collections Department since 2004. HPL left his own amateur journalism collection to Smith for the Library of Amateur Journalism.

33. When he registered for the draft on 5 June 1917, Horatio Lawrence Smith (b. 2 September 1889, Binghamton NY) was living at 26 Arthur Street in Binghamton NY and working as an agent for Adams Express Company. In the 1900 U.S. census, he had been recorded in the home of his parents Charles R. and Jennie Smith at 87 Prospect Street in Binghamton NY, along with a brother Charles H. and sisters Georgiana and

[72*] Louis C Smith,[34] 1908 98th Ave, Oakland Calif
[73*] Truman J. Spencer,[35] 2525 Whitney Ave, Hamden, Conn.

Clarissa. He was still residing in the paternal home in Binghamton NY when the 1910 U.S. census was taken. In the 1930 U.S. census, Horatio L. Smith, age 40, born NY of a NY-born father and a MA-born mother, was living with his wife Iola, age 39, born PA of Welsh-born parents, at 36 Dodd Street in Montclair, Essex County, NJ. Horatio was working as a clothing salesman. In their household in that year were son Lawrence W., age 9, and daughters Evelyn R., age 9, and Shirley A., age 4. When he registered for the draft in 1942, Smith repeated the date and place of birth which he provided in his 1917 registration. He was living at 66 Dodd Street in Montclair, Essex County, NJ, and was working at the offices of Boston-based A. S. Tower Company at 66 Worth Street in New York City. His wife Iola was listed as his closest relation. SSDI has a record for an Horatio Smith (SSN issued NY before 1951) who died August 1966 in Sarasota FL; the date of birth (2 September 1889) of this Horatio Smith matches the date of birth of Horatio Lawrence Smith from the 1917 and 1942 draft registrations. I wonder if Horatio Lawrence Smith might have been a relation of either Charles W. ("Tryout") Smith or Edwin Hadley Smith. Haden (185–86) has a better identification of Horatio Elwin Smith (1886–1948).

34. Louis C. Smith was an early collecting fan, mentioned in Sam Moskowitz's *The Immortal Storm*. He may be the Louis C. Smith, age 8, born CA, recorded in the 1920 U.S. census in the Bernicia, Solano County, CA, home of his parents Benjamin F. Smith, age 46, born CA of OH-born father and MO-born mother, a locomotive engineer, and Margaret (Cunningham) Smith, age 41, born Scotland of Scottish-born father and Irish-born mother. Also in the household that year were sisters Marie, age 11, and Lois, age 9, both born in CA, and grandfather Alex Cunningham, age 68, widower, born Scotland. This Louis C. Smith may be identified with SSDI's Louis O. C. Smith, born 15 June 1912, died 26 August 2000, Downey, Los Angeles County, CA. Louis C. Smith, age 55, married Stella G. Anderson or Harrington in Madera CA on 9 August 1967. Another SSDI Louis C. Smith was born 16 September 1918 and died 3 January 1999, Irvine, Orange County, CA. Haden (184–85) has a better identification for Louis C. Smith.

35. Truman Joseph Spencer (1864–1944) was a longtime amateur journalist whose most famous journal was the *Investigator*. He published a 512-page collection of writing by various amateur journalists under the title *A Cyclopedia of the Literature of Amateur Journalism* in 1891 and was well known for his own writings on the works of William Shakespeare. He served as president of The Fossils in 1934–35 and as official editor of the

[74*] Helm C Spink,[36] 513 Belgravia Court, Louisville Ky
[75] Kenneth Sterling Room A-11, Lionel Hall, Harvard College
[76*] Corwin F Stickney[37] 21 Jefferson St, Belleville, NJ
[77*] Carl F. Strauch,[38] 812 Washington, Allentown Pa
[78*] C. L. Stuart[39] 17 Brockett St, E Milton, Mass

Fossil from 1934 until his death. His own collection of amateur journals was bequeathed to the American Antiquarian Society in Worcester, MA. His work *The History of Amateur Journalism* was posthumously published by The Fossils in 1957; an index volume followed in 1959.

36. Helm C. Spink was born 22 March 1909, the son of Thomas F. and Juliet B. Spink. His father, a medical doctor, had been involved in amateur journalism in Indiana in 1880–83. While working as printing foreman for George G. Fetter in Louisville KY, Spink supervised the printing of HPL's *Further Criticism of Poetry* (1932). In the 1940s Spink moved to Cleveland to work as managing editor for William Feather, a magazine printer/publisher. In 1948 Spink married fellow amateur journalist Bernice McCarthy, the niece of Vincent and Felicitas Haggerty. Spink served the National Amateur Press Association as official editor for three terms: 1929–30, 1930–31, and 1935–36. He became president of The Fossils in 1963 but had to retire following a debilitating stroke. He died in Cleveland in September 1970. His obituary appeared in the *Fossil* dated July 1970 (apparently released later).

37. Corwin F. Stickney was born 10 October 1921 and died 15 November 1998 in Glen Ridge, Essex County, NJ. He knew HPL through science fiction fandom. August Derleth attacked his use of HPL material in the commemorative chapbook *HPL* (1937).

38. HPL's letters to Carl Ferdinand Strauch (1908–1989) are in *JVS*.

39. Clara Louise Stuart (b. 19 October 1875 Boston, d. May 1951 Cambridge) was the daughter of policeman George G. Stuart (b. 7 April 1830 Mount Desert [or Deer Island], Hancock County, Maine, d. 24 December 1887 Boston) and Mary A. (Butler) Stuart (b. 29 September 1841 Baltimore, d. 16 January 1914 Boston) and worked as a secretary and stenographer. For many years she shared her household with teacher Bertha L. Peirce (b. 2 December 1866 Roxbury, d. 25 April 1933 Boston), the daughter of William Frederick Peirce (1838–1901) and Martha Ann (Leonard) Peirce (1842–1922). Peirce and Stuart hosted Lovecraft for a roast beef dinner at the Women's City Club at 40 Beacon Street in Boston on 3 July 1930 (*LFF* 867). Lovecraft was in town for the annual convention of the National Amateur Press Association. Clara was buried at Mount Auburn Cemetery in Cambridge on 16 May 1951, in lot 3298 on Walnut Avenue,

[79*] Edw. F. Suhre,[40] 3641 Juniata St, St Louis Mo
[80*] Sutton-Morgan,[41] 505 W 167 NYC

with her friend Bertha Peirce and Bertha's parents. Peirce and/or Stuart presumably had some connection with the amateur journalism hobby.

40. Edward Frederick Suhre was born 24 March 1879 in St. Louis MO, the son of Herman Suhre. A longtime amateur journalist, he was a founding member of the United Amateur Press Association in 1895 and served as Edith Miniter's successor as president of the National Amateur Press Association in 1910–11. He died 18 August 1939.

41. HPL's surviving letters to Mayte Sutton are in *LFF*. Mrs. Sutton can probably be identified with SSDI's Mayte Sutton (SSN issued NY 1957–59), born 7 July 1879, died September 1968 Ithaca NY. Her first husband John L. Morgan was born in Scotland in March 1877, the son of William and Margaret (Duncan) Morgan. John and a younger brother James came to the United States with their mother in 1883, a year after their father arrived. Mayte married John L. Morgan about 1905, and the 1910 U.S. census found the couple at 606 Bessemer Avenue in East Pittsburgh PA, with their daughters Christine M., age 3 years, born NJ, and Terrace [Jerrace?] F., age 3 months, born PA. Mayte E. Morgan was recorded as born NJ of a NY-born father and a ME-born mother. Mayte became a widow and remarried between the 1910 and 1920 U.S. censuses. The 1920 U.S. census recorded Mayte and her new husband Frank M. Sutton at 5707 Warrington Street in Philadelphia PA (ward 40). Frank M. Sutton, age 53, born in PA of PA-born parents, was working as traffic manager for an electric company. His wife Mayte E. Sutton, age 38, was recorded as born NJ of a VT-born father and a NY-born mother. With them in their household were Frank's stepdaughters Margaret Morgan, age 13, born NJ, and Terrace Morgan, age 9, born PA, both with Scottish-born father and NJ-born mother. In the 1930 U.S. census Mayte E. Sutton, age 48, once again widowed, was recorded in Dryden, Tompkins County, NY, as a dormitory house mother in a private school. The 1930 U.S. census recorded Mayte Sutton as NJ-born, with ME-born father and NY-born mother. HPL's letters to his aunt Annie E. P. Gamwell written from the Long family home in NYC during the 1933–34 Christmas holiday recorded several meetings with Mayte E. Sutton and her daughter. Mayte E. Sutton was the author of "The Cursed Peach Orchard," published under the heading "Student Lore" in the *New York Folklore Quarterly* (17:4) for Winter 1961. Perhaps the 1940 U.S. census will reveal more concerning these NYC friends of HPL. I am indebted to David E. Schultz for assistance on Mayte E. Sutton and her daughter Margaret Morgan.

[81] Margaret Sylvester, 612 W115 NYC
[82] W B Talman, 135 E 42 NYC
[83] Donald Wandrei
[84*] Howard Wandrei
[85*] Henry Geo. Weiss Bx 190, Route 4 Tucson Ariz—*Weiss, a Red, had many vast political tussles with HPL, whose changing social views are probably embodied in letters if they've been preserved—*
[86*] Frederick A. Wesley, 6 Hammond St, Providence
[87*] Lee White, Jr.[42] 2834 Bush Blvd, Birmingham Ala.
[88*] Eola P. Willis[43] 72 Tradd St, Charleston SC
[89*] D A Wollheim 801 West End Ave NYC
[90*] N H Wooley[44] 18 S Mill St, Rosedale, Kansas

---

42. HPL's letters to Lee McBride White, Jr. (1915–1989) are in *JVS*.

43. HPL made the acquaintance of artist and author Eola P. Willis (b. 1856 Decatur GA; d. 1952 Charleston SC) on one of his visits to Charleston. She was the author of *The Charleston Stage in the XVIIIth Century: With Social Settings of the Time* (Columbia, SC: State Co., 1924; rpt. New York: S. Blom, 1966). She was also the author of *A Pretty Mocking of the Life* (New York: Godey, 1893) and *Isle of Palms, Charleston, S.C.* (Charleston, SC: Lucas & Richardson, c. 1910–19); St. Julien Grimké was her co-author for the second title. Her article on "The Dramatic Careers of Poe's Parents" appeared in the *Bookman* in 1926. No work by Eola Willis appears in Lovecraft's library.

44. In the 1925 KS state census, Natalie Wooley, age 20, born KS, was recorded in the Kansas City KS household of her husband George H. Wooley, age 24, born MO, a sheep driver in the stockyards. In the 1930 U.S. census, their household was recorded in Kansas City MO on 8 April 1930. George H. Wooley, age 29, born MO of IL-born father and German-born mother, was working as a teamster for a grading company. His wife, Natalie, age 25, was born KS of a KS-born father and a MO-born mother. Also in their household that year was a son George A. Wooley, age 6, born MO. Natalie Wooley was well-known as a poet in the amateur journalism hobby in the 1930s. Records on Ancestry.com associate her with Natalie Ashburn (SSN 573-07-2921), born 11 November 1904, who died in April 1973 in Houston TX. TX death records recorded Natalie Ashburn's marital status as single. Refer to *An H. P. Lovecraft Encyclopedia* for additional information regarding Natalie Wooley.

note: Marion [sic] Bonner,⁴⁵ and Miss Staples,⁴⁶ *two elderly women fond of cats, have letters on the subject, likely amusing. Write % AEP Gamwell, she'll locate them in Providence*

Entries in HPs 1937 diary⁴⁷

[The "death diary" entries as transcribed by Barlow are published in the locations indicated in note 47 and are not reprinted here.]

---

45. Marian F. Bonner (b. 6 September 1883, Providence RI; d. 13 May 1952, Providence RI), daughter of Robert and Marian Bonner, spent her working career in the periodicals department of the Providence Public Library. In the 1930 U.S. census, she was a boarder in the rooming house at 55 Waterman Street. By 1947, she resided at 167 Evergreen. Her final Providence address (recorded in the 1952 city directory) was 303 Benefit Street. Her letters from HPL are in the Lovecraft Collection at Brown University. Refer to *An H. P. Lovecraft Encyclopedia* for additional information regarding Marian Bonner.

46. Evelyn M. Staples (b. 1 October 1860, Barrington, RI; d. 10 June 1938, St. John, New Brunswick, Canada) was the daughter of Henry Staples, a paper merchant, and his wife Mary H. Staples. Providence historian Judge William R. Staples (1798–1868), the author of *Annals of Providence* (1843), was her paternal grandfather. She began her career as a primary school teacher in her home town of Barrington RI, but was teaching in Providence by 1900. She boarded at 47 Camp Street in 1900, 118 Lexington Avenue in 1910, and 34 Mawney Street in 1920, and was teaching at the Charles Street School no later than 1910. By 1930, she was residing at 55 Waterman Street, in the same rooming house as Marian F. Bonner. She continued to be listed at 55 Waterman Street in City Directories through 1938. Evelyn Staples died during a visit to her niece in St. John, New Brunswick, Canada. No HPL letters to Miss Staples are known to survive. Like Marian Bonner, her fellow resident at 55 Waterman Street, Miss Staples was the owner of some of the cats belonging to the Kappa Alpha Tau feline fraternity whose headquarters was located atop the shed adjoining HPL's last home at 66 College Street.

47. For the diary entries transcribed by Barlow (the so-called "death diary") see *CE* 5.241–42. These transcribed entries were earlier published in Everts, *The Death of a Gentleman* (1987), 25–28.

Works Cited

Everts, R. Alain. *The Death of a Gentleman: The Last Days of Howard Phillips* Lovecraft. Madison WI: The Strange Company, 1987.

Haden, David, "Additions and Corrections for 'Lovecraft's 1937 Diary,'" *Lovecraft Annual* 7 (2013): 178–86.

Joshi, S. T., and David E. *An H. P. Lovecraft Encyclopedia.* 2001. New York: Hippocampus Press, 2004.

PLACES

Providence's Poe Street

In "Walks with H. P. Lovecraft," C. M. Eddy, Jr. wrote that H. P. Lovecraft was unfamiliar with Providence's Poe Street when the subject first arose in a discussion with Eddy of Poe's Providence connections. Two nights later, after the trolleys had ceased to run, Lovecraft and Eddy walked down Eddy Street to Rhodes Street, and from thence to Poe Street, to conduct their own exploration. Eddy recalled:

> At the time we made our pilgrimage, Poe Street ran for approximately fourteen city blocks, ending at Lehigh Street, which turned sharply left and went down to the river. Poe Street was an unpaved road, much overgrown on both sides by unsightly weeds that added to its look of desolation. There were only three or four houses to be seen for the entire length of the street, long abandoned to the years, and harking back to the early existence of the street. Perhaps the city fathers of that early time visualized an expansion of the area all the way to the banks of the nearby river, but such an expansion did not take place. (243)

Eddy's and Lovecraft's exploration, which consumed two hours from departure to return to the Eddy household, probably occurred sometime during the period 1918–24, most likely in 1921–23.

In fact, no street named for Edgar Allan Poe existed at the time of the poet's own visits to Providence in 1845 and 1848. From an early date, Allens Avenue followed the original harbor line all the way to the Cranston line. In fact, Poe Street did not appear in the Providence house directories until 1901.[1] It was a

---

1. According to Britni Gorman of the Providence City Archives, Camm St. was renamed as Poe St. on 7 December 1899. The renaming probably took a little time to be reflected in the city directories.

renaming of Camm Street, which first appeared in the 1869 Providence directory. In this directory, Camm Street ran from Hellen [*sic*] Street to Autumn Street. It paralleled Allens Avenue for its length. Hellen ran from Allens Avenue to 644 Eddy Street, while Autumn ran from Camm, crossed Eddy at 789, and ended at 360 Plain. Camm, Hellen, and Autumn were all then in ward 9. Residents were first listed on Camm Street in the 1899 Providence House Directory. Over the years, tenements were listed at numbers 6, 8, 10, 40, 42, and 61 Poe Street. The even numbers occupied the east (harborward) side of the street; the odd numbers, the west (cityward) side.

The 1870 Rhode Island Atlas depicted Camm Street commencing on the north end at O'Connell and ending on the south end at Lehigh. From north to south, it crossed Bay, Sherburne, Swan, Sayles, Mutual, Square, Oxford, and Seymour before ending at Burgess Cove. The 1895 Providence City Atlas showed that Camm Street had been extended north four blocks, to cross Helen, Public, and Eudora, and to end at Rhodes Street. Pleasure Street now ran east from Camm to Allens Avenue between Oxford and Seymour. Allens Avenue had by now been straightened, and Burgess Cove (which would be drained by 1918), was a cut-off body of water. Square and Autumn Streets had apparently disappeared or been renamed between 1870 and 1895. Briggs Street joined Camm Street just north of Burgess Cove, while Haswell Street ran from Eddy Street to the Cove. The 1918 Providence Atlas showed the southern terminus of Poe Street on recovered land owned by Fred L. Pearce and by Fred L. Pearce and Abraham Bazar jointly, north of Thurbers Avenue. The Macdonald and Corbett Stone Yard occupied the block between Seymour and Lehigh between Poe Street and Allens Avenue. Large businesses on Allens Avenue included the American Radiator Company between Bay and Sherburne and the Dutee

W. Flint Ford Service Station between Sherburne and Swan.

Eddy was correct about the working-class demographic of Poe Street. The 1911 Providence House Directory enumerated only two tenement houses, at numbers 6 and 8 Poe Street:

6 Poe Street
    Bird, Edward, laborer, h.
    Thompson, Isaac, stevedore, h.
    Anderson, James, laborer, h.
    Snead, Louis, laborer, h.

8 Poe Street
    Jennings, William B., laborer, h.
    Vanwinkle, ——, laborer, h.
    Shavers, Donald, hostler, h.

In the 1921–22 and 1923–24 house directories, Poe Street still ran from 136 Rhodes to Lehigh in ward 6. The fourteen blocks enumerated by Eddy included Rhodes, Eudora, Public, Helen, O'Connell, Bay, Sherburne, Swan, Sayles, Mutual, Oxford, Pleasure, Seymour and Lehigh. In 1921–22, residences on Poe Street comprised:

Right Hand Side[2]
    61 Poe Street
        O'Neill, William F., jeweler
        Duffy, John J., machinist
        Trolle, Herlof, music teacher

Left Hand Side
    Eudora begins
    Public crosses

---

2. From the perspective of a pedestrian walking from the northern to the southern terminus of the street. The right-hand side would have been the westward (cityward) side, while the left-hand side would have been the eastward (harborward) side.

8 Poe Street—Vacant
10 Poe Street—Vacant
10 Helen St. crosses
O'Connell St. crosses
Bay St. crosses
40 Poe Street
        Bell, John, laborer
        Anderson, James H., foreman
42 Poe Street
        Craighead, Ernest, truckman
        Shavers, William, jeweler

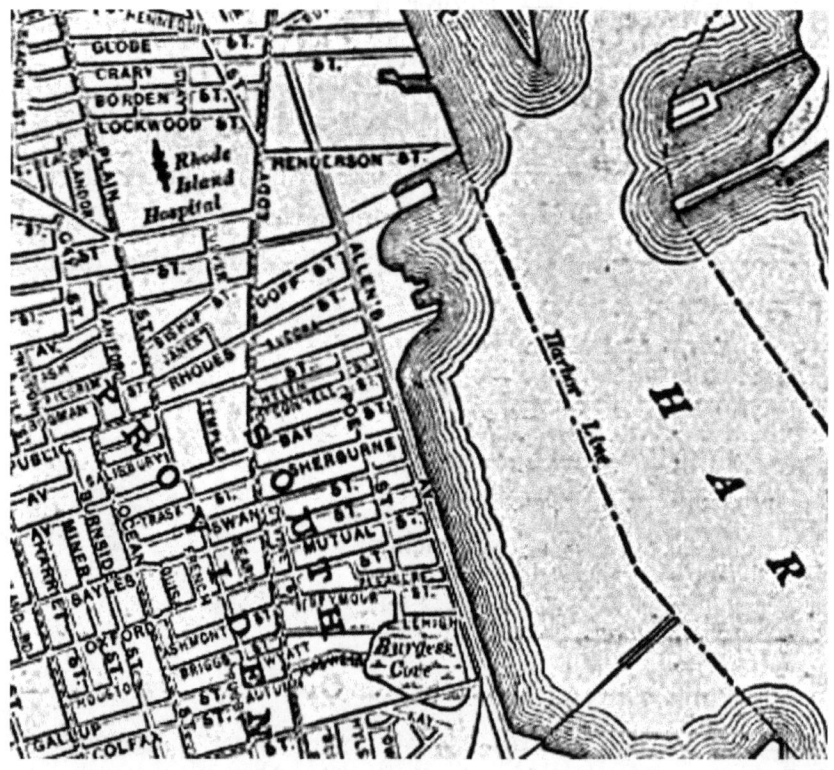

The listings in the 1923–24 house directory were not much changed. Bernard McNeil, janitor, had joined William F. O'Neill and John J. Duffy at 61 Poe Street, while music teacher Herlof Trolle had departed. Numbers 8 and 10 Poe Street, between Public and Helen Streets, vacant in the 1921–22 directory, had apparently been torn down by the time the 1923–24 directory was compiled. Clifford H. Peterson, porter, had joined John Bell and James H. Anderson at 40 Poe Street in 1923–24. William Shavers had left 42 Poe Street by 1923–24, and Mary Brown, widow, and Robert Bailey, laborer, had taken up residence there. The 1923–24 directory also took note of the Modern Auto Spring and Forge Company between Pleasure and Seymour.

Bernard McNeil (1902–1943) and his wife Eva M. (Girard) McNeil (1906–2014) were two of the most persistent residents of Poe Street for the next forty some years, although they were not listed at 61 Poe Street in every year. The 1933 directory enumerated the street about a dozen years after Eddy and Lovecraft made their exploration:

Eudora begins
    Public crosses
    00 Poe Street—Mexican Petroleum Company garage
    40 Poe Street
        Busher, Isabella, Mrs., domestic
        Mason, Grover, laborer
        Williams, Hazel A., Mrs., domestic
    42 Poe Street
        Silva, Rachel, Mrs.
        McNiff, Peter, laborer
        Frazier, Walter, laborer
        Madden, John, laborer
    Helen crosses
    O'Connell crosses
    61 Poe Street

Curtis, Rose, Mrs. Cleaner
Perry, Mary L., Mrs.

Bay crosses
Swan crosses
Sayles crosses
Mutual crosses
Oxford crosses
Pleasure crosses
Cor. Pleasure, Miller Forge Company
165 Poe Street—M. H. Borland Steam Engine & Machine Co.
175 Poe Street—Modern Auto Spring & Forge Co.
183 Petroleum Heat & Power Co.
Seymour crosses

Bernard Francis McNeil, Jr., age 41, died on 15 December 1943, and was buried in St. Francis Cemetery in Pawtucket. He was the son of Bernard Francis McNeil, Sr. (1874–1945), and Margaret (McMahon) McNeil (1869–1952). John J. McNeil and his wife Sophie joined Bernard and Eva at 61 Poe as early as 1941, and remained there as late as 1956. The widow Eva McNeil held out at 61 Poe through at least 1960. Donald N. McNeill [sic], packer, and Richard E. McNeill [sic], USAF, joined Eva, John and Sophie there in 1954. Eva M. McNeil, had been born in Woonsocket on 24 January 1906, the daughter of Zophir Girard and Amanda Giroux. She was the mother of Bernard, Donald, Richard, Margaret, Kathleen, Barbara and two still-surviving children. She died at the magisterial age of 108 years in Providence on 18 February 2014. So a Poe Street resident whom Lovecraft and Eddy might have encountered in 1923–24, did not pass from among us until nearly ninety years after the Lovecraft–Eddy expedition.

By 1948, the household of Mrs. Eva M. McNeil and John J.

McNeil at 61 Poe Street, between O'Connell and Bay, was in fact the only private residence remaining on the street. The American Oil Company garage was at 25 Poe Street, between Eudora and Public. The following additional commercial enterprises were listed on Poe Street: 165, M. H. Borland Ship & Engine Company; 175, Miller Forge Company (blacksmiths); 183, storage—all between Seymour and Lehigh. The configuration was virtually the same in 1956, except that 73 Poe Street, between Bay and Swan, vacant in 1948, was occupied by C. R. & E. R. Pickett, electrical contractors, in 1956.

As late as 1956, Poe Street still ran from Rhodes Street on the north to Lehigh Street on the south. However, the construction of I-95 eliminated the stretch of Poe Street between Rhodes Street and O'Connell Street. The former Helen Street, still extant in 1956, has completely disappeared. The satellite view of Poe Street and environs available on Google Maps gives a good idea of the current configuration. The construction of I-95 through Providence in the 1960s doubtless changed the relationship of the neighborhood with the rest of Lower South Providence to the west. When Poe Street takes its sharp turn into Lehigh Street at its southern end, it is now the expressway which looms beyond the embankment. While some commentators may have expected that the "Chinese wall" of the expressway would facilitate the development of Poe Street and its environs, the commercial character of the lower Providence harbor, combined with the somewhat seedy nature of the adjoining stretch of Allens Avenue, have probably inhibited any residential revival on Poe Street.[3]

On the other hand, there has been some commercial renaissance along Poe Street in recent years. Providence Welding is on

---

3. Crime in the area in recent years may also have posed a deterrent. The *Providence Journal* has reported arrests for drug dealing and sexual assault on Poe Street.

the west side of Poe Street between Bay and Swan (101 Poe Street). Coletta's Collision Center is now on the east side of Poe Street between Swan and Sayles (283 Allens Avenue). U-Haul Moving & Storage of Providence now occupies the west side of the street between Mutual and Oxford (35 Oxford Street). Platforms Dance Club occupies part of the western side of the street in the next block south at 165 Poe Street. The former stretch of Seymour Street east of the expressway has been renamed Warren Way for Warren Equities on the east side of Poe Street north of Lehigh (27 Warren Way).

Across the expressway on O'Connell Street, the Big Blue Bug Solutions (formerly New England Pest Control), with its gigantic rooftop Nibbleswoodaway statue, is a near neighbor of Poe Street (161 O'Connell Street). A less welcome neighbor is the former Cheaters adult entertainment club (once painted a garish pink) on the southwest corner of O'Connell Street and Allens Avenue (245 Allens Avenue). The club, once a notorious site for prostitution,[4] has now been repainted gray and renamed Wild Zebra Gentlemen's Club. Another adult entertainment club, Saints and Sinners, is only a block south on the southwest corner of Allens Avenue and Bay Street (257 Allens Avenue).

On the plus side, the Seaplane Diner, which generally gets

---

4. For prostitution at Cheaters, see Katie Mulvaney, "Ex-manager at Cheaters club tells of problem with prostitution," www.providencejournal.com/article/20150717/NEWS/150719307. Former club manager Paul Calligano testified that dancers employed by the club had to sign a statement acknowledging that they would be asked to leave if they engaged in prostitution. However, the club was provided with five curtained cubicles with small love seats. Dancers were charged $35 to work a shift and had to charge $10 for a lap dance, $35 for a private dance, and $10 for access to the fully nude Godiva Room. Presumably, at least some of these charges went to the house. Thus the dancers had motivation to contract with patrons for sex acts in order to make up for the $35 they were charged for the use of the facilities for each shift.

good reviews, occupies the northwest corner of Allens Avenue and Mutual Street (307 Allens Avenue). Providence Community Health (375 Allens Avenue) occupies the southwest corner of Warren Way and Allens Avenue. Looking to the east of Allens Avenue, it is apparent that heavy industry and shipping still dominate the lower harbor. The section of the harbor to the east of Lehigh Street is still known as Burgess Cove, although there is barely any inlet any longer detectable, apart from a narrow channel which runs westward from the harbor to Thurber's Avenue.[5] A tank "farm" lies immediately south of the channel; Honeydew Donuts (460 Allens Avenue) is to the west of the tank farm.

H. P. Lovecraft and C. M. Eddy, Jr. would probably have a hard time recognizing Poe Street today. For one thing, the street was paved some time after they made their exploration in 1921–23. In addition, none of the sparse tenement residences they observed on their visit survive today. Instead, there has been a renaissance of commercial enterprises along the street. Even as compulsive a Poe site compiler as J. W. Ocker in his *Poe Land* (Countryman Press, 2015) completely omits any discussion of Providence's Poe Street. Of course, neither Poe Street nor its predecessor Camm Street existed when Poe visited Providence in 1845 and 1848. Whether any substantive record of the renaming of Camm Street as Poe Street in 1901 survives is a matter still requiring resolution. Perhaps some local literary figures suggested that the visits of Poe to Providence and his romance with Sarah Helen Whitman (1803–1878) be honored by the renaming of Camm Street. There seems to be no suggestion that Hellen

---

5. Google Maps identifies this channel as the remains of Corliss Cove. Of the three coves that once existed in the Providence harbor—Burgess, Corliss, and Sassafras—Sassafras is probably the most identifiable today. John H. Cady's map of the harbor (see *Civic and Architectural Development of Providence* 220) shows the configuration of the harbor in 1918, with the former coves indicated by dotted lines.

Street, when laid out ca. 1869, was named in honor of Sarah Helen Whitman. It seems doubtful that Mrs. Whitman ever saw either Hellen Street or Camm Street. There would have been no reason for her to venture down to the lower harbor.

Clifford Eddy's "Walks with H. P. Lovecraft" did send me on my own exploration of Poe Street, while I was a student at Brown University, probably sometime during the summer of 1971. (Unlike Lovecraft and Eddy, I made his expedition by day, rather than by night.) I remember best of all the abutment that ends the street when it makes its sharp turn into Lehigh. All things considered, Poe Street has probably had a considerable revival of sorts since I trekked its length more than fifty years ago. Poe Street will certainly never make the list of "top ten" places for fans of Edgar Allan Poe or of H. P. Lovecraft to visit in Providence. Whether a café or restaurant or club named "Edgar" could ever flourish on the street is a question that only the future can resolve. For now, we will shortly celebrate the centenary of Lovecraft's and Eddy's exploration of Poe Street in 1921–23. It is amazing that one contemporary resident, Eva McNeil, only left our company in 2014. That she ever saw Lovecraft and Eddy—given the late hour of their visit—is certainly doubtful. However, we can still speculate that their shades may still appear occasionally, shrouded by the midnight darkness on Poe Street. Perhaps some startled patron of Wild Zebra or Saints and Sinners may yet encounter them.

Works Cited

Cady, John Hitchens. *The Civic and Architectural Development of Providence, 1636–1950*. Providence, RI: Book Shop, 1957.

Eddy, C. M., Jr. "Walks with H. P. Lovecraft." In H. P. Lovecraft et al. *The Dark Brotherhood and Other Pieces*. Sauk City, WI: Arkham House, 1966. 242–45.

Lovecraft's Travelogues of Foster, Rhode Island

In Memory of Foster Historian Margery I. Matthews (1923–2000)

Introduction

Most readers will associate the name of Howard Phillips Lovecraft with stories of cosmic alienage and the supernatural. It is proper that his fame should rest primarily upon these works, since, as he wrote to the members of the Transatlantic Circulator in 1920–21, his creative impulse was limited to this domain.

But there was another aspect to Lovecraft the writer—the private world of his letters, of which a very generous selection was published by Arkham House in five volumes between 1965 and 1976. More letter groups have since been edited by S. T. Joshi and David E. Schultz, for publication by Necronomicon Press, Hippocampus Press, and Night Shade Books. In his letters Lovecraft may be seen as a "whole man," with interests ranging far beyond the outré to encompass literature, philosophy, and the physical and social sciences.

The mind of Lovecraft the private man was never very far from his native city of Providence, Rhode Island. Here his maternal grandfather, Whipple V. Phillips, had come in the mid-1870s to pursue his business career, and here he himself was born in his grandfather's house at 454 Angell Street on 20 August 1890. He developed an extensive knowledge of the antiquities of his native city, buttressed by reading the complete file of the *Providence Journal* at the Providence Public Library. His neighbor Addison P. Munroe, who served in the Rhode Island General Assembly, commented to Winfield Townley Scott that the young Lovecraft knew more of the issues before the Assembly than most of its members. Lovecraft's knowledge of the antiquities of his native city can be appreciated by any reader of his great short novel *The Case of Charles Dexter Ward*. Fittingly, the marker on Lovecraft's grave at Swan Point Cemetery bears the legend: "I Am Providence."

However, if there was a second topographical locus that fascinated the author, it was certainly the western reaches of rural Rhode Island where his mother's family, the Phillipses, settled in the latter portion of the eighteenth century. Sarah Susan (Phillips) Lovecraft's great-grandfather Asaph Phillips (1764–1829) had purchased property on Howard Hill in the newly established town of Foster between 1788 and 1790. Here he farmed on a property that remained in the family through its Cole and Henry lines well into the twentieth century. Asaph and his wife Esther Whipple (1767–1842), married in 1787, raised a family of four sons and four daughters born between 1788 and 1807. Their son Jeremiah Phillips (1800–1848) purchased the Blanchard Mill on the Moosup River from the estate of William Blanchard at auction on 22 December 1834,[1] and died when caught in its machinery fourteen years later. Since his wife, Roby (Rathbone) Phillips (1797–1848), had died the previous summer, their two surviving sons, James Wheaton Phillips (1830–1901) and Whipple Van Buren Phillips (1833–1904), and two surviving daughters, Susan Esther Phillips (1827–1851) and Abbie Emeline Phillips (1839–1873), were left as orphans to be cared for by their relative Nancy Stanton when the 1850 census was recorded. Both sons eventually married into the Place family: James married Jane Ann Place (1829–1900) in 1853 and Whip-

---

1. Jeremiah Phillips was the winning bidder for the mill property at $280. Communicated to the editor by Margery I. Matthews, 31 May 1994, citing Foster Town Records, Book 9, p. 228.

ple married Robie Alzada Place (1827–1896) in 1856. James and Jane inherited the Johnson Road farm of Jane's uncle Abraham (whose wife was another Rathbone sister Nabby), which they farmed through the end of the century, while Whipple and his family removed to Greene, in Coventry, Rhode Island, after several years of keeping store in Foster.

Howard Phillips Lovecraft first came to know Foster when he and his mother Sarah Susan (Phillips) Lovecraft (1857–1921) spent two weeks as boarders in the Johnson Road farmhouse of his great-uncle James Phillips around the time of his sixth birthday in August 1896. The boy must have been impressed with this new rural domain, for a number of his memories of his great-uncle's farmhouse and the surrounding countryside are clearly etched in his fine story "The Silver Key," written shortly after he and his aunt Mrs. Gamwell paid a one-day visit to Foster in October 1926. He was probably a less willing visitor to Moosup Valley Church, where his great-uncle was one of the elders, but doubtlessly sat politely through the sermons of his remote relation, Rev. George W. Kennedy (1824–1900), then in his final years of service. Lovecraft and his mother returned to Foster for a brief one-day visit in 1908, and there is a surviving photograph of fifty-year-old Sarah Susan in front of the James Phillips farmhouse, then owned by James's elder son Walter Herbert Phillips (1854–1924).

Lovecraft was not to return to Foster until the autumn of 1926. By this time, Sarah Susan (Phillips) Lovecraft was dead, and Lovecraft was accompanied by his younger aunt, Annie Emeline (Phillips) Gamwell (1866–1941). Having learned that the original Asaph Phillips farmhouse had been destroyed by fire earlier in the century, Lovecraft and his aunt resolved upon a program of tracing the family roots and visiting ancestral burial grounds. His own interest in family history, originally evinced in his 1905 copying of paternal records compiled by his great-aunt Sarah Allgood, had been reawakened by his young friend Wilfred Blanch Talman, an ardent devotee of genealogical research. The development of motor coach service from Providence to western Rhode Island and points beyond finally facilitated the pursuit of Lovecraft's interest, and with Annie Gamwell he traversed the Plainfield Pike westward from Providence to the hamlet of Rice City on an October day in 1926. Through the graciousness of one of their local relatives, Lovecraft and Annie Gamwell were able to visit not only Tyler and Place sites in the Moosup Valley vicinity but also the village of Greene, where Whipple V. Phillips got his start as a businessman and served as first master of the Masonic lodge. Talking to old-time residents like Squire G. Wood, who had known Whipple V. Phillips personally, and viewing the portrait of Whipple V. Phillips still on display in the Masonic lodge must have made a pleasant ending to a day's exploration for Lovecraft and his aunt.

They were not to return to western Rhode Island for nearly three years. Their second expedition occurred on Wednesday, 26 August 1929, when they disembarked from the motor coach in the tiny hamlet of Mount Vernon and ascended Howard Hill Road to explore their more direct Phillips ancestry. Here Lovecraft viewed for the first time the graves of his great-great-grandparents, Asaph Phillips and Esther (Whipple) Phillips. Providence engineer William A. Henry (1867–1941) and his wife Emma Isadore (Phillips) Henry (1866–1929) had erected a summer home in colonial style on the Asaph Phillips farmstead, which they inherited through Mrs. Henry's grandmother Esther (Phillips) Cole (1807–1881), the youngest daughter of Asaph and Esther Phillips.

Mrs. Henry had died the April before the visit of Lovecraft and Annie Gamwell, who were greeted by her daughter Maud

Esther (Henry) Shelmerdine and her young sons. After enjoying "coffee, cordiality and pears from a tree planted by Asaph Phillips" at the Henry home, Lovecraft and his aunt departed to revisit the Stephen Place homestead in Moosup Valley. Lovecraft's account of his own and his aunt's traversal of the "Moosup Valley short-cut" (shown as "Whippoorwill Lane" in *Foster Map 1971*) is surely his most lyrical paean to the Foster countryside. Despite some rough going through swampy lowland on the abandoned Moosup Valley side of the road, Lovecraft and his aunt emerged in the vicinity of the Job Place and James Phillips farms on Johnson Road, and made their way again to the Stephen Place home. During this visit, Lovecraft and his aunt had the good fortune to see not only the exterior but the interior of the home in which Sarah Susan (Phillips) Lovecraft, her mother Robie Alzada (Place) Phillips, and her grandfather Stephen Place, Jr., had been born. This home, which passed from the Place family to the Battey family after the death of Stephen Place, Jr.'s widow Sarah (Rathbone) Place in 1868, was of great sentimental value to the author. For many years, a crayon drawing of the home that his mother had made after a painting by her aunt Sarah Place Vaughan adorned his study. Lovecraft liked to imagine the peaceful rural existence of Stephen Place, Jr. (1783–1849), and his father, Stephen Place, Sr. (1736–1817). Doubtless there was much more hard work and toil than he imagined; but more reliably he appreciated the understated beauty of the rural countryside that had formed an important part of his ancestors' lives.

It is our misfortune that Lovecraft never carried out his stated intention of exploring even earlier ancestral sites in Foster and elsewhere in Rhode Island. It is possible that he was frustrated by the lack of reliable information relating to his direct paternal line. It is known that Asaph Phillips's father was James Phillips, but his burial place is not known and his date of death (1807) as provided by Lovecraft unproven. Pardon Tillinghast Howard (1839–1925), a great-grandson of Asaph Phillips through his daughter Betsey (Phillips) Howard, believed that James was the son of Jeremiah (1695?–1779) of Glocester, the grandson of Joseph (1669?–1719) of Providence, and the great-grandson of Michael (1630?–before 1676) of Newport. Lovecraft himself, however, believed that Asaph's father James was the son of James and the grandson of Michael, thus skipping a generation. Further, by 1929 Lovecraft was claiming that Michael was himself the son of Rev. George Phillips (d. 1644) of Watertown, Massachusetts—a claim not supported by any genealogical evidence known to me. The persistence of the given name "Jeremiah" in Lovecraft's branch of the Phillips family provides some circumstantial evidence in favor of Pardon Tillinghast Howard's account of Asaph Phillips's ancestry. Lovecraft expressed an intention to consult with his remote relation Frank Darius Phillips (1872–1958) of Potterville, Scituate, R.I., on the matter of the earlier Phillips generations and their burial places, but he is not known to have pursued his expressed intention. Mrs. Gamwell's increasing age and ill health in the 1930s may have also militated against further explorations in her company, while Lovecraft's natural modesty may have militated against solo expeditions that would have required social calls.

Thus we are left with Lovecraft's accounts of his one-day expeditions of 1926 and 1929. While we certainly wish that the author had had further opportunity to explore his western Rhode Island origins in Foster, we must also be appreciative of the wonderful accounts that he left of his two actually accomplished expeditions. These accounts are not unmarred by the author's prejudices: the hard-working Finnish immigrants who helped Foster maintain its viability as an agricultural community in the twentieth century come in for their share of criticism—perhaps Lovecraft recalled his friend Edith Miniter's account of Polish immigrants in *Our Natupski Neighbors* (Henry Holt, 1916)—and there is one unfortunate reference to the "mongrel" Jewish population of New York City (where Lovecraft lived in 1924–26), which he would surely have lived to regret had he survived the Second World War to become familiar with Hitler's Holocaust. Lovecraft's racial prejudices are an unfortunate part of the man, but we should not allow them to detract from his appreciation of his family origins in the Rhode Island countryside.

I do not believe that Lovecraft would have found the Foster of 1825 of his great-grandfathers Jeremiah Phillips (1800–1848) and Stephen Place, Jr. (1783–1849) a very congenial place. The author, like most of the rest of us, had become very dependent upon the comforts provided by modern "machine" civilization. But setting aside the harsh practicalities of making a living in a nineteenth-century agricultural environment, one can contemplate Lovecraft's identification with the cultural and emotional heritage that he received through his ancestors. He had some twenty of the books of his great-grandfather Stephen Place, Jr., in his own library, including the 1802 Abner Alden *Reader* that so influenced his own development as a writer. His collection of the *Farmer's Almanack* began with issues collected by his great-great-grandfather Stephen Place, Sr., who had made marginal notes in some of his copies.

While his immediate family had ceased to be direct owners of real estate with the sale of Whipple V. Phillips's Providence home following his death in 1904, Lovecraft continued to hold (with pride) throughout his life a small mortgage on a Providence quarry, which Whipple V. Phillips may have acquired from his nephew Jeremiah Wheaton Phillips (1863–1902); the mortgage, in fact, was the only asset listed in the inventory of

Lovecraft's estate made by his executor Albert A. Baker (1862–1959). In the 1920s, Lovecraft's friend James Ferdinand Morton, Jr. (1870–1941), became the curator of the Paterson, New Jersey, museum, and Lovecraft took "squirearchical" delight in presenting Morton with rock specimens from the family quarry, then operated by Mariano de Magistris.

One may well dream of the life that might have been Howard Phillips Lovecraft's had he not died prematurely of cancer in 1937 but lived to witness the Second World War and subsequent events. While his grandfather Whipple Phillips and his great-uncle James Phillips both died at about seventy, Lovecraft's Place ancestors were long-lived. Had he attained economic success as an author of science fiction in the postwar world, one wonders if he might have acquired the Whipple Phillips house at 454 Angell Street before its ultimate demolition and restored it to its former grandeur. Had Lovecraft lived to witness the celebration of his centenary in 1990, perhaps he might have been a resident of Halsworth House, able to look out from the window of his room onto his beloved St. John's Churchyard on the steep hillside ascent. But would Providence have been his most likely "retirement" haven? The sunny south with its cultural traditions and warm climate—particularly Charleston, South Carolina—would certainly have beckoned. Of course, there would always be the New England villages where his ultimate cultural roots and personal sympathies lay. His regret for the American Revolution, while idiosyncratic, was nevertheless real.

From my perspective, however, it is difficult to envision a more appropriate retirement haven for Lovecraft than the farmhouse of his great-uncle James Phillips in Foster, Rhode Island[2]—

---

2. Regrettably, this farmhouse on the west side of Johnson Road was destroyed by fire in the first decade of the 21st century and was replaced by a modern structure.

where he awakened to view the dewy morn from the small-paned windows of his bedroom and rose to explore the beautiful countryside with a boy's energy and fascination for two glorious summer weeks in 1896. Perhaps in later life a hired female helper from Moosup Valley might have made life comfortable for the author in the James Phillips farmhouse. Perhaps he might have taken his exercise on each clement day by strolling from his home along the country lanes, visiting family burial grounds and other familiar sights. Doubtless he would have ranged as far as the energies of old age would allow, for in middle age he was a walker of great endurance, especially if motivated by an antiquarian, topographical, or aesthetic quest. It is indeed possible that an "alternative universe" life of Howard Phillips Lovecraft might have ended in quiet retirement in Foster, Rhode Island. His life of course did not end in the Foster he so loved, but the Foster travelogues of 1926 and 1929 that the author left to us permit us to reconstruct and to participate in part in his cultural identifications with this ancestral topography.

I have not provided full citations for vital records. The vast majority, with exceptions as noted, have come from the Ancestry.com, FamilySearch.org (LDS), and AmericanAncestors.org (NEHGS) websites. The editor wishes to thank the Rhode Island State Archives, the late Margery I. Matthews, the late Violet E. Kettelle, and other individuals and institutions who assisted him in his research; however, he retains full responsibility for all errors and opinions contained in his annotations. All occurrences of the Rathbone surname have been normalized to that form; however, the author has let stand variations of the Harrington surname like Herenden, etc.

10 Barnes Street,
Providence, R.I.,
Octr. 26, 1926.

Young Man:—

In replying to your keenly appreciated communication, I must begin in something of my old-time travelogical vein; for the past week has witnessed a pilgrimage on my part, more impressive that [*sic*] any I can recall taking in years. This excursion, on which I was accompany'd by my youngest daughter Mrs. Gamwell, was to these rural reaches of Rhode-Island from whence our stock is immediately sprung; and is design'd to be the first of several antiquarian and genealogical trips covering the Phillips-Place-Tyler-Rathbone-Howard country, and including inspection of as many of the original colonial homesteads as are yet standing. This devotional survey is naturally a recreation of the keenest interest; covering as it does those forms of landscape whose images are permanently burnt into my pastoral soul, and those actual scenes from which my personality was moulded—scenes whose spirit and atmosphere are ineffaceably stamped on the quintessential germ-plasm bequeathed to me down a long line of rustick progenitors. I had previously been in that region but twice in my life; in 1896, when I spent two weeks at the colonial farmhouse of my great-uncle James Phillips,[3] and in 1908, when I took a very casual single day's jaunt with my mother;[4] this infrequent

---

3. James Wheaton Phillips (1830–1901) was the elder brother of HPL's grandfather Whipple V. Phillips (1833–1904). In 1853 he married Jane Ann Place (1829–1900), daughter of Job W. Place (1795–1879) and Asenath (Pierce) Place (1793–1881). Jane's uncle Abraham Place (1800–1852) and his wife, Nabby (Rathbone) Place (1794–1854), were childless, so James and Jane took over their farmhouse on Johnson Road and farmed there through the end of the century.
4. Sarah Susan (Phillips) Lovecraft (1857–1921), who married Winfield Scott Lovecraft (1853–1898) in Boston in 1889.

visiting being due to difficulties of transportation only just solved by means of one of those new-fangled motor stage-coach lines.

On this occasion we started at 9 a.m. from the Eddy Street coach terminal over the antient Plainfield Pike, noting in due time the historick Fenner farmhouse (1677)[5]—homestead of one of Rhode-Island's greatest old families—and later on the region devastated to create the new Scituate reservoir.[6] In less than an hour we reach'd the general section associated with our lineage, and were delighted with some of the late Georgian doorways around Clayville.[7] At length we disembarked at the quaint hilltop village (with a *gorgeous* view!) oddly known as "Rice City",[8] and struck northward along a back road[9] across the town line from

---

5. The Thomas Fenner house is located at 43 Stony Acre Drive in Cranston RI, less than 500 feet south of RI Route 14 (Plainfield Pike). HPL may have had a less obscured view from the Pike in 1926 than is available today. With the Clemence-Irons house in Johnston and the Eleazar Arnold house in Lincoln, the Thomas Fenner house is one of three surviving 17th-century "stone-ender" houses in Rhode Island, and is the least altered of the three. See Jordy 184–85 [item CR12] and Isham and Brown frontispiece, 31–35 and plates 12–18.
6. The Scituate Reservoir covered 14,800 acres and was constructed 1915–25 (Wolf-3 7).
7. The village of Clayville is situated on the Foster-Scituate town line on RI Routes 14–102. Clayville was a mill village but lost its two mill buildings in 1923 during the construction of the Scituate Reservoir (Jordy 263, Downing 35). An 81-acre historic district, admitted to the National Register of Historic Places in 1988, is still preserved in the village.
8. In the late 18th century, Samuel Rice kept a tavern in the vicinity and named the hamlet "Rice City." Elder Douglass Farnum preached a revival in Rice City in November 1812, and in January 1813 Samuel Rice and others received baptism. Rice later removed to Ohio, where he named another hamlet after himself. The Christian Church in Rice City continued to thrive, and in 1870 46 members received dismissal to join the Moosup Valley Church founded by Elder George W. Kennedy in 1868. See Matthews-3 28 et seq. and Jordy 339–40 [CO13].
9. HPL and Mrs. Gamwell probably took Vaughan Hollow Road north

Coventry into Foster, and toward the brookside hamlet of Moosup Valley, "metropolis" of our hereditary rural region.

As we followed the antique highway past copse and mead, cottage and stream, gentle slope and shady bend, I was destin'd to be surpris'd by the loveliness of the countryside. I had known before that it was pretty, but having seen it only twice—once thirty and once eighteen years ago—I had never properly appreciated it. Now, in my old age, I was forcibly struck with its incomparably graceful lines of rolling hill and stone-walled meadow, distant vale and hanging woodland, curving roadway and nestling farmstead, and all along the route the crystal convolutions of the upper Moosup River, cross'd here and there by some pleasing rustick bridge. At one bend in the stream I paus'd with proper pensiveness; for there in 1848 my great-grandfather Capt. Jeremiah Phillips met an untimely end in his own mill, (now demolish'd)[10] being dragg'd into the machinery by the skirts of his voluminous frock coat as a malign wind blew them against some wheel or belt. Whenever we enquir'd the way we found that our names were well known to the inhabitants, and I doubt if any person we saw was not related to us in some more or less distant fashion—such being the universal consanguinity of an antient pastoral community. Finally we beheld across the meadows at our left the distant roofs and white church belfry of

---

from Rice City, and then the right fork where Vaughan Hollow Road divides into Barb's Hill Road (left fork) and Potter Road (right fork). They would have followed Potter Road to Moosup Valley Road and then proceeded west to the hamlet of Moosup Valley.

10. Jeremiah Phillips (1800–1848), the father of Whipple V. Phillips, purchased the mill on the Moosup River originally constructed (c. 1796) by William Blanchard following Blanchard's death in 1833 and operated it until his own accidental death in its machinery on 20 November 1848. A new mill was built on the site in 1867 by Leonard Hopkins and destroyed by a freshet in 1886. The ruins of both mills may still be seen at the sharp bend of Potter Road. See Downing 69.

Moosup Valley,[11] and were soon descending to it past the idyllick farmhouse at the bend of the road—once the seat of "Aunt 'Rushy"—Jerusha Foster[12]—who used to give candy to my mother and aunt[13] when they came to see her back in the early 'sixties—but now occupy'd by a fashionable Providence man[14] who has married into the old local stock—Arthur Dexter's daughter, who lived a piece up the hill.

Crossing the rushing Moosup by another of those deliciously Arcadian bridges, we were soon in the pine-shaded village cemetery,[15] where for some time the colonial slate slabs kept us busy. There were scores of our kindred there—Tylers, Howards, Fryes, Hopkinses, Rathbones, and Places—although our closest relatives all rest in private burying grounds near their respective

---

11. This meeting house for Moosup Valley Christians was originally erected in 1864–65. The Moosup Valley Christian Church was organized in 1868 under Rev. George W. Kennedy (1824–1900), who served as its first pastor for thirty years until retirement in 1898. See Matthews-3 49–56 and Downing 64.

12. Rusha (Potter) Foster (1800–1867) was the wife of Otis Foster (1808–1887) (Faig-1 81). In Foster Map 1870, O. Foster was located on the east bank of the Moosup River, south of Moosup Valley Road. William Kennedy was at this location in Foster Map 1895.

13. The reference is to HPL's elder aunt, Lillian Delora (Phillips) Clark (1856–1932).

14. Margery I. Matthews wrote to me on 29 February 1992: "#2 house which HPL says was occupied by the scion of a well-connected Providence family—well that was true. However 'Nick' was an easy-going, unambitious fellow not well regarded by the high society branch of the family!" I wish I had asked Mrs. Matthews for the surname of the Providence gentleman, but I did not. I have not been able to determine which of Arthur Dexter's three daughters was his wife. In Foster Map 1971 R. Salisbury resides on the southeast corner of Potter and Moosup Valley Roads.

15. Moosup Valley Cemetery (Foster Historical Cemetery #83) lies immediately east of Moosup Valley Church on the north side of Moosup Valley Road. In addition to the persons mentioned by HPL, Clarke Howard Johnson (1851–1930) and Casey B. Tyler (1819–1899) are also buried there.

homesteads. We now walkt through the "civick centre" of the village, noting the church, schoolhouse, grange, and publick library—all of which is family 'property' through association. A distant relative—the Rev. George Kennedy[16]—built the church and was its first pastor, whilst my grandmother's cousin[17] Casey B. Tyler (a local writer and historian, also notary publick, town clerk, and State Senator 1850–51)[18] left his private library to the village to form the present Tyler Free Library—which has some 5000 volumes and is annually aided by the state.[19] The village formerly contain'd a smithy, two shops, a slaughter-house, and a tannery; but commerce declin'd when the old stage route left, and the omnipresent Ford has driven out all that could support a blacksmith. Beyond the "civick centre" we climbed the hill to the old Casey Tyler house[20] where my aunt Mrs. Clark was born,[21]

---

16. Rev. George Waldron Kennedy (1824–1900) was the founding pastor of Moosup Valley Church.

17. Robie Alzada Place (1827–1896) and Casey B. Tyler (1819–1899) were third cousins through common descent from Adam(2) [Thomas(1)] Casey. Robie Alzada Place was the granddaughter of Sarah(4) Casey (1755–1813) [John(3) Adam(2) Thomas(1)] and John Rathbone (1750–1810). Casey B. Tyler was the grandson of Nehemiah Potter (1739–1812) and Eunice(4) Casey (1745–before census date 1790) [Edward(3) Adam(2) Thomas(1)].

18. For the relevant vital statistics on Casey B. Tyler, see Holman 24–26. Faig-1 60–113 reprints Tyler's "Historical Reminiscences of Foster."

19. Since the time of HPL's visit, the Tyler Free Library, originally built on the north side of Moosup Valley Road in 1900, was moved (1965) across the street and joined to the Moosup Valley Schoolhouse (originally built in 1811) (Downing 64 [#236]). The entire structure is now operated as the Tyler Free Library. Many of the publications of the Foster Preservation Society are available for purchase at the Tyler Free Library.

20. This is the Tyler Store on Plain Woods Road, which runs west from Moosup Valley Road (Downing 68 [#244]). Photographs of the house may be found in Colwell 64 and Wolf-1 88. This section of Foster was known as Tylerville, from the Tyler family, which settled there by 1728. Casey B.(6) Tyler [John(5) James(4) John(3) Lazarus(1) John(1)] was the son of John Tyler (1784?–1860), the grandson of James Tyler (1736–1813),

and here we were literally enchanted with the beauty of the landscape. Across the road a wooded valley dips magnificently to the lower meadows, while to the east and north are incredibly lovely vistas of stone-walled rolling pastures, clumps of forest, bits of stream, and purple ranges of hills beyond hills. The house itself, a large three-story structure, is of the early 19th century origin; but beside it is the still intact (though inhabited by a newcomer named Dunbar[22] who has only lived there twenty-five or thirty years) colonial homestead of a story and a half which housed James Tyler (Casey's father)[23] before he built it. The house of Casey[24] was establish'd in the patriarchal Narragansett Country, where large slaveholding was the rule, and was connected with the great Newport house of Wanton, which gave the Province three Royal Governors and some spectacular privateer captains.[25] The marriages of James Tyler and of John Rathbone to Caseys[26]

---

and the great-grandson of John Tyler (b. 1688–93, Portsmouth RI, d. 21 September 1778, Foster RI), who settled in Foster c. 1728. William(4) Tyler (b. 4 April 1718, Warwick or East Greenwich, R.I.) came with his father John(3) to Foster in 1728. See Holman 1–7 and Sherman 220–25.

21. Lillian Delora Phillips was born here on 20 April 1856. Whipple V. Phillips operated the Tyler Store for about two years commencing in 1855 (Faig-1 101).

22. Albert Jarvis Dunbar was born 16 November 1892 in Eastham MA, the son of George E. Dunbar and Mary (Hartley) Dunbar. By 1925, the family had relocated to Moosup Valley Road in Foster, where they remained through the 1940 census. Albert J. Dunbar was working as a public road inspector when the 1935 RI census was enumerated. Albert J. Dunbar died on 4 March 1942, age 49, in Rutland, Worcester County, MA. At the time of his death his residence was Greene RI.

23. James(4) Tyler (1736–1813).

24. Thomas(1) Casey (1637?–1711).

25. William Wanton (1670–1733) and John Wanton (1672–1740) were brothers who served as Governors of Rhode Island in 1732–33 and 1734–40, respectively (both died in office).

26. John Tyler (1784?–1860) married 20 December 1807 Abigail (Nabby) Potter (1787–1838), the daughter of Nehemiah Potter and Eunice(4)

give us an interesting link with the Newport Tories—God Save the King! (One branch of Samuel Casey's[27] descendants left the U.S. at the close of the Revolution, & is still existent at Colborne, Ontario, Canada.) I told my aunt upon reaching home that she had certainly chosen an ideal spot to be born in!

From there we retraced our steps to the village, this time stopping to see a cousin, Mrs. Nabby (Abigail) Tyler Kennedy,[28] whom Mrs. Clark asked us to look up, and who lives in the oldest homestead of all—the antient Judge Tyler Tavern[29] whose

---

Casey [Edward(3) Adam(2) Thomas(1)]. (Casey 7) Eunice was born in Warwick RI on 7 July 1745, the daughter of Edward and Hannah (Bowen) Casey. Her husband Nehemiah Potter was born 13 April 1739 in Coventry RI, the son of Job Potter (born 4 March 1720), and grandson of Abiel and Martha Potter. The couple married in 1763 and Eunice was apparently deceased by the time of the 1790 U.S. census. Nehemiah Potter died on 12 September 1812 in Scituate RI. In addition to daughter Abigail (b. 1787), Nehemiah and Eunice (Casey) Potter had daughters Rhoda (b. 1764), Rachel (b. 1766), and Eunice (1771–1848) and sons Russell (1769–1832) and Nehemiah, Jr. (1773–1810). In 1776 John Rathbone (1750–1810) married Sarah(4) Casey (1755–1813) [John(3) Samuel(2) Thomas(1)] (Casey 27). Their daughter Sarah ("Sally") Rathbone (1787–1868) married HPL's great-grandfather Stephen Place, Jr. (1783–1849). Their daughter Rhoby Rathbone (1797–1848) married HPL's great-grandfather Jeremiah E. Phillips (1800–1848). Another daughter, Abigail (Nabby) Rathbone (1794–1854), married Abraham Place (1800–1852).

27. Casey 34–35 notes that William(4) Casey [Samuel(3) Samuel(2) Thomas(1)] and his brother Willett(4) Casey, the sons of silversmith Samuel(3) Casey, settled in Adolphustown, Canada. Perhaps the fact that these two sons located in Canada may point to the ultimate destination of their father after he was freed from the Kingstown RI jail on 3 November 1770. Willett(4)'s son Samuel(5) Casey continued to reside in Adolphustown, Canada, and served as a member of the Canadian parliament (Casey 39).

28. Nabby Emogene (Tyler) Kennedy (1854–1945) was a third cousin of Lillian Delora (Phillips) Clark (1856–1932) through common descent from Enoch(3) Place. Nabby descended from Enoch(3)'s daughter Mary(4) Place (d. 1787), who was the first wife of James Tyler (1736–1813). Lillian descended from Enoch(3)'s son Stephen(4) Place (1736–1817), who married Martha Perkins (1747–1822).

29. The Tyler Tavern Stand on Moosup Valley Road (Downing 64

oldest parts date back to 1729, (according to some, 1728) when William Tyler, Gent.,[30] made the region his family seat, and took up most of the land in sight. That land, call'd the "Tyler Purchase", was later divided amongst other colonial proprietors; and a hearteningly large part of it still remains in the hands of blood descendants. The region is the most truly American and wholesomely colonial I have ever seen; for there seems to be no break or alteration in the steady stream of hereditary habits and traditions which dates back to the times when Col. Thomas Parker[31] married 'Squire Tyler's daughter and knocked the local raw recruits for the French and Indian Wars into shape on the training-field back of the old Tavern. The reigning Tyler of Revolutionary times was a magistrate, and in his day a formidably business-like whipping-post stood in front of the house. Much of the Tavern, by the way, was blown down in the great gale of 1815; so that the house at which we stopt is really a composite, with its final form dating from 1816. The room in which we sat, however, was part of the original house; and had the immense floor-boards, exposed corner-posts, and panelled overmantel which

---

[#239]) was erected by William Tyler, Jr. [William(5) Tyler (b. 1750)] about 1780. It was damaged and rebuilt following the Great Gale of 1815. HPL claims that the oldest part of the house was built in 1728 or 1729. The oldest Tyler house (Downing 68 [#246]) stands on the south side of Plain Woods Road and is dated to c. 1740 by Downing and her researchers. It was reconstructed from a shell in 1972.
30. William(4) Tyler [John(3) Lazarus(2) John (1)] was born in Warwick or East Greenwich RI on 4 April 1718 and was the son of original Foster settler John(3) Tyler. Casey B. Tyler erroneously described early Foster settler William Tyler as the brother, rather than the son, of original Foster settler John(3) Tyler (Faig-1 60).
31. A Thomas Parker was born to George and Warwick Parker in RI on 20 May 1725. Another Thomas Parker, possibly his son, married Rosanna Tyler (1756?–1832). This Thomas Parker (1755?–1814) died in Foster on 7 May 1814 in his sixtieth year. His widow Rosanna (Tyler) Parker died in 1832, in her seventy-seventh year. See Faig-1 68.

told authentically of the early Georgian period. Our cousin, tho' only 72 years of age, is now the oldest inhabitant;[32] and I was astonish'd at the amount of family lore she has preserv'd. She has much better genealogical records than ours, and will be a mine of information if ever I start the close research I have long plann'd. She reaches the time of William the Conqueror direct through two lines, Tyler and Foster; and believes she could do so through others with a little additional compiling. Her mother[33] was my grandmother's closest confidante and associate in the 1840's, so that she knows as much about my particular branch as about her own. All in all, I was very glad to run across this manorial family Sibyl, with whom my immediate kindred had been wholly out of touch since the 'seventies, when she attended a seminary with my elder aunt.[34] She was, indeed, able to unlock the present as well as the past; being custodian by right

---

32. HPL refers specifically to the hamlet of Moosup Valley. Nabby Emogene (Tyler) Kennedy (1854–1945) did survive long enough to hold the Boston Post gold-headed cane as the oldest inhabitant of the town of Foster. She was presented with the cane by the Foster Town Council on 3 June 1944, following the death of Caroline Johnson Carroll, and held it until her own death on 16 March 1945 at the age of ninety. Her successor as holder of the gold-headed cane was Jennie Foster (Place) Bennis (1859–1948), the daughter of Christopher and Nancy (Blanchard) Place and widow of James M. Bennis (1851–1912). For the Boston Post cane, see Matthews-6 24–25 and Wolf-1 121–27.

33. Waity Ann Foster was the wife of James E. Tyler (1817–1879), brother of Casey B. Tyler (1819–1899).

34. Nabby Emogene (Tyler) Kennedy (1854–1945) was a member of the graduating class of the Rhode Island Normal School in June 1875. I do not find the name of Lillian Delora Phillips among the graduates of the Rhode Island Normal School listed in Thomas W. Bicknell's *A History of the Rhode Island Normal School* (1911). Lillian Delora Phillips and her sister Sarah Susan Phillips attended the Wheaton Seminary in Norton MA. This institution was founded as a female seminary in 1834 and became Wheaton College in 1912. It is possible that Nabby Emogene Tyler attended Wheaton Seminary before she went to the Rhode Island Normal School.

of seniority and ancestral position of all the keys in the village. Kindly enough, she took us through the old church—where her husband's father[35] had preach'd sulphureous damnation—the grange in which she is an active worker, and the Tyler Free Library, which her kinsman founded and of which her daughter[36] (who now lives in my grand-uncle James Phillips' homestead where I visited in 1896) is the present librarian. The latter building is simple, but the collection is astonishingly good. I have a new respect for the taste of my bygone cousin, whose old desk occupies a place of honour at the end of the main room. He used to have historical and antiquarian articles in the papers, "cutely" signed "K.C."[37] Many specimens repose in our old family scrapbooks, but I can't truthfully say that the Gibbonesque style impressed me overpoweringly. The recent library accessions are as well chosen as Casey Tyler's original private stock, and if the natives read many of them, they will be in no danger of retrograding toward a state of yokelry.

Now leaving Moosup Valley, we climb'd another hill past

---

35. Rev. George W. Kennedy (1824–1900), founding pastor of Moosup Valley Church and father of Alvero A. Kennedy (1853–1936), husband of Nabby Emogene (Tyler) Kennedy (1854–1945).

36. Jessie Helen (Kennedy) Bennis (1889–1974), the wife of Albert John Bennis (1887–1971), served as librarian of the Tyler Free Library between 1907 and 1965 (Holman 136–37). Jessie's sister Bertha Tyler Kennedy (1893–1974) married Ellis Blake Bennis (1890–1976), the brother of Albert John Bennis. It is possible that Ellis and Bertha (Kennedy) Bennis were the occupants of the James W. Phillips farm in 1926, in which case HPL mistakenly stated that Bertha was the librarian of the Tyler Free Library. It seems equally possible that Albert and Jessie (Kennedy) Bennis were the occupants of the James W. Phillips farm in 1926, in which case HPL correctly stated that Jessie was the librarian of the Tyler Free Library. In *Foster Map 1971* the households of both Albert and Ellis Bennis are on Moosup Valley Road.

37. Tyler's "Historical Reminiscences of Foster" was reprinted in Faig-1 60–111.

"Aunt 'Rushy's" homestead (which them city folks a-stayin' thar dew keep up in right peart shape!) and enter'd the especial territory of the Places[38]—encountering on our right the well-beloved homestead[39] whose crayon picture by my mother you may have noticed on my wall.[40] I had seen this twice before—in 1896 and 1908—but had really never given it the appreciation it deserves. Now, in my sunset years, I can accord greater credit to that vanish'd Place who built it—or its predecessor—for truly, I never saw an house so intelligently adjusted to make the most of all the aesthetick features of the landscape. In front, across the road, one sees on the right the ascent of rocky meadow extending to the James Phillips house and later to the Job Place[41] estate atop the

---

38. The stretch of Moosup Valley Road around the intersection with Johnson Road was in fact often called "Placetown" because of the predominance of the Place family in the vicinity. Enoch Place (1704–1789) first settled in this vicinity in 1751. For the name "Placetown," see Matthews-2 31 and Faig-2a xxiii [letter of Vivian E. (Phillips) Kinnecom to Lyman T. Place, 15 December 1947].

39. The Place-Battey farmhouse on Moosup Valley Road (1769 et seq., Downing 64 [#234]). Originally constructed by Stephen Place, Sr. (1736–1817), it was the birthplace and subsequent home of his son Stephen Place, Jr. (1783–1849). HPL's mother Sarah Susan (Phillips) Lovecraft (1857–1921) and maternal grandmother Robie Alzada (Place) Phillips (1827–1896) were both born in this house, which probably accounts largely for its sentimental importance to the author. The house was purchased by Henry Battey (1832–1919) after the death of Stephen Place, Jr.'s widow Sarah [Sally] (Rathbone) Place (1787–1868).

40. I do not believe that this crayon drawing is among the HPL relics preserved in the Lovecraft Collection in the John Hay Library at Brown University. Whether it survives in family or other hands is not known to me. I am unable to ascertain whether the crayon drawing can be detected in the photographs of HPL's study at 66 College Street taken by Robert H. Barlow following HPL's death in 1937, which were reproduced in *Marginalia* (Arkham House, 1944).

41. Job W. Place (1795–1879) and his wife Asenath (Pierce) Place (1793–1881) were the parents of James Phillips's wife Jane Ann Place (1829–1900). After their deaths, their home became the residence of their son

hill; this slope balanc'd by a breathlessly lovely valley panorama on the left, in which the stone-wall'd meadows descend in terraces to the gleaming bends of the river, whilst the white village belfry peeps alluringly thro' embowering verdure (now turn'd to the riotous red and gold of autumn) and sets off the endless undulations of purple hills beyond. Behind the house and its attendant orchard a sparsely wooded ravine winds gently down to lower pastures, and forms a background worthy of any artist's brush. Altogether, I was prodigiously imprest with the beauty of the whole picture; and wisht ardently that I might buy back the place, which pass'd from the family some half-century ago. The Vale of Tempë[42] here finds its reincarnation, and the very birds pipe Theocritus[43] and the Eclogues and Georgicks of Maro.[44] The house, in which my own mother and her mother and mother's father[45]

Henry Lester Place (1839–1902). The house on Johnson Road (Downing 63 [#269]) was originally constructed c. 1760 by Stephen Place, Sr.'s brother Benajah Place (1742–1815), the father of John Place (1763–1846), and the grandfather of Job W. Place and Abraham Place (1800–1852).

42. The Vale of Tempe is a valley in northern Thessaly that runs from Olympus on the north to Ossa on the south, through which the river Pineios (Peneus) flows to the Aegean Sea. Its length is 10 kilometers; its width is as narrow as 25 meters. The poets of antiquity described the vale as a beautiful location as noted by John Lemprière in his *Classical Dictionary* (1788). In mythology, it was noted as the domain of Apollo and the Muses. Laurels for the winners of the Pythian games were gathered in a temple dedicated to Apollo that stood on the banks of the Pineios. Here Aristaeus, the son of Apollo and Cyrene, pursued Eurydice, the wife of Orpheus, until she was killed by a serpent's bite. The cities of Tempe, Arizona (USA), and Tempe, New South Wales (Australia), are named after the Vale of Tempe.

43. Theocritus was a Greek poet of the third century B.C.E. He was most noted as a writer of pastoral or bucolic poetry.

44. HPL refers to the Roman poet Publius Vergilius Maro (70–19 B.C.E.), most commonly known as Virgil or Vergil.

45. Sarah Susan (Phillips) Lovecraft (1857–1921), Robie Alzada (Place) Phillips (1827–1896), and Stephen Place, Jr. (1783–1849).

before her were born, is of the prettiest New-England farm type; and dates from a late colonial period when the larger Georgian homestead on the same site was burn'd down. It is now tenanted by the parvenu newcomers who took it fifty years ago, (anyone around Moosup Valley is a stranger and newcomer unless his family has a good two centuries of settlement there!) and has quite sadly deteriorated since our forbears had it. I can even see a marked falling-off since 1908, when I was last there. We paus'd at length in the family burying-ground,[46] separated by a bank wall and iron gate from the roadside, and admir'd several comely skulls and cheerful cherubs—to say nothing of urns, fountains, and weeping willows—on the many slabs of slate and marble. No fragments, unfortunately, were *conveniently loose;* (I *do* want a paperweight of New-England slate instead of New-Jersey red sandstone!) tho' I was strongly tempted by an entire slab of the 1840 period, remov'd from the grave of Stephen Place Jr. in 1903, when a Western relative erected a finer stone, and now lying against the wall at the rear of the enclosure. Epitaphs were abundant, but I found nothing really quaint or grotesque. The rural 'squires of that region were too much in town, and too well train'd in taste at the village academies, to blossom forth with the engaging illiteracy found in other parts of New-England. Time has not been kind to the antient slate, and moss has play'd its obscuring part; so that the earliest epitaph I could read was that of my great-great-grandfather Stephen Place, (there were endless Stephens![47]) who died in 1817. His stone (topt by a willow weeping over an urn) reads thus:

---

46. The Place-Blanchard lot (Foster Historical Cemetery #90) stands next to the Moosup Valley Fire Station (Downing 64). It contains the graves of Stephen Place, Sr., Stephen Place, Jr., and their wives, among others.
47. HPL refers to Stephen(4) Place (1736–1817) [Enoch(3) Thomas(2) Enoch(1)], who married Martha Perkins (1747–1822) and had a large family.

"The dust must to the dust return,
And dearest friends must part and mourn;
The gospel faith alone can give
A cheering hope, the dead shall live."

Inane, but hardly *quaint* in the truest sense. His wife Martha,[48] who departed this life in 1822, revels in equal inanity:

"Hail, sweet repose, now shall I rest,
No more with sickness be distress'd;
Here from all sorrows find release,
My soul shall dwell in endless peace."

We now proceeded to the old James Phillips place,[49] scene of my 1896 visit, and here again I was astonisht by the beauty of the landskip. The antient white house nestles against a side hill whose picturesque rocks and greenery almost overhang the north gable end, while across the road is a delicious combination of hill and vale—hill to the left, with the Job Place estate and its burying ground at the top, (James Phillips, having married Job Place's daughter Jane, lies there)[50] and to the right the exquisite

---

48. Martha (Perkins) Place (1747–1822).
49. The Place-Phillips farmhouse (c. 1810, Downing 63 [#270]). However, the house, constructed for Abraham Place, probably dates to 1826 or later, since a deed of that year describes the 30-acre property as vacant (letter of Margery I. Matthews to editor, 22 July 1992, citing Foster Deed Book 8, p. 226). John(5) Place (1763–1846) [Benajah(4) Enoch(3) Thomas(2) Enoch(1)] deeded the property to his son Abraham(6) Place (1800–1852) in this 1826 deed. This house on the west side of Johnson Road was burned to the ground in the first decade of the twenty-first century and replaced by a modern dwelling. I had the good fortune to examine the interior of the original Place-Phillips farmhouse with Marc A. Michaud, Daniel W. Lorraine, and others in 1990, when the property was offered for sale.
50. The Place-Phillips lot is Foster Historical Cemetery #86. An enumeration of the burials there, abstracted from the records of James N. Arnold and Grace G. Tillinghast, may be found in Faig-2 231–34. James W. Phil-

"lower meadow" with its musical winding brook. The only flaw in the picture is a recent social-ethnic one—for FINNS, eternally confound 'em, have bought the old Job Place house![51] This Finnish plague has afflicted North Foster for a decade, but has hardly secured a real foothold in Moosup Valley, only two families marring the otherwise solid colonialism. They are seldom seen or heard—but it does make me crawl to think of those bovine peasants in the house where my great-uncle's wife was born—and tramping about an antient Place graveyard! Maybe a *hand* will reach up thro' the rocky mould some day.... Well— after this I fancy people will be careful about how they dispose of their real estate![52] Entering the James Phillips house—which has not alter'd since 1896—we were welcom'd by its present inhabitants—a distant kinsman (whose mother was Christopher Place's daughter) named Bennis, and his wife, daughter of Nab-

---

lips (1830–1901) and his wife Jane Ann (Place) Phillips, three of their early-deceased children, and their son Walter Herbert Phillips (1854–1924) are all buried in this lot. In addition, Jane Ann's parents Job Wilcox Place (1795–1879) and Asenath (Pierce) Place (1794–1881) and paternal grandparents John Place (1763–1846) and Lydia (Wilcox) Place (1773?–1856) and numerous other Place relatives are buried here. Janet (McCallum) Phillips (d. 1987), the widow of James W. Phillips's grandson Ellston Corey Phillips (1890–1977), left a bequest for the maintenance of Foster Historical Cemetery #86.

51. Grass 30, 32, 38, 39 notes four Finnish households on Johnson Road: Oscar and Ida Johnson (with children Taimi, Arno, Anne, Arnie, and Art); Vaino and Minnie Lehto (with children Sylvia and Onni); Minnie (Lehto) Taskinen; Sylvia (Basset) Taskinen (with two daughters). I do not know which of these families farmed the former Job W. Place farm on Johnson Road.

52. Actually the Finnish settlers added significantly to the value of Foster agriculture when 50 families settled in the western part of the town between 1919 and 1926. There are still a significant number of families of Finnish descent resident in Foster. For the Finns in Foster, see Grass and Downing 41.

by Tyler Kennedy and librarian of the Tyler Free Library.[53] News of our presence in the region had travelled ahead of us; and I was greeted with two bygone letters of my mother's, which Mrs. Bennis had found among Uncle James's old papers in the attick! This pastoral "grapevine telegraph" (or rather, Bell Telephone) is really quite amusing—for we were heralded in advance wherever we went. Even our first casual inquiry at Moosup Valley caused us to be overtaken at the Tyler Tavern by an honest housewife bearing a newspaper cutting of my grandfather's obituary, which the village thought might be of interest! At Uncle James's place I continued some observations on the feline part of the population which I had begun in Moosup Valley, and decided that the prevalence of tailless Manx Cats was mark'd enough to constitute a distinct local feature. Evidently the breed—about which you must tell Felis[54]—secur'd a strong foothold at an early date; diffusing its blood throughout the continuously settled territory adjacent, but stopping when the distances became extreme. These uncaudal creatures are lively and graceful, and one soon forgets the handicap impos'd upon them by

---

53. Jennie Foster Place (1859–1948) was the only daughter of Christopher Perry Place (1820–1897) and his second wife Nancy (Blanchard) Place (1824–1911). She married James Matthew Bennis (1851–1912) in 1876 and had six children. Two of their sons, Albert John Bennis (1887–1971) and Ellis Blake Bennis (1890–1976), married Jessie Helen Kennedy (1889–1974) and Bertha Tyler Kennedy (1893–1974), daughters of Alvero A. Kennedy (1853–1936) and Nabby Emogene (Tyler) Kennedy (1854–1945). If HPL is correct, Albert John Bennis and his wife Jessie Helen (Kennedy) Bennis were the occupants of the James W. Phillips farmhouse on Johnson Road when HPL and his aunt visited in 1926. Since Vivian E. (Phillips) Kinnecom states in a 1947 letter to Lyman T. Place that her brother Ellston Corey Phillips sold the James W. Phillips farmhouse to Ellis B. Bennis, it is possible that HPL mistakenly identified Ellis's wife Bertha (Kennedy) Bennis as the librarian of the Tyler Free Library.

54. Latin for "cat"; also the name of the then-current feline pet in the household of Frank Belknap Long, Jr.

Nature—an handicap, indeed, which we poor featherless bipeds are not asham'd to share! (Yet how would Felis look without that glorious vulpine brush?) The house pleas'd me as much as it did in 1896, and I envy'd afresh the rag carpets and the wealth of colonial furniture.[55] The Dyckman cottage[56] in New-York will illustrate the atmosphere of the place better than anything else in your benighted metropolitan reach—allowing of course for the difference betwixt Dutch and New-England designs. I was permitted to revisit the corner room where I slept thirty years ago, and where I used to see the green side hill thro' the archaick small-pan'd windows as I awoke in the dewy dawn. Certainly, I was drawn back to ancestral sources more vividly than at any other time I can recall; and have since thought about little else! I am infus'd and saturated with the vital forces of my inherited being, and re-baptis'd in the mood, atmosphere, and personality of sturdy New-England forbears. A pox on thy taowns and decadent modern notions—one sight of the mossy walls and white gables of true agrestick America, and pure heredity can flout 'em all! An health to His Majesty's Province of Rhode-Island and Providence-Plantations! GOD SAVE THE KING!

Later in the afternoon my good 333d cousin Bennis[57] took us

---

55. Some elements of the James Phillips farmhouse are reflected in HPL's description of the Randolph Carter house in "The Silver Key," which HPL wrote shortly after his 1926 visit to Foster (Connors 30ff.).

56. Located at Broadway and 204th Street in Inwood section of Manhattan, the Dyckman Cottage was built in 1784 and deeded to New York City in 1910.

57. Albert John Bennis (1887–1971) and his wife Jessie Helen (Kennedy) Bennis (1889–1974) and Ellis Blake Bennis (1890–1976) and his wife Bertha Tyler (Kennedy) Bennis (1893–1974) were all HPL's fourth cousins, through common descent from Enoch(3) Place [Thomas(2) Enoch(1)]. Jessie's and Bertha's great-great-grandfather James(4) Tyler (1736–1813) married for his first wife Mary(4) Place (d. 1787), the daughter of Enoch(3) Place. The editor is not sure whether Albert John Bennis or Ellis Blake Bennis greeted HPL and his aunt at the James W.

in his car to another scene of our family history—the village of Greene,[58] across the town line in Coventry, where my grandfather establish'd himself and his enterprises in early manhood, and where his last two children (including Mrs. Gamwell) were born. He found the place a tiny crossroads hamlet call'd "Coffin's Corner", but at once proceeded to build a mill, a house, an assembly hall, and several cottages for employees—finally renaming the village after Rhode Island's arch-rebel, Genl. Nathanael Greene.[59] All his edifices are still standing, tho' some of them are diverted from their original uses. The house—a capacious Victorian affair of 16 rooms—remains in the hands of those distant kinsfolk (the Tillinghasts, descendants of old Pardon Tillinghast who founded the Providence sea-trade in 1681) to whom it pass'd when my grandfather came to Providence for good in the 'seventies;[60] whilst the mill is broken up into shops and tenements. The hall retains its pristine impressiveness; its lofty rooms forming the present home of Ionick Lodge, the Masonick branch founded by my grandfather, and of which he was the first Grand Master. It did me good to see his picture there, enshrin'd in proper state.[61] All the population speak of him with affection, and I was espe-

---

Phillips farmhouse and took them to visit Greene.

58. Greene and vicinity are discussed extensively in Wood. See particularly p. 35 for Whipple V. Phillips's business enterprises, p. 12 for his home, and pp. 61–66 for his Masonic connections. Whipple V. Phillips and his wife Robie Alzada (Place) Phillips originally attended the Rice City Christian Church. In the 1880s Robie Phillips and her daughters became members of the First Baptist Church in Providence RI; however, Whipple V. Phillips and his son Edwin E. Phillips never joined the First Baptist Church.

59. Nathanael Greene (1742–1786) was a major general of the Continental Army during the Revolutionary War.

60. Daniel Tillinghast purchased Whipple V. Phillips's home and lived there until his death. It was subsequently owned by Albert W. Cleveland. See Wood 12.

61. Whipple V. Phillips was the first Master (1870–71) of Ionic Lodge No. 28. His portrait still hangs in the lodge hall.

cially pleas'd to talk with those who knew him in person—the old folks like 'Squire Gardner Wood,[62] and Col. Brown the local G.A.R. leader,[63] and the antient cracker-box senate in the gen'ral store, many of whose bearded or stubbly patriarchs worked for him some sixty years ago. One old boy named George Scott[64] shed actual tears of sentimental reminiscence at being confronted with Whipple Phillips' darter an' gran'son!

Well, by that time it was night, and we had to take the 6:12

---

62. Squire G. Wood 3rd was born on 11 March 1861, the son of Caleb Thomas Wood and Ellen P. (Tillinghast) Wood. He died in 1932. He was the author of *A History of Greene and Vicinity,* published posthumously in 1936.

63. HPL probably refers to Curnel Seth Brown, born 17 June 1845, who served in the Navy during the Civil War and married Sarah Jane Case (1847–1927) in 1864. He was recorded in Voluntown CT in the 1870 U.S. census and in West Greenwich RI in the 1880 U.S. census. Brown arrived in Greene in 1882 and opened a grocery (Wood 12). Beginning in 1885, he served as postmaster of Greene for twenty-seven years, with one gap of eighteen months (Wood 30). (The gap apparently ended when Brown was reappointed to the office by the Cleveland administration on 14 October 1893.) Brown died in 1935. Curnel S. Brown and his wife had at least two sons: Elmer E. Brown (1871–1875) and Irving Elmer Brown (1890–1959) [m. Amy Martin Barrows (1890–1981)]. They are all buried in Woodland Cemetery, Coventry, R.I. (Edelman and Sterling CY066 AE0016). G.A.R. refers to Grand Army of the Republic, a Union Civil War veterans' organization.

64. George W. Scott was born June 1856 in RI, the son of Lyman Scott (1813–1894) and Olive (———) Scott. In the 1900 U.S. census, he was living with his wife Sarah W. (born January 1866, R.I.) and his son Harold W. (born December 1892 RI) in Cranston RI, working as a grocer's clerk. By 1920, he was divorced from his wife and living with his sister Sarah Smith in Greene RI, where he worked as a farm laborer. His situation remained the same in the 1930 U.S. census, except that his former spouse Sarah Scott, 64, single, was also living in his household in that year. In the 1940 U.S. census, he was living in the home of his son Harold W. Scott (1891–1947), a postal clerk, and his daughter-in-law Ellen F. Scott (1898–1983) in Greene. George W. Scott died later in 1940 and was buried in Hopkins Hollow Cemetery (Edelman and Sterling CYO12 A0054).

stagecoach home. We had had a great day, but even so had hardly scratched the surface of what we wish to see. The territory cover'd was more Place and Tyler than Phillips or Rathbone country, and a first sight of the antient Phillips burying ground (near the old Asaph Phillips homestead—which my aunt has just learned by telephone was burned down some five years ago[65]) still lies ahead of me. Asaph Phillips, by marrying Esther Whipple of Providence,[66] brought us the blood of that damn'd prophane ruffian Capt. Abraham Whipple,[67] ringleader in the lawless burning of His Majesty's arm'd schooner Gaspee on Nanquit Point in 1772. I hope to take this Phillips pilgrimage before winter—but if I don't, I shall have something to live till next summer for. Anyway, I have definitely adopted the bucolick squirearchical ideal—or confirm'd myself in its adoption—and am already acquiring a distinctly provincial accent—such as Foster folks ought to use, although they don't seem to. Had I not renounc'd literature, I shou'd compose a pastoral poem in the heroick couplet, intitul'd, "Moosup-Valley; an Eclogue".[68]

---

65. This reference dates the burning of the Asaph Phillips farmhouse (c. 1788–90) about 1921. However, note that HPL's 1929 travelogue dates the burning of the farmhouse fifteen years earlier (c. 1914). The editor does not know which date is correct.

66. Esther Whipple (1767–1842) was the daughter of Benedict Whipple (1739–1819) and Elizabeth (Mathewson) Whipple (1736–1802) of Scituate, R.I. Scituate separated from Providence as early as 1731.

67. Captain Abraham(5) Whipple (1735–1819) [Noah (4) Noah(3) Samuel(2) John(1)] was most famous as one of the leaders of the group of Rhode Island colonials who burned the grounded ship HMS *Gaspee* on 9 June 1772. Numerous individuals commented that HPL resembled the portrait of Captain Whipple (now lost) once owned by Brown University; however, HPL was not a descendant of Captain Whipple but rather a third cousin at four removes. His great-great grandmother Esther(5) Whipple (1767–1842) [Benedict(4) Benjamin(3) Benjamin(2) John(1)] was a third cousin of Captain Abraham Whipple through common descent from John(1) Whipple (1618–1685) of Providence.

68. Insofar as I am aware, no such work by HPL has survived. An eclogue

Well—be a reasonably good young man.

Yr obt GRANDPA THEOBALD.[69]

Providence, Rhode-Island,
Septr. 1, 1929.

Young Man[70]:—

Well, Sir, once more you must prepare your sophisticated soul for boredom; for your grandpa hath another travelogue coming on! This will be really a direct continuation of one which I writ you three years ago next month; for like that it deals with a day's journey into my ancestral countryside of Foster, in western Rhode-Island. You may recall that my treatise of 1926 dealt wholly with the Place-Tyler-Casey region of Moosup-Valley—representing my grandmother's rather than my grandfather's streams of heredity—and that I outlin'd therein a design of making further ancestral pilgrimages to cover the more predominantly Phillips regions. Little did I think that three years wou'd elapse ere I took the next trip of the series; but such hath been the crouded programme of an indolent old gentleman that this indeed turn'd out to be the case! Incidentally, I presume I told you last month, as I guided your gaudily painted Essex on the Plainfield Pike, that you went directly through that antient Theobaldian countryside on your way from Providence to your next pausing-place. Had you but diverged on some of the winding, rutted roads which cross the Pike beyond Clayville, you might have seen all that I describ'd in 1926 and shall describe today—yet I doubt not but that

---

is a poem in traditional form on a pastoral subject.

69. HPL took the pseudonym Lewis Theobald, Jun. in remembrance of Alexander Pope's literary foe Lewis Theobald (1688–1744). Pope and Theobald published rival editions of the works of William Shakespeare and were severely critical of each other's editorial work. Pope parodied Theobald as Dulness in his *Dunciad*.

70. The addressee was Frank Belknap Long, Jr. (1901–1994).

the beaches of Connecticut offer'd many more attractions to spirited youth than the stone-wall'd meads and embower'd farmhouse gables of archaick Foster cou'd have done!

My own trip was made last Wednesday,[71] in the company of that selfsame aunt Mrs. Gamwell who shared the memorable trip of 1926. The day was glorious, and as our scene of action we selected the region next to Moosup-Valley—Howard Hill, where the later Phillipses and Howards are thickest—in order to follow out our plan of working backward through our ancestral stream. The lovely slopes of Howard Hill do not form the oldest Phillips country; for that terrain, containing the very antient homestead now falling to ruin, lies to the south, on the old abandon'd section of the Plainfield Pike,[72] and is being sav'd by me as a climax. In the graveyard there I shall find the cherub-carven slate slab of my great-great-great-grandfather James Phillips (d. 1807)[73] and

---

71. 26 August 1929.
72. The Plainfield Pike originally ran more or less directly southwest from Providence RI to Plainfield CT. The construction of the Scituate Reservoir in 1915–25 necessitated the rerouting of a section of the pike. The modern pike is designated as RI Route 14 in Rhode Island. The Old Plainfield Pike runs from Route 14 in Foster RI, eastward to Route 12 (Tunk Hill Road) in Scituate. (A gated private roadway that forms part of the reservoir property runs further eastward until it submerges in the reservoir.) Foster historian Marjorie I. Matthews wrote to me that there are no Phillips burial grounds along the Foster section of the Old Plainfield Pike. Perhaps the road that HPL was referring to was a completely different one. HPL's hoped-for informant on earlier Phillips family burials, his remote cousin Frank Darius Phillips (1872–1958), lived in the village of Potterville, on the Scituate section of Old Plainfield Pike. Like Tylerville and Placetown in Moosup Valley, Potterville was doubtless named because of the onetime predominance of the Potter surname in its immediate vicinity. See Faig-2 (241–59) for a discussion of HPL's beliefs concerning his Phillips ancestry. For Potterville, see Scituate Map 1964 and Jordy 269–70.
73. HPL's letters appear to be the only source for the year of death of James Phillips. I am not aware that any James Phillips matching this year of death is recorded in John Sterling's cemetery database.

probably that of his father James (d. 1746)[74] as well; things I have never seen, but whereof I have heard accounts. For this present trip we chose a region easier of access, (known to my aunt, but never beheld by me) where between 1788 and 1790 my great-great-grandfather Asaph Phillips (1764–1829) settled, and where his descendants are represented both by permanent residents and by persons who spend only their summers there for old heritage's sake. Catching the stagecoach in good season, we travers'd a route at first lying along the old Danielson Pike and including the pleasing village of North-Scituate, but later reaching the Plainfield Pike at Clayville—a small hamlet which you may recall as lying just beyond the extensive reservoir country, and straggling up an hill from the water, with two abandon'd factories along the shoar. Thereafter we duplicated your route of last month as far as Mount Vernon—a semi-abandon'd settlement of two or three houses whose chief edifice[75] has a splendid Georgian doorway with festoon'd fanlight, (I hope you notic'd it!) and which still harbours the crumbling cellar walls of the ruin'd bank of which my great-uncle Raymond Place[76] was

---

74. No son James is recorded for James(2) Phillips (d. 1746) [Michael(1)] of Smithfield, R.I. Pardon Tillinghast Howard (1839–1925), a great-grandson of Asaph and Esther (Whipple) Phillips, recorded Asaph(5)'s ancestry as James(4) Jeremiah(3) Joseph(2) Michael(1) (Faig-2 241–59).

75. HPL probably refers to the Mount Vernon Tavern (Downing 68 [#224]). It is curious that he does not mention that this edifice was in the Fry family from 1842 until 1888, when George Fry (1824–1899) and his family removed to Oregon. George Fry was the son of Richard Fry (1789–1855) and Waite (Phillips) Fry (1791–1883); his mother was the second daughter of Asaph and Esther (Whipple) Phillips. See Faig-2 49–52 and 302–4.

76. Raymond Gardiner Place (1813–1902) was the son of Stephen Place, Jr. (1783–1849), and his wife Sarah (Sally) (Rathbone) Place (1787–1868) and the brother of HPL's maternal grandmother Robie Alzada (Place) Phillips (1827–1896). He married Eliza Lyon Fry (1813–1894), the daughter of Richard Fry (1789–1855) and Waite (Phillips) Fry (1791–1883), the

cashier in the 1830's. Helpful rusticks—who remember'd my grandfather well—directed us to the proper road toward Howard Hill,[77] and we were soon rambling northward along one of the loveliest country lanes I have ever seen—a lane which now and then dipt into dark coppices, and now and then emerg'd to grassy heights whence one might survey the countryside for miles around, spying distant farmhouse gables, lines of stone walls, winding brooks, and gnarl'd hillside orchards whose combined glamour produc'd a picture finer than anything in any eclogue I ever read. This lane at length debouch'd upon the Howard Hill Road thro' a picturesque farmyard with an old mill and mill-stream close by. Then came a walk along the hill's crest, where every lane ended in a noble prospect of distant horizons and where sentinel elms and pines, stone walls and bars, swinging meadow gates, and a little old white schoolhouse[78] with bel-

second daughter of Asaph and Esther (Whipple) Phillips. Raymond G. Place was appointed cashier of the Mount Vernon Bank in 1844 and continued in that office after the bank removed to Providence about 1855. He succeeded Judge Daniel Howard, Jr. (1787–1879), husband of Asaph's and Esther's eldest daughter Betsey (Phillips) Howard, as Foster town clerk in 1852 and continued in that office until 1854. He subsequently served as cashier of the Westminster Bank (1858–61) in Providence and served three terms as a city councilman representing the Eighth Ward. His principal business, like that of Whipple V. Phillips, was coal and lumber. When he died at the age of eighty-eight he was a resident of the Home for Aged Men on Broad Street in Providence. See Faig-2 45–47.

77. HPL and his aunt probably walked north on Howard Hill Road from the Plainfield Pike (RI Route 14) in Mount Vernon. Curiously, he does not mention Foster Historical Cemetery #87 (Downing 62) on the east side of the road. Asaph and Esther (Whipple) Phillips's daughter Waite (Phillips) Fry (1791–1883), her husband Richard Fry (1789–1855), and their son Alfred Casey Fry (1816–1836) are buried in this cemetery. Their headstones can be seen readily from Howard Hill Road.

78. Not far north of the Randall-Howard wheelwright shop, Howard Hill Road takes a jog to the east; most automobile travelers will miss the jog and continue north on Walker Road. However, if one examines Foster Map 1895 and Foster Map 1971 it appears likely that HPL and his aunt

fry and small-pan'd windows, help'd to promote the pastoral beauty of the scene.

At last the site of the burn'd-down Asaph Phillips homestead hove in sight, (recognis'd by my aunt, who had been there before) and we knew we had arriv'd at the focal point of our journey. The old house, built about 1790, perisht some fifteen years ago;[79] but the present owner of the estate, William Henry, Esq., a civil-engineer of Providence (husband of the late great-granddaughter of Asaph Phillips)[80] who dwells there summers,

---

followed the eastward jog of Howard Hill Road. This jog soon turns north and the stretch from the northward turn to Briggs Road probably represents the walk along the rim of the hill which HPL describes. At the intersection of Howard Hill Road and Briggs Road formerly stood Foster School no. 5—probably the schoolhouse referred to by HPL. From this point, HPL and his aunt would have followed Briggs Road eastward to its intersection with Luther Road. The home shown as occupied by W. Bennett in Foster Map 1895 is the site of the original Asaph Phillips farmhouse (c. 1788–90); it was inherited in turn by Asaph's daughter Esther (Phillips) Cole (1807–1881) and her husband Israel Cole (1807?–1886) and by their daughter Waite (Cole) Phillips Bennett (1843–1911) (Faig-2 225–26). Through Mrs. Bennett the home was inherited by her daughter Emma Isadore (Phillips) Henry (1866–1929) and her husband William Alan Henry (1867–1941). The Phillips-Cole cemetery (Foster Historical Cemetery #73) lies in the meadow immediately east of the site of the Asaph Phillips farmhouse (c. 1788–90).

79. Note the conflict between HPL's 1929 and 1926 travelogues on this point. The 1929 travelogue says the original Asaph Phillips farmhouse burned about fifteen years ago (c. 1914), while the 1926 travelogue says the farmhouse burned about five years ago (c. 1921).

80. William Alan Henry (1867–1941) married Emma Isadore Phillips (1866–1929) on 23 June 1889. Emma Isadore Phillips was the daughter of Waite Anne Cole (1843–1911) and her first husband Harley Colwell Phillips (1843–1911) (Faig-2 144–46). Emma Isadore Phillips had died in Providence on 18 April 1929, four months and eight days before HPL and Mrs. Gamwell made their visit to the homestead on 26 August 1929. Arthur Phillips Henry (1892–1967) and Walter Earl Henry (1898–1954), sons of William Alan and Emma Isadore (Phillips) Henry, were operating the farm at the time of the 1920 U.S. census, and the story of their operation was told in the Providence *Sunday Journal* for 9 January 1921.

hath erected a new house of antient design, with interior woodwork taken from demolisht colonial buildings of the region. There are sightly orchards, picturesque old barns and byres, rambling stone walls, stately groves, and magnificent vistas on every hand; so that, recalling that my grandfather (Whipple V. Phillips) and great-grandfather (Capt. Jeremiah Phillips) were both born here, and that the seat of my Place ancestors down the slope toward Moosup-Valley is equally beautiful, (cf. 1926 travelogue, plus subsequent parts of this) I again assur'd myself that I come naturally and honestly by my pastoral predilections and love of fine bucolick landskips. The old Phillips graveyard,[81] which I have long'd to see for years, is situate on the crest of a meadow hill which drops abruptly to an exquisite wooded valley with a brook.[82] It is girdled by a low drest-stone wall, and commands a splendid prospect of meads and groves—one particularly impressive cluster of giant trees lying shortly westward. On its hillward side it drops to a lower terrace which juts boldly out from the slope and ends in a high bank-wall—a terrace devoted to the newer interments, and maintain'd in as elegant and sophisticated a state as your own Woodlawn;[83] with close-shav'd greensward, trim beds of

---

81. Foster Historical Cemetery #73 (Cole-Phillips lot). The somewhat conflicting information from the Benns and Tillinghast transcriptions of this cemetery is reproduced in Faig-2 228–30. The cemetery may be approached from the yard of the adjoining home or from a path cut south from Briggs Road.
82. The newer portion of the cemetery is built on an embankment overlooking Westconnaug Brook.
83. Woodlawn Cemetery was founded in the Bronx NY in 1863. After temporary interment in an indigent grave, Frank Belknap Long [Jr.] (1901–1994) was himself reburied in a family lot [Lot East Middle Part 55 L.L.P. Sec. 57 Plot Prospect] in Woodlawn Cemetery on 17 November 1994, and his name subsequently inscribed on the lot's central monument. *Moshassuck Review* (February 1995) contains an account of Long's reburial and a reproduction of the lot plat. Foster Historical Cemetery #73 containing the graves of Asaph and Esther (Whipple) Phillips and

gay flowers, tasteful urns, and polisht granite monument and markers of the most metropolitan pattern. In this lower terrace area are interr'd many Providence Phillipses who cherish a wish to lie on ancestral soil despite their lifetime separation from the ancestral scene. It is very attractive in its way, but forms a rather incongruous element in the agrestick Foster landskip. Naturally, my chief interest lay in the upper and older burying-ground with its Georgian slate slabs bearing weeping-willows, cinerary urns, and glibly rhym'd epitaphs, and its white marble slabs of the 1840's with their brief, pious, and sentimental observations. This place was much like the old Place cemetery in Moosup-Valley, which I describ'd in my 1926 travelogue. I now copy'd with great pains several ancestral epitaphs—in some cases having to clear away moss, earth, and creepers in order to reach the bottom lines. I was reminded of my delightful day's trip through the New-Netherland Dutch region of Rockland County with Talman in 1928,[84] when he took me to scores of similar places containing his ancestors. He has all his family burial-grounds at his finger-tips—as indeed I hope to have mine after the completion of my series of expeditions. But here are a few of the Phillips epitaphs:

---

other family members is maintained twice a year through a bequest left by their great-great-granddaughter Maud Esther (Henry) Shelmerdine (1893–1958), who with her two young sons entertained HPL and Annie Gamwell when they visited the cemetery and the site of the Asaph Phillips homestead in 1929. When I visited this cemetery in 1990, the upper section with the older graves was in poor condition, while the lower, banked section containing later graves was reasonably well maintained. Daniel W. Lorraine took the photographs of Asaph's and Esther's markers that served as the frontispiece for Faig-2 but contracted a serious case of poison ivy in the endeavor. For burials in Foster Historical Cemetery #73, see Faig-2 228–30.
84. HPL visited his friend Wilfred B. Talman at his home in Spring Valley, Rockland County, NY, on 24 May 1928 (*IAP* 709).

ASAPH PHILLIPS
(my gt-gt-grandfather; 1764–1829)

The sweet remembrance of the just
Shall flourish when they sleep in dust.

ESTHER PHILLIPS, wife of Asaph Phillips (1767–1842)

Blessed are the pure in heart, for they shall see God.

CAPT. JEREMIAH PHILLIPS (Asaph's son, 1800–1848.)

(Kill'd in his own mill—he was inspecting it on Nov. 20, 1848, and caught the skirts of his voluminous frock-coat in a whirling belt. This was 4 months after the death of his wife, so that my grandfather grew up an orphan.[85])

This mortal shall put on immortality.

---

85. In the 1850 federal census, Nancy Stanton was caring for the four surviving children of Jeremiah and Roby (Rathbone) Phillips in their home in Foster: Susan Esther Phillips (1827–1851), James Wheaton Phillips (1830–1901), Whipple Van Buren Phillips (1833–1904), and Abbie Emeline Phillips (1839–1873). Nancy Stanton was probably a relation by blood or marriage of Roby (Rathbone) Phillips (wife of Jeremiah), Sarah (Sally) (Rathbone) Place (wife of Stephen, Jr.), and Nabby (Rathbone) Place (wife of Abraham), through their sister Ruth Rathbone (1787–1838), who married John Stanton, son of Joseph Stanton, of Voluntown, Conn., in 1812. Cooley 181 shows daughters Mary E. Stanton (born 3 May 1812) and Sally Stanton (born 10 February 1820) for this marriage. Perhaps Nancy Stanton was a sister or other relative of John Stanton. Writing to Lyman T. Place on 15 December 1947, Vivian E. (Phillips) Kinnecom (1884–1963), a granddaughter of Whipple V. Phillips's elder brother James W. Phillips (1830–1901), recalled that the three Rathbone sisters (Sarah, Nabby, Roby) from West Greenwich RI visited so frequently that they wore paths among their respective homes in Moosup Valley (Faig-2a vii).

RHOBY RATHBONE
(wife of Capt. Jeremiah Phillips; 1797–1848)

(Whose sister Sarah Casey Rathbone,[86] marrying Capt. Stephen Place Jun., was the mother of my grandmother Rhoby Place—named for her, and later marrying her son Whipple Phillips.)

> O ye mourners, cease to languish
>   O'er the grave of those you love;
> Pain and death and nights of anguish
>   Enter not the world above.

SUSAN ESTHER PHILLIPS
(dau. of Capt. Jeremiah: 1827–1851)

(My grandfather's favourite sister,[87] who dy'd at 24, and after whom my mother was given her middle name of Susan.)

---

86. HPL refers to his great-grandmother Sarah Casey Rathbone (1787–1868), the daughter of John Rathbone (1750–1810) and Sarah Casey (1755–1813). HPL's ancestor John(3) Casey (1723–1794) [Samuel(2) Thomas(1)] was the father of Sarah Casey (1755–1813).

87. Whipple Phillips also had a younger sister, Abbie Emeline Phillips (1839–1873), who married Henry D. Dixon (1835–1905) in Sterling CT in 1859. They had four sons, three of whom lived to maturity, while one son, Whipple Van Buren Phillips Dixon, died as an infant in a scalding accident in 1872. The Benns and Tillinghast transcriptions of the Cole-Phillips lot (Foster Historical Cemetery #73) disagree as to whether there was yet a third sister Anna M. Phillips; Tillinghast lists such a child dying on 10 January 1829 at the age of 3 years 7 months 22 days, while Benns lists no such child but a child Seth dying on 10 January 1829 at the age of 7 months 22 days (Faig-2 228–30). It seems clear that Tillinghast and Benns must have interpreted a worn or fragmentary stone or stones differently. It seems that barring further evidence HPL's earlier transcription of the stone for Seth Whipple Phillips ought to have the greatest authority, combined as it is with a bit of family tradition concerning the boy. The commonplace book of Sarah Susan (Phillips) Lovecraft as preserved in the Lovecraft Collection in the John Hay Library at Brown University lists yet

Thou art gone to the grave, but we will not deplore thee,
   Tho' sorrows and darkness encompass the tomb;
The Saviour has pass'd thro' the portals before thee,
   And the lamp of his love is thy guide thro' the gloom.

SETH WHIPPLE PHILLIPS
(Son of Capt. Jeremiah: 1825–1829)

(Dy'd at the age of 3yrs. 7mo. 22d., before my grandfather was born. When—in 1833—my grandfather did appear, he was given the first name of Whipple—the middle name of this tiny brother he had never known.)

    Parents, weep not for thy son,
      Who is early call'd away;
    His better life is now begun,
      Where youth will ne'er decay.

ZILPHA ANN PHILLIPS (dau. of James,[88]
the son of Asaph and bro. of Jeremiah)
(died Sept. 23, 1824, aged only 10 mo. 20d.)

    Our short-liv'd idol, our sweetest flow'r,
    Is call'd by death's all-conquering pow'r

---

another child of Jeremiah and Roby (Rathbone) Phillips: a son Wheaton, presumed to have died early.

88. James Phillips (1794–1878) was the second son of Asaph and Esther (Whipple) Phillips. Zilpha Ann Phillips was his daughter by his second wife, Mary Ann Phillips (1803–1852). James and Mary Ann (Phillips) Phillips had another daughter, Emily Esther Phillips (1830–1895), who lived to maturity and married Charles W. Greene (1829–1901). James and Mary Ann Phillips and their family removed in 1844 to Delavan IL, where James Phillips prospered and became prominent in local affairs. For James Phillips, see Faig-2 13–19.

To leave a world of grief and pain:
We part, but soon shall meet again.

Tho' the head of the Henry household[89] was absent in town, his visiting daughter (my third cousin) from New-Jersey[90] and several grandsons extended pleasing hospitality. I had met none of them before, and was very favourably imprest by their unaffected kindliness and quiet cultivation. They produc'd some genealogical data—books and charts—which help'd me very materially in defining my exact relationship to several collateral Phillips lines, and I in turn was able to tell them much they did not know about various links and coats-of-arms. Here the incentive given me by Talman two years ago bore useful fruit!

Having been regaled with cordiality, coffee, data, and pears from a tree planted by Asaph Phillips, we departed over Howard Hill in quest of a short cut to Moosup-Valley and the Place country, insomuch as I wisht to behold again the antient and sightly birthplace of my mother, grandmother, and Place great-

---

89. William Alan Henry (1867–1941), widower of Emma Isadore (Phillips) Henry (1866–1929), a great-granddaughter of Asaph and Esther (Whipple) Phillips.
90. Maud Esther (Henry) Shelmerdine (1893–1958) was the daughter of William Alan Henry (1867–1941) and Emma Isadore (Phillips) Henry (1866–1929). She married William A. Shelmerdine (1888–1966) in Providence in 1914. They had sons William A. Shelmerdine, Jr. (1916–1978) and Alan Gordon Shelmerdine (born 11 February 1926), undoubtedly the grandsons of William and Emma (Phillips) Henry whom HPL and his aunt met in 1929. For Maud Esther (Henry) Shelmerdine, see Faig-2 184–85. Alan Gordon Shelmerdine resided with his parents in Summit, Union County, NJ, when the 1930 and 1940 U.S. censuses were enumerated. He enlisted in the armed forces at Fort Dix NJ on 22 March 1944 and subsequently attended Oberlin College in Oberlin, Ohio. He married Betty Jean Stevens, whom he divorced in Marin County, CA, in November 1975. In 1993 he resided in Bellevue, WA. It does not seem likely that he would have retained any memory of HPL's 1929 visit, since he was only three years old at the time.

grandfather. At the top of the hill we paus'd at the newer Howard homestead, where we made ourselves known to the gentleman of the estate, Whipple Howard, Jun.,[91] a descendant of Judge Daniel Howard, whose wife was Asaph Phillips' next-youngest daughter Anna[92]—my third cousin by that link, and a remoter cousin by an earlier link. He prov'd a man of middle age, wide information, and much affability; who remains on his ancestral soil in the manner of those who went before him. His house is of early 19th century date, and in fine repair—one of the most pleasing New-England rural places I have ever beheld. I am proud to bear his family name as my first. By his directions we found the Moosup-Valley short cut, and at once plung'd into a deserted countryside of utterly dreamlike loveliness.

The lane we follow'd[93] was formerly the main highroad to Moosup-Valley and the country westward, but was abandon'd

---

91. Whipple Howard (1834–1910) was the son of Martin Howard (1790–1865) and his wife Ruth Lockwood (Whipple) Howard (1803–1881). Whipple Howard lived all his life on his father's farm (c. 1783, Downing 62 [#262]) about a mile and quarter south of Foster Center, and his home is readily located on Howard Hill Road in *Foster Map 1895*. Whipple Howard married Esmeralda Evelyn Cole (1853–1904), daughter of George Cole. However, according to Howard 69–70, their son Whipple Howard, Jr. died in infancy in 1873. Perhaps HPL in fact met one of their other sons, Almond Ormond Howard (1881–1954), Everett Martin Howard (1883–1968), or William Albert Howard (1885–1949).
92. HPL errs here. The wife of Daniel Howard, Jr. (1787–1879) was Asaph and Esther (Whipple) Phillips's eldest daughter Betsey Phillips (1789–1848). Their daughter Ann Phillips (1804–1845) married Gardner Lyon (1804–1849). Daniel Howard, Jr. and his wife Betsey (Phillips) Howard are buried in Foster Historical Cemetery #71 across from their home on Howard Hill Road. Gardner Lyon and Ann (Phillips) Lyon are buried in Foster Historical Cemetery #103 (the Lyon lot) located westward from Howard Hill Road (along what is labeled "Whip-Poor-Will Lane" in *Foster Map 1971*). HPL and Mrs. Gamwell skirted, but did not visit, the Lyon lot in their traversal of the "Moosup Valley short-cut" during their 1929 visit to Foster.
93. I believe that this lane was almost certainly "Whip-Poor-Will Lane" as

about the time of the revolution in favour of the present route. During its existence houses had been built upon the Howard Hill half of it, so that the perpetuation of that part as an accessible lane was necessary. The other half, in the valley beyond the Lyon burying-ground[94] and toward the James Phillips place, was suffer'd to fall into desuetude; to such extent that today not a trace remains of it. Entering the still-preserv'd part of the route from the top of Howard Hill, we found ourselves in the most marvellous and magical colonial territory it hath ever been my good-fortune to behold. Other old roads have such signs of modern decadence as telegraph-poles and mail-boxes, but here nothing of the kind had intruded. Just the quaint, narrow, stone-wall'd line of the antient road, now carpeted with soft, delicate grass and mosses and rambling in curves and twists through an incredibly exquisite variety of meadows, orchards, woods, valleys, and sleepy Georgian farmsteads. Birds sang, and the westering sun pour'd a flood of almost unreal and theatrical witchery over the graceful verdure and undulant pastures. The feeling that one walkt in a sheer vision became more and more intense as the chromatick pageantry of fresh greenery, deep-blue sky, and fleecy cumulus clouds spread more and more thoroughly within one's consciousness. The charm of the antient seats with their white-gabled houses, old-fashion'd gardens, stone walls, sloping orchards, and picturesque lines of barns and sheds became so overwhelmingly pervasive that one felt almost opprest for lack of opportunities for instant lyrical utterance. Here, indeed, was a

---

shown in *Foster Map 1971*. Note that this lane ends in marshy land just west of the G. Hollis sawmill site and the Lyon lot (Foster Historical Cemetery #103). Today this gravel lane enters Howard Hill Road at numbers 43–43A. Once the marshy land has been traversed, it is an easy walk to the Job Place homestead, the James Phillips homestead and Moosup Valley.

94. Foster Historical Cemetery #103.

small and glorious world of the past *completely* sever'd from the sullying tides of time; a world *exactly* the same as before the revolution, with *absolutely nothing* chang'd in the way of visual details, currents of folk-feeling, identity of families, or social and oeconomick order. Where Howards or Lyons or Phillipses or Places settled in the first half of the 18th century, there Howards and Lyons and Phillipses and Places live now—tilling the same fields in the same way, living in the same houses and thinking the same thoughts. Horse-drawn vehicles preponderate still, and the drowsy hum of summer is unvext by any discordant note of urbanism or mechanism. A gentle, elusive fragrance unknown either to towns or to ordinary countrysides pervades the whole scene, and so stimulates the imagination that even I, whose fancy is so disproportionately visual, found myself living with several senses rather than with only one. Certain appropriate lines from Milton came spontaneously into my head, and I found myself muttering:

> "As one who long in populous city pent,
>   Where houses thick, and sewers, annoy the air,
>   Forth issuing on a summer's morn, to breathe
>   Among the pleasant villages, and farms
>   Adjoin'd, from each thing met conceives delight:
>   The smell of grain, or tedded grass, or kine,
>   Or dairy, each rural sight, each rural sound."[95]

Verily, I told my aunt, there is no need to marvel at that circumstance noted by Horace, when he said:

> "Scriptorum chorus omnis amat nemus et fugit urbes."[96]

---

95. From Milton's *Paradise Lost* 9.445–51.
96. From Horace's *Epistles* 2.2.77: "The entire band of writers hates the town and loves the country."

Such, without the least difference in aspect or mood, is the agrestick realm thro' which my forefathers rov'd in the golden age of the Georges. It is beyond question that young Asaph Phillips must have strid along its length on many a sunny afternoon whilst bound for his kinsfolk's abodes in the valley beyond, and here my great-grandfather Jeremiah must often have pluckt blossoms and lain on the sward looking up at the mysterious sky and elfin clouds and fantastick treetops in the days just after 1800, when as a little boy he play'd truant from the trim white schoolhouse with its neat belfry and small-pan'd windows.[97] Today either young Asaph or little Jerry and his brothers and sisters—Benoni, Betsey, Waity Ann, James, Whipple, Anna and Esther[98]—cou'd roam thro' these selfsame meads and lanes and groves without finding anything amiss or thinking that anything had happen'd to their small, simple, Arcadian world in the interim. For after all, the antient New-England of the Magnalia,[99] the Pilgrim's Progress,[100] the Bible, the Farmer's Almanack,[101] the New-

---

97. HPL certainly paints an idealized view of life, even child life, in the Foster of 1800. For a more realistic description of rural life at this period, see Jones.

98. The children of Asaph and Esther (Whipple) Phillips were Benoni Phillips (1788–1850) (m. Lucy Fry); Betsey Phillips (1789–1848) (m. Daniel Howard, Jr.); Waite Phillips (1791–1883) (m. Richard Fry, brother of Benoni's wife); James Phillips (1794–1878) (m.1 Susanna Paine, m.2 Mary Ann Phillips, m.3 Annie M. Davidson); Whipple Phillips (1797–1856) (m. Eliza W. Gardner); Jeremiah Phillips (1800–1848) (m. Roby Rathbone); Anne Phillips (1804–1845) (m. Gardner Lyon); and Esther Phillips (1807–1881) (m. Israel Cole). For the children of Asaph and Esther (Whipple) Phillips, see Faig-2 7–30.

99. *Magnalia Christi Americana* by Cotton Mather (1663–1728) was originally published in London in 1702. HPL owned a family copy of the first edition, inherited from his uncle Dr. Franklin Chase Clark (1847–1915). After HPL's death, Robert H. Barlow (1918–1951), as directed by the "Instructions in Case of Decease" left behind by the author, sent HPL's copy of the first edition to James Ferdinand Morton, Jr. (1870–1941).

100. This famous work by John Bunyan (1628–1688) was first published in 1678. HPL owned an 1817 edition of this work (*LL* 152).

England Primer,[102] and the elder poets *is not dead*. It hath meerly *retreated from visibility* and from oeconomick predominance—from the dirty fringe of foreignised cities and the squalid length of cement state roads with their billboards, roadhouses, tourist cabins, and hot-dawg stands. Quietly, in the tranquil and lovely by-roads where vulgar wealth and aimless progress never intrude, it still lives on in its own old way—with narrow winding roads, smiling rock-and-turf slopes, gnarl'd brooding apple-trees, and massive, smoak-wreath'd farmhouse chimneys. There is no paradox or deception in the statement that the old Foster scene shrin'd in my ancestral memories is likewise a reality of the 20th ventury, [*sic*] and that the pil'd-up squares and rectangles on my genealogical charts represent not a dynasty and milieu that are extinct, but a breed and life which exist today as truly as they existed in those glamourous 1700's and early 1800's. The only difference is in *the relative place which these people and this life occupy in the nation and world as a whole*—and as you may easily imagine, this difference is trifling indeed to an old gentleman who repudiates *in toto* both the entire machine culture of the present, and the personality-stunted Babbitt-warren[103] of North-American com-

---

101. HPL's main collecting interest was *The [Old] Farmer's Almanack*, begun by Robert B. Thomas in 1792. ("Old" was added to the title in 1832, to distinguish the publication from competitors like *The Farmer's Almanack*, first published in 1818 from Morristown NJ by Jacob Mann with David Young as editor.) *The Old Farmer's Almanack* was acquired by Robb Sagendorph of Yankee, Inc. in 1939 and continues to be published today. HPL owned a fine collection, which Robert H. Barlow sent to the author's friend W. Paul Cook following HPL's death, in accordance with his "Instructions in Case of Decease." HPL discussed his holdings of *The Old Farmer's Almanack* in his letter to Walter J. Coates of 13 October 1927 (*WH* 112).

102. *The New-England Primer* was first published in 1687–90 by Benjamin Harris from Boston. The earliest surviving edition dates from 1727. For the three different editions HPL owned, see (*LL* 738).

103. HPL refers to the protagonist of *Babbitt* (1922) by Sinclair Lewis (1885–1951).

mercialism, size-worship, and time-table servitude to which that accursed bastard-culture hath now reduc'd these once-glorious colonies. God Save the King! I am happy to say that the peril of Finnish immigration, which was an active threat to Foster when I writ my travelogue three years ago, is waning rather than increasing. The intruding Finns were mainly summer pests who spent their winters in diverse labours around the wharves of New-York, and as time goes on, they seem to gravitate more toward New-York than toward Foster. It was their old Finland peasant heritage which made them seek the soil upon first reaching America; but as they become assimilated into the mongrel proletariat of the usurping machine civilisation of this continent, they gradually adopt its rat-like urbanism. Many farms, Finn-own'd a decade ago, have lately return'd to Anglo-Saxon hands. Howard Hill never had other than its old colonial stock, and now the whole South Foster region seems assur'd of an indefinite English future. The Italian wave from Providence stops ten miles east of this terrain, with a great reservoir system and barren belt as a buffer. Most of the home-keeping old folk have never seen a foreigner save for the few intruding Finns, and are inclin'd to call all foreigners "Finns"—just as you Manhattanites find all alienism summed up in the ratty Mongoloid Jew. If any ingulphment ever comes, it will probably be from the towns of Connecticut across the state line rather than from Providence—but even that menace is obviously far remote. At present, Foster is an all-Yankee colonial town carrying on the original New-England tradition of agricultural simplicity. There is less danger of change now than in the middle 19th century, when everyone flockt to the cities and dreaded the notion of being thought countrify'd. The good Foster families send their sons to Providence schools and Brown University, and sometimes (as in the case of Mr. Henry aforemention'd) engage in business of professional occupations in town; but their anchorage always remains on their paternal soil—they are on their old farms all summer, and chuse (as the lower terrace of the Phillips burying-ground attests) to be laid to rest in the end beneath the calm skies and waving grasses of the meadows their fathers knew and lov'd. For two hundred years these people and these lands have always been the same—and I hope they will always be. The sort of stock they produce is well display'd by typical sons who have caught some notice from the world—Pres. James Burrill Angell[104] of the U. of Mich., who sate next my grandmother at the Smithville Seminary;[105] U.S. Senator Nelson Wilmarth Aldrich;[106] Chief-Justice Clark Howard Johnson[107] of the R.I. Supreme Court (distant cousin and close friend of my grandfather—executor of his will); Pres. Gilbert Anthony Phillips[108] of the Prov. Bank (my grandfather's 3d cousin); and so on. I am sorry that my direct personal line did not stay on the antient soil; for as it is, my affection and

---

104. James Burrill Angell (1829–1916) served as president of the University of Michigan from 1871 to 1909.

105. Smithville Seminary was established in North Scituate RI in 1839. It became the Lapham Institute in 1863 and survived until 1876. Thereafter, a series of religious and vocational schools and summer camps—including the Pentecostal Collegiate Institute in 1902–19, the Watchman Institute in 1923–38, and the Watchman Summer Camp in 1938–74—occupied the premises until 1974, when the building was converted to private apartments. See Jordy 266–67. The village of Smithville or North Scituate is located at the intersection of Danielson Pike (RI Route 6) and West Greenville Road. The village historic district was enrolled in the National Register of Historic Places in 1979. HPL's maternal grandmother Robie Alzada (Place) Phillips (1827–1896) was a student at the Smithville Seminary in the 1840s.

106. Nelson Wilmarth Aldrich (1841–1915) served as one of Rhode Island's U.S. senators from 1881 to 1911.

107. Clark[e] Howard Johnson (1851–1930) was a close friend and business associate of HPL's grandfather Whipple V. Phillips (1833–1904).

108. Gilbert Anthony Phillips (born 30 June 1843, Foster; died 25 November 1908, Providence) rose to become a prominent banker in Providence.

loyalty are necessarily divided betwixt these pastoral meads of ancestral memory, and the antient hill and Georgian spires and roofs of that Old Providence to which my own infant eyes were open'd. By birth urban, I am by every hereditary instinct the compleat rural squire. God Save the King!

Well—having loiter'd as long as possible along the old road, we finally came to the hilltop farm of the Lyons[109] which marks the end of its accessible part. Inquiring the way to Moosup-Valley of a kindly, antient gentlewoman, we struck out across thinly-path'd hills and dales of the greatest conceivable beauty; skirting the Lyon burying-ground[110] and traversing the pastures where the kine of Howard Hill and Moosup-Valley meet on common territory. The way became more and more difficult as we proceeded, paths being obscure and thorn-choak'd, and valleys being exceeding marshy. At one point an enormous black snake glided across our path, causing my aunt to advance with added caution. The last barrier was a brook which separated a wooded swamp from a rising meadow—and having edg'd across this on planks, we stood at the edge of Moosup-Valley, where the exquisitely beautiful James Phillips place dreams on as of old at the road's bend; nestling in the lee of its rocky hill, and looking across the elm-arcaded way at the green lower meadow, where graceful alders nod above a crystal, convoluted stream. Of this place I spoke at some length in my 1926 travelogue, telling how I visited there for two weeks in August 1896, when my grand-uncle James Phillips (my grandfather's brother—Capt. Jeremiah's eldest son) was alive, and how

---

109. Shown as home of George P. Lyon in Foster Map 1895. S. P. Lyon in Foster Map 1862 and Foster Map 1870. Probably same as John Lyon House (Downing 62 [#294]). The address of the Lyon farmhouse is 43–43A Howard Hill Road.

110. Foster Historical Cemetery #103. Asaph and Esther (Whipple) Phillips's daughter Anne (Phillips) Lyon (1804–1845) and her husband Gardner Lyon (1804–1849) are buried in this cemetery.

it is now in the hands of an agreeable couple named Bennis,[111] both collateral kinsfolk of mine. On this occasion we paus'd only for brief civilities, proceeding at once to the neighbouring Place homestead whose picture (a crayon drawing by my mother, after an oil-painting by my late great-aunt Sarah Place Vaughan[112] of East-Greenwich, R.I.) you have often seen on your grandpa's wall, and beneath whose roof my mother, my grandmother Rhoby Place, and my great-grandfather Stephen Place Jun. were born. Of the loveliness of this house, landskip, and roadside burying-ground I have spoken in the earlier travelogue; so that I need not describe in detail my pleasure at beholding the time-mellow'd gables, the climbing ivy, the stone-wall'd road, the verdant vale behind, and the downward-sloping meadows to the northwest, where the modest white belfry of the Moosup-Valley village church gleam'd thro' embowering boskage. Despite the mediocre newcomers who have inhabited the place since it left our family in 1870,[113] we on this occasion decided to inspect the interior; which I had not seen since my sixth birthday, Aug. 20, 1896, and which my aunt *had never seen in her life*—at least, with conscious eyes, since her only entrance to the house was as a toddling infant in the last days of its Place tenure.

Beholding it thus as a relative novelty, we were very much

---

111. Either Albert John Bennis (1887–1971) and his wife Jessie Helen (Kennedy) Bennis (1889–1974) or Ellis Blake Bennis (1890–1976) and his wife Bertha Tyler (Kennedy) Bennis (1893–1974), all four of whom were HPL's fourth cousins, by common descent from Enoch(3) Place [Thomas(2) Enoch(1)].
112. Sarah Ann (Place) Vaughn [Vaughan] (1824–1901) was the older sister of HPL's grandmother Robie Alzada (Place) Phillips (1827–1896). They were both daughters of Stephen Place, Jr. (1783–1849), and his wife Sarah [Sally] (Rathbone) Place (1787–1868).
113. Henry Battey (1832–1919) purchased the Stephen Place, Jr., homestead after the death of Stephen, Jr.'s widow Sarah [Sally] (Rathbone) Place (1787–1868).

prepossess'd by the evidences of what had been—tho' the present inhabitants are rather slovenly householders with far from old-Novanglian standards of neatness and decoration. The elder Stephen Place, (1736–1817)[114] who built the house toward the end of the 18th century after an older one just across the road had burn'd down, must have had something of the mediaeval-manorial in his taste; insomuch as he provided an enormous central room or "great hall" with fireplace, out of which many smaller rooms open'd—a design which I have never seen in any other old New-England farmhouse. The interior woodwork, though not treated as well during the last sixty years as it deserves, is still excellent; and I wou'd give much to have the carv'd white Georgian mantel in the great room to sit by of an evening with logs blazing behind colonial andirons—perhaps a pair of marching iron Hessians with bristling muskets and tall grenadier hats. The six-panell'd doors are finely wrought, and equipt with latches and hinges of a type already old-fashion'd when the house was built. Old Stephen was a man after my own heart, and I have reason to know that he fully appreciated his exquisite rural environment. It is his file of Farmer's Almanacks which begins my own collection, and in those numbers publisht toward the close of his life I find marginal notes in his hand, indicating timid poetick attempts bas'd upon the agrestick scene—or more, perhaps, on the conventional literature of agrestick scenes. In the 1815 issue I find the following not very original bit—

> "Hark, from the copse a tuneful sound,
>   My ears attend the cry"

---

114. Stephen's father Enoch(3) Place (1704–1789) [Thomas(2) Enoch(1)] settled in Foster RI in 1751. He married Hannah Wilcox (1710?–1802).

which makes me regret that no more of the text is accessible. He was evidently unwilling to have any of his manuscripts survive for the edification of his posterity, since I have never seen any compleat poem of his. Incidentally—the rhetorical textbook us'd by his son Stephen Jun. (my great-grandfather) at the old Kent Academy[115] in the early 1800's (The Reader, by Abner Alden, A.M. Boston, 1797[116]) is the very volume out of which I first pickt up the rules of prosody myself—by coincidence, in the same year of 1896 wherein I visited Foster. I found it tuckt away with other Georgian reliquiae in a windowless attick room of my birthplace—454 Angell St.—and was fascinated by its long s's, well-stated precepts, and Dryden-Pope-Thomson-Addison-Johnson selections. I have it before me as I click these lines[117]—faithful guide and companion of my youth and old age alike! God bless it—a worthy preparation for my present task of revising and shaping Moe's "Doorways to Poetry"![118] Such were the influences which made old Grandpa Theobald what he is! How I lapt this up in '96 and '97—and how little Stevie Place Jun. must

---

115. The East Greenwich Academy (originally named the Kent Academy) survived from 1802 to 1943. In addition to his Place great-grandfather Stephen Place, Jr. (1783–1849), HPL's grandfather Whipple V. Phillips was also educated at the East Greenwich Academy. Foster historian Margery I. (Harrington) Matthews (1923–2000), the daughter of Herman Battey Harrington and Mary (Griffiths) Harrington, was a 1941 graduate of the East Greenwich Academy.

116. HPL owned an 1808 third edition of *The Reader: Containing the Art of Delivery, Articulation, Accent, Pronunciation* [etc.] by Abner Alden (1758?–1820). *LL* 25.

117. HPL uncharacteristically typed both the 1929 travelogue and the 1926 travelogue; perhaps he made carbon copies for his files. The 1929 travelogue also exists as a holograph letter to Maurice W. Moe dated 1 September 1929 (see *MWM* 231–45). The 1926 and 1929 typescript letters to Frank Belknap Long are used herein for the text.

118. HPL worked extensively on this book-length manuscript written by his friend Maurice Winter Moe. It was never published.

have lapt this same material up at the academy a century and a quarter ago! Same stuff—same book—same spirit—and here was your grandpa in the same house on a glorious August afternoon; the house where little Stevie was born, where he grew up, and where he dy'd full of placid rural memories in 1849—the year after his brother-in-law Jeremiah Phillips was kill'd in the old mill down the Moosup-Valley Road. Old days—old days—and old ways! Here I sit a century later with Steve's old book before me, a score of his other books on my shelves,[119] his file of *Farmer's Almanacks* (following his father's) in my lower table drawer, his blood in my veins, and the glowing memory of his house and native landskip in my mind and fancy. God Save the King! Who says the Georgian past is gone? Bring on your damn'd years—a helluva lot they can modernise this tough old Georgian bird!

> Nor can decadent change unchalleng'd thrive
> While Foster and Old Theobald both survive![120]

Well—we broke away from the hallow'd spot at last, and walkt amongst lengthening shadows in the golden light down

---

119. A few books from HPL's library bearing the signature of Stephen Place, Jr. have been offered in the rare book trade. Chris Perridas (www.chrisperridas.blogspot.com) identifies one such title (and reproduces images from its eBay offering) in his post dated 4 February 2007: *The Analogy of Religion, Natural and Revealed, to the Constitution and Course of Nature* by Joseph Butler (1692–1752) (*LL* 163). HPL owned an 1822 New Haven edition of this work, originally published in 1736. This book contains ownership signatures of Stephen Place (Foster RI, 1833), HPL and Annie E. Phillips Gamwell (7 July 1924). (Perhaps HPL gave the book to his aunt following his relocation to New York City in March 1924.) Unfortunately, it does not seem possible to identify with certainty which score of HPL's books were originally owned by his great-great-grandfather Stephen Place, Jr.

120. Could these be surviving lines from the apparently non-extant poem "Moosup Valley: An Eclogue," which HPL mentions in his 1926 Foster travelogue?

the old road, the narrow, stone-wall'd road, the bending, mead-flankt road, thro' vary'd rustick vistas to the huddle of old gables and chimneys, barns and byres, elms and orchards, that is antient Mount-Vernon on the Plainfield Pike. There, as twilight stole upon us, we took the Providence stage-coach; thereafter rumbling back thro' the fine old villages of Clayville and North-Scituate, and finally entering the mongrel chaos of the urban penumbra. Jangling, bustling down-town was a sad anticlimax after Foster—but balm came when I turn'd toward the antient hill and saw the Great Square of Pegasus[121] shimmering over the shadowy Georgian roofs and steeples on the wooded crest. Old Providence! Here, too, the antient colonial life and spirit survive amongst the hillside lanes where double flights of steps rise from mellow brick sidewalks, and the early lights of evening gleam soft and yellow from arching fanlights and small-pan'd windows.[122] God Save the King! If one must dwell in a town, then surely there's no place like Old Providence, round which all the memories of my youth are cluster'd. Thank Heav'n I reside in a quiet byway[123] on the crest of the hill; where all is as it used to be, and no sight or sound suggests anything that one might not find in a placid New-England village of 2000 or 3000 souls!

My next ancestral pilgrimage will cover the *earlier* Phillips re-

---

121. Pegasus is a north sky constellation first listed by Ptolemy in the second century C.E. Alpha, Beta, and Gamma of Pegasus plus the Andromedae form the "great square."

122. Refer to Cannon for further discussion of this type of imagery in HPL's work.

123. Between 1926 and 1933 HPL resided at 10 Barnes Street. His aunt Lillian Delora (Phillips) Clark (1856–1932) (widow of Franklin Chase Clark, M.D.) also lived at this address. In 1933, HPL and his younger aunt Annie Emeline (Phillips) Gamwell (1866–1941) combined households in a second-floor apartment at 66 College Street, just west of Brown University's John Hay Library, which today houses HPL's papers.

gion south of Howard Hill—on the *old* Plainfield Pike;[124] a section cut off from offensive traffick when the highway was relocated to banish a bend. Here I hope to find living and discursive a very distant cousin nam'd Frank Phillips,[125] who I am told can shew me where my great-great-great-grandfather James (Jun.—d. 1807) (Asaph's father) is bury'd—in the old God's-acre which may possibly harbour *his* father as well. (d. 1746)[126] This elder James's father Michael (1642–1686)[127] rests at antient Newport, whereof he was made a freeman in 1668; and I still hope to find his mortal remains amidst the populous slate acreage of the Farewell St. burying-ground.[128] Mike was a townsman—I'm asham'd of him!—for Newport was a great and cultivated seaport in his day. His father Rev. George[129] (prais'd in Cotton Mather's

---

124. See note 78.
125. Frank Darius(8) Phillips [Darius Olney(7) Matthew Colvin(6) Joseph(5) David(4) John(3) Richard(2) Michael(1)] was born 27 September 1872, the son of Darius Olney Phillips (1832–1916) and Malina Stone (Colvin) Phillips (1834–1896). He married Gertrude Elizabeth Howard (1872–1949), the daughter of Whipple Howard (1834–1910), on 1 November 1891. HPL was a sixth cousin at one remove of Frank Darius Phillips.
126. Pardon Tillinghast Howard (1839–1925) gave the ancestry of Asaph(5) Phillips as James(4) Jeremiah(3) Joseph(2) Michael(1). Joseph(2) Phillips died in 1719.
127. Michael(1) Phillips was already referred to as deceased in a letter written by Francis Brinley of Newport RI to John Whipple of Providence dated 13 August 1676 (*Early Records of the Town of Providence*, 15.151). Family historian Dean Crawford Smith believes that Michael may have died shortly after he became a freeman of Newport on 28 October 1668, since all his children are believed to have been born between 1651 and 1667 (Smith 368). Austin 152 shows Michael Phillips's year of death as 1689 or earlier. See Faig-2a (xvii) for more discussion of the date of death of Michael(1) Phillips.
128. The Newport Common Burial Ground is located on Farewell Street. Established in 1665, it contains over 7500 burials in its 500-by-500-foot area. No stone or marker for Michael(1) Phillips (1630?–before 13 August 1676) is known to survive.
129. Rev. George Phillips, originally of Rainham St. Martin's in Norfolk,

Magnalia) dy'd in 1644, and is bury'd where he preach'd, in Watertown, in Y^e Massachusetts-Bay,—a place I have never seen, but which I have all my life been meaning to visit. On with the epitaph chase! . . . . tho' back of Rev. George it will lead me far, since his father, Christopher Phillips, Gent.[130]—and all the still earlier fathers—Tudor and Plantagenet gentlemen of OLD ENGLAND—sleep on holier soil—beneath the ivy'd and crumbling parish church of Rainham St. Martin's in Norfolk. They never saw New-England—and with lov'd, blest *Old England* stretching delectably about them they never needed to!! The main line—by primogeniture—of these Norfolk Phillipses now sports a baronetcy, as I found during my Talman-born[131] researches of 1927; the present baronet being Sir Lionel Phillips of Boxford,[132] unless he was kill'd in the war or somehow return'd to dust since the publication of the book I found him in. And so it goes! Now back to curst revision—but with hopes of another and more early-Georgian ramble thro' Foster's pastoral meads before the chill of winter sets in. It's a great sport, really. Had you been wise, you

---

died in Watertown MA in 1644. There does not seem to be any support for HPL's assertion that his ancestor Michael(1) Phillips (1630?–before 13 August 1676) of Newport was a son of Rev. George Phillips. Albert M. Phillips's 1885 Phillips family genealogy (Phillips) devotes many of its pages to the descendants of Rev. George Phillips; perhaps HPL decided that he wanted to claim this illustrious cleric as an ancestor.

130. Christopher Phillips was buried 3 February 1620/21 in Rainham St. Martins, near Rougham in the hundred of Gallow in Norfolk, England. Savage (3.409–10) makes the assertion that Christopher was the father of Rev. George Phillips (1593–1644), whom he states to have been born in the same parish in which his father died.

131. HPL refers to his friend Wilfred B. Talman, an avid genealogist.

132. Sir Lionel Phillips (1855–1936), created 1st Baronet in 1912, spent most of his life in the mining business in South Africa. He was succeeded in the baronetcy by his grandson Sir Lionel Francis Phillips, 2nd Baronet. It seems likely that these Phillipses are very distant relatives of HPL, if they are related at all.

wou'd have made your recent Connecticut stopping place New-Haven instead of some colourless beach—for 'tis there I believe you can find the Doty and Mansfield epitaphs[133] which you really need in order to establish a perfectly harmonious terrestrial orientation!

Well—be a good young man! Here are some cuttings and oddments which may amuse you. Please return Moe's transcript of the Sirenica[134] extract. Isn't that prose a thing to marvel at and revere?

Yr obt. GRANDPA

Works Cited

Austin, John Osborne. *The Genealogical Dictionary of Rhode Island*. Albany, NY: Joel Munsell's Sons, 1887. Rpt. Baltimore: Genealogical Publishing Co., 1969.

Bayles, Richard M., et al. "The Town of Foster." In *History of Providence County, Rhode Island*. New York: W. W. Preston & Co., 1891. 2.626–39.

---

133. The parents of Frank Belknap Long, Jr. (1901–1994) were Frank Belknap Long (b. 18 October 1870, New York, d. 28 February 1940, New York) [the son of Charles C. Long (1845?–1904) and Julia A. Long (1845?–1914)] and May Mansfield Doty (b. 13 October 1870, New York, d. 22 September 1951, New York) [the daughter of Charles Edmund Doty and Emma Augusta Mansfield]. Long's maternal grandparents were both born in 1846 and married in New Haven on 15 September 1869. Long's father was a New York City dentist; he and his wife frequently entertained the members of the Kalem Club in their home. "Doc" Long's Essex automobile enabled his son to stop to visit HPL on several family vacation trips to Cape Cod and other New England tourist destinations. The Longs sometimes took HPL along for part of their journeys.

134. HPL probably refers to *Sirenica* (John Lane, 1913) by W. Compton Leith [pseudonym of Ormonde Maddick Dalton (1866–1945)]. Mark Valentine and Douglas Anderson have some useful information on this work and its author on the Wormwoodiana website (wormwoodiana.blogspot.com/2010/12/w-compton-leith.html). Perhaps Maurice W. Moe had made a transcription of parts of this work, available today in its entirety for reading on Google Books.

Bucknum, Shirley E. *The Place Family Research Aid*. Portland, OR: Published by the author, [n.d.].

Cannon, Peter H. *"Sunset Terrace Imagery in Lovecraft" and Other Essays*. West Warwick, RI: Necronomicon Press, 1990.

Casey, Thomas Lincoln [T. L.]. "Early Families of Casey in Rhode Island." *Magazine of New England History* 3, No. 2 (April 1893): 83–128.

Colwell, Heidi, et al. *Foster, 1781–1981: A Bicentennial Celebration*. Foster, RI: Foster Bicentennial Committee, 1981.

Connors, Scott, ed. *A Century Less A Dream: Selected Criticism on H. P. Lovecraft*. Holicong, PA: Wildside Press, 2002.

Cooley, John C. *Rathbone Family*. Syracuse, NY: Published for the Author, 1898. A photocopy reprint of this work was published by the New England Historic Genealogical Society in 1992.

Downing, Antoinette F., et al. *Foster, Rhode Island: Statewide Historical Preservation Report P-F-1*. Providence, RI: Rhode Island Historical Preservation Commission, 1982. Sometimes referred to as "the green book" because of the color of its front cover.

Eddleman, Bill, and John E. Sterling. *Coventry Rhode Island: Historical Cemeteries*. Baltimore: Gateway Press, 1998.

Faig, Kenneth W., Jr., ed. *Early Historical Accounts of Foster, Rhode Island*. Glenview, IL: Moshassuck Press, 1993. Contains "Sketches of Foster" by Charles C. Beaman (1799–1883) and "Historical Reminiscences of Foster" by Casey B. Tyler (1819–1899). Sometimes referred to as "the yellow book" because of the color of its covers. [Faig-1]

———. *Some of the Descendants of Asaph Phillips and Esther Whipple of Foster, Rhode Island*. Glenview, IL: Moshassuck Press, 1993. [Faig-2]

———. *Corrections and Additions for Some of the Descendants of Asaph Phillips and Esther Whipple of Foster, Rhode Island.* Glenview, IL: Moshassuck Press, 1994. [Faig-2a]

Folsom, John R., Jr. *Place Families of Southwest Oswego, N.Y., Volume I: The Descendants of Samuel, Hazard, and Dr. Simeon G. Place.* Orlando, FL: John R. and Charlotte W. Folsom, 1994. [Folsom-1]

———. *Place Families of Southwest Oswego, N.Y., Volume II [Draft]: Other Descendants of Enoch Place of Kings Town, R.I. and Unconnected Families.* Orlando, FL: John R. Folsom, Jr., 1995. [Folsom-2]

Foster Map 1799. Isaac Davenport (with corrections and additions by Theodore Foster). *Plan of the Town of Foster, June 20, 1799.* Redrawn by Sandra J. Campbell. Foster, RI: Foster Preservation Society, 1974.

Foster Map 1862. Henry F. Walling. *Portion of Henry F. Walling Map: Providence, R.I., 1862.* Foster portion reprinted by Foster Preservation Society (Foster, RI, 1974).

Foster Map 1870. D. G. Beers and Company. *Foster, Providence Co., R.I.* Philadelphia, 1870. Reprinted by Foster Preservation Society (Foster, RI, 1974).

Foster Map 1895. Everts & Richards. *Town of Foster.* Philadelphia, 1895. Reprinted by Foster Preservation Society (Foster, RI, 1974).

Foster Map 1971. George E. Matteson. *Foster Rhode Island Directory Map.* Coventry, RI: Matteson Map Service, 1971.

Grass, Walter W. *This Finnish Episode: Recalling the Finns in Foster, Rhode Island and Its Surrounding Areas.* Foster, RI: Parable Studio, 2005. Distributed by Foster Preservation Society.

Holman, Susan Tyler. *The Family of James Tyler, Descendants of John Tyler of Portsmouth, Rhode Island.* Farmington, CT: Published by the Author, 1997.

Howard, Daniel. *A History of Isaac Howard of Foster, Rhode Island and His Descendants Who Have Borne the Name of Howard.* Windsor Locks, CT: Published by the Author, 1901.

Isham, Norman M., and Albert F. Brown. *Early Rhode Island Houses.* Providence, RI: Preston & Rounds, 1895.

Jones, Daniel P. *The Economic and Social Transformation of Rural Rhode Island, 1770–1850.* Boston: Northeastern University Press, 1992.

Jordy, William H. *Buildings of Rhode Island.* New York: Oxford University Press, 2004.

Matthews, Margery I. *By My Kin: Stories of Foster.* Foster, RI: Foster Preservation Society, 1991. [Matthews-1]

———. *Chronicles of Foster.* Foster, RI: Foster Preservation Society, 1995. [Matthews-2]

———; Benson, Virginia I.; and Wilson, Arthur E. *Churches of Foster: A History of Religious Life in Rural Rhode Island.* Foster, RI: North Foster Baptist Church, 1978. [Matthews-3]

———. *Foster and the Patriots' Dream.* Foster, RI: Foster Preservation Society, 1976. [Matthews-4]

———. *Peleg's Last Word: The Story of The Foster Woolen Manufactory.* Foster, RI: Foster Preservation Society, 1987. [Matthews-5]

———. *So I've Been Told: Stories of Foster.* Foster, RI: Foster Preservation Society, 1985. [Matthews-6]

Miller, William Davis. *The Silversmiths of Little Rest.* 1928. Concord, MA: Joslin Hall Publishing, 1992.

Phillips, Albert M. *Phillips Genealogies: Including the Family of George Phillips.* Auburn, MA: Privately published, 1885.

Pierce, Frederick Clifton. *Foster Genealogy.* Chicago: Published by the Author, 1899.

Savage, James. *A Genealogical Dictionary of the First Settlers of New England.* 1860–62. Baltimore: Genealogical Publishing Co., 1986.

Scituate Map 1964. George E. Matteson. *Scituate, Rhode Island Directory Map*. Hope, RI: Matteson Map Service, 1964.

Sherman, Ruth Wilder, F.A.S.G. "Descendants of John Tyler of Portsmouth, RI." *American Genealogist* 52 (1976): 220–25. [Sherman]

Smith, Dean Crawford. *The Ancestry of Emily Jane Angell, 1844–1910*. Boston: New England Historic Genealogical Society [NEHGS], 1992.

Sowa, Iona Ingram. *The Phillips and Associated Families of Early New England, 1630–1810*. Santa Clara, CA: Published by the Author, 1988. A successor volume was published, but not seen by the editor.

Wolf, Raymond A. *Foster*. Charleston, SC: Arcadia Publishing. 2012. [Wolf-1]

———. *The Lost Villages of Scituate*. Charleston, SC: Arcadia Publishing, 2009. [Wolf-2]

———. *The Scituate Reservoir*. Charleston, SC: Arcadia Publishing, 2010. [Wolf-3]

Wood, Squire G. *A History of Greene and Vicinity*. Providence, RI: Privately published, 1936.

Boy in Summer

Foster, Rhode Island
August 1896

The soft morning song of the birds in the grove just north of his bedroom window gradually woke the boy from his dreams. And vivid dreams they were, centering on his exploits in the narrow passages of the John Harrington Cave a few days before. That day he had pilfered matches from the match-safe in Uncle Jim's and Aunt Jane's parlor and, after eating a hearty breakfast of hotcakes, disappeared out the screen door, ignoring old Paris Shippee's admonitions that he listen for the dinner bell. Heading across the open meadows to the land of his grandpa's friend Judge Johnson, the young boy had known in his heart that the explorations planned for that day wouldn't allow him to listen for the dinner bell. And in the dream all the marvelous discoveries he made in the narrow passages of the Harrington Cave, lit by the matches pilfered from his aunt and uncle, were magnified a hundred times until a rusty old key—which had perhaps once opened a can of sardines—opened the door to vast interior caverns of hidden mysteries. Even the boy had been somewhat alarmed to find dusk already well settled when he emerged from his explorations, and as he ran home across the open fields he could hear the voices of old Paris Shippee and of his uncle calling for him.

"Whar yew ben, boy?" said old Paris as the boy ran into view. "Thank God you're safe," contributed Uncle Jim, summoned by Paris's cries that the prodigal had returned. But it wasn't until he

---

Fictional account of H. P. Lovecraft's 1896 Foster visit. While used fictionally, all the characters except Paris Shippee are real people.

came into the kitchen and found his mother in tears that the boy had nearly broken down himself. "In my day," said Uncle Jim, "I'd a bin razor-strapped good for sech an exploit," but kindly Aunt Jane just gave the boy a hug and said she'd known he'd be all right all the time. "Now, Jim Phillips, you just treat our guests as you ought," said Aunt Jane. "Howard sees how much he's upset his mother, and I'm sure he won't offend again." And then, addressing the boy, she said, "Now, Howard, I was afeared we'd have to eat without you, but now you're here we shall all sit down gratefully to a fine supper." And so they did. Afterward the boy slept well, despite all the excitement and emotion of that day of exploration. Uncle Jim would talk about his young nephew's explorations for years afterward. "He'd a dun thet wild old fust John Harrington well—out amongst the bears and Injuns," he'd say of his young nephew.

And what a wonderful two weeks it had been with Uncle Jim and Aunt Jane. The Phillips household in Providence had been in mourning for Grandma Robie since her death in January, and the invitation from Uncle Jim and Aunt Jane to Howard and his mother had been a godsend. Uncle Jim had even sent the pony cart into the city to fetch them from the handsome edifice his younger brother Whip Phillips had acquired on the corner of Elmgrove and Angell. In spite of the open fields that still bordered the Seekonk River to the east of his home, the young boy would have more space to roam on his uncle's farm. Besides, the city was becoming a dangerous place, and one couldn't be sure any longer that a person met along the street would be a kindly neighbor. So the boy and his mother had plunged into two weeks of rural retreat. Not that the small hamlet of Moosup Valley couldn't be lively: only a few days after his arrival, the boy had been treated to a Grange supper and introduced to more relatives—Howards and Whipples and Tylers and Fosters and Places and Kennedys—than he could ever remember. Despite being relatively poor, the country folk seemed to enjoy life just as well as people in the city—and the boy had certainly relished all the attention paid to Whip Phillips's grandson and the luscious country ham and fresh boiled corn served at the Grange supper, topped off with strawberry shortcake and fresh whipped cream.

Most of the vacation was his very own—exploring the countryside and playing with his newfound friends, the Dexter sons and daughters, themselves from the Providence metropolis. The beauty he found in the city, along the unspoiled banks of the Seekonk River, was quieter and deeper here: the little brooks and tributaries of the Moosup River, the swampy places and frequent rock outcroppings, were all tinged with quiet mystery. Perhaps the mystery was deepened by an aura of ancestral presence that even a six-year-old could feel. For here were the boy's roots—where, five generations back, his Place grandmother's ancestor Enoch had settled, some forty or fifty years after wild old John Harrington first arrived here. And as for the Phillipses, this was their ancestral territory, too—an ancestor known as "Great Jeremiah" having once owned much property to the north.

Along the Moosup Valley road one might still find the memorials of the past generations—the private burial grounds of the Places, once so thick in this area, according to Uncle Jim, that the entire stretch of Moosup Valley Road and the hamlet itself had once been known as "Placetown." The young boy found these secluded and sometimes neglected burial grounds places of fascination, and his mother pointed out to him with especial pride the handsome banked lot in which her grandfather and great-grandfather Place, both named Stephen, rested. Both Uncle Jim and Grandpa Whip Phillips could remember the younger Stephen well—and the kindly Batteys, who now lived in the Stephen Place household where the boy's mother had been born, allowed the visitors to tour the home, which they had kept up well.

Both of Uncle Jim's boys—Walt and Jerry Phillips—and their families managed to pay calls while the boy and his mother were visiting; but the boy found most poignant the graves of the little boys and girls of Uncle Jim and Aunt Jane who had not survived to have their own families, in the little plot up the steep slope opposite Uncle Jim's farmhouse. When Uncle Jim told the boy that he and his wife would also be buried there, the boy, only recently introduced to mortality by the death of his grandmother, began to cry. Aunt Jane scolded her husband, and the tears were soon dried. Most of the loved ones of former generations had died before photographers had swarmed over the land, but Aunt Jane's parents, old Job Wilcox Place and his wife Asenath Pierce Place, had lived well into their eighties, and their photographs looked down on the old familiar rag carpets from the parlor walls. Uncle Jim told the boy that this had been the home of Job's brother Abraham; he and his wife Nabby were without children and had left this home to their niece Jane and her husband.

Indeed, few Places were now left in the vicinity of Moosup Valley. Aunt Jane's younger brother Henry and his family had moved to the Providence metropolis a few years ago. Their cousin Job D. Place and his family farmed way up north of Foster Center. The only Places left along Moosup Valley road were old Christopher Place and his wife Nancy Blanchard Place. Christopher and Nancy now lived in the household of their only daughter Jennie and her husband Jim Bennis. Despite his seventy-six years, old Christopher still helped Jim and Jennie Bennis and their children with the farm work. And the boy came to visit him—this old man who had spent all his years working the rocky soil of his native town and hardly been to Providence more than a dozen times.

"So yew be Whip Phillips's gran'sun," the old man had greeted the boy with his rough, raspy voice. (Uncle Jim told the boy that old Chris Place was not a well man.) "Yer mom thar I dew re-call well; she war a lively gal back when she cum ter visit here over summers in the seventies and eighties. Married up ter Bostun, I heered—always sed she shudda chusen a Moosup Valley feller." At this even the quiet Nancy Place ventured to reproach her husband. "I knowed Whip and Jim's pa and ma real well—them boys wuz left orfins when Robie died of the fever in the summer of '48 and Jerry was kilt in his mill thet same winter. Mary Stanton cum in and tuk keer of them boys and thar sisters—did yew know yer gran'pap an' Uncle Jim hed two sisters? Sadly gone these many years—Susan, who war a stunning gal and tha favrite of all, of a fever jest three years arter her ma, in '51, afore she cud even marry, and Abbie, in the prime of her life, in '73. Abbie married a Dixon feller over Connectycut way and ef yew stay long enuff by Uncle Jim, ye'll meet yer Dixon cuzins, fer sure."

It seemed old Christopher wanted to tell the boy things. "Yew know, I kin re-member futher back lots then even Jerry and Robie Phillips wot owned ther mill. I dew re-member Jerry's pa Aseph Phillips, wot took over the farm of his pa Jim over whar tha Luther Road hez ben cut, and married Ben Whipple's dawter Esther. I member him personal, fer when he wuz an olt man in the summer of '27 and I wuz a boy uv seven—jest a year older than yew—he lernt me to cut swamp hay. Thet summer and the next three or fur I wukked as a hand—which is ter say, did chures—on old Aseph's farm, though by '28 and '29 he wuz too sick to wuk hisself. I 'member, he died jest a few days arter the Fourth of July in '29. He enjuyed his last Fourth as well as a sick man cud; I 'member he wuz in some considrabul pain and eased it with his likker jug. I 'member well when he was laid out in his home and then buried ter the fambly yard, fer I wer thar. His widder Esther—I 'member her well, too. She muster lived ten er fifteen mur years. Even young blades like Jim an' Whip kin member her.

"I wuz mighty sorry, tew, young feller, ter hear uv the passin' of yer Gramma Robie this past winter—ez fine a womun ez yew might wish. Ez fer her side uv yer fambly, I knowed 'em all well, tew. I wukked fer Robie's father, young Stephen, in tha thirties and forties, arter Aseph died. Did yew know thet young Stephen Place an' Jerry Phillips married sisters—Sally an' Robie Rathbun? Uncle Jim's Aunt Nabby war thar sister and Mary Stanton wot keered fer Jerry's and Robie's orfins war thar niece, the dawter of tha sister Ruth. So yew see ez haow we're all fambly out here by Moosup Valley. Here in Placetun, as they uster call it, the woods wuz thick with Places—we had mur Stephens than yew could shake er stick at, an' I knowed must uv 'em. Old Stephen died afore I wuz born, but they dew tell me I wuz tuk ter the fun'ral uv his widder Martha in '22. Preacher Stephen wuz a mur remut relashun, but I heared him preach onct—same summer I lernt swamp haying from yer two times great gran'pa Aseph. I think it may ev bin the last time he ever preached, fer he wer woful decrepit and died soon arter. Even today thar's a shoemaker Stephen in thar township."

"Naow, Chris," offered old Nancy, "I think yew have bored thet poor boy enuff with tales of tha past. Let's say we let him play with yer gran'chilrun."

"That's wot chilrun's ot ter dew—play," said the old man. "Naow, young feller, yew be getting along and see yew don't go pulling thar har o' my gran'dawters. And dew bee-have when yew go ter meeting with Elder Kennedy this Sunday. He dew be my kinsman and wun uv thar few uv my generashun left herebaouts."

And the boy flew out the door to leave the old sick man to visit with the adults. He did indeed comport himself well in Elder Kennedy's meeting and he even liked it better than the services at the Baptist Church in Providence. There was much to tell his Grandpa about his wonderful two weeks with Uncle Jim and Aunt Jane—and Grandpa even presented him with a book once owned by Stephen Place the younger. The boy grew in strength and in wisdom, but he never forgot his summer in Moosup Valley. Later he wrote of it and kept its memory alive. But much more of that magical summer in the life of the boy remains to be told.

Written to mark the centennial of Howard Phillips Lovecraft's visit to Foster, Rhode Island, 20 August 1996.

EARLY RECOGNITION

The First Public Lecture on H. P. Lovecraft

The end of 1943 and the beginning of 1944 were exciting times for the legacy of H. P. Lovecraft in his native city, Providence, Rhode Island.

After the author's death in 1937, his friends August Derleth and Donald Wandrei resolved that his work ought to be preserved in hardcover. They explored various publication possibilities, but finally decided to publish his work on their own, under the name Arkham House. Their first collection of Lovecraft's work, entitled *The Outsider and Others*, was published in a limited edition in 1939. A second, titled *Beyond the Wall of Sleep*, followed in 1943.

During his lifetime Lovecraft made several appearances in the "Sideshow" column conducted by *Providence Journal* literary editor B. K. Hart. But publication of *The Outsider and Others* went unnoticed in the *Journal*. Hart died in 1941 and was succeeded as literary editor by Winfield Townley Scott (1910–1968), who had been working as his assistant since 1931.

Scott had no basic affinity with Lovecraft's literary work but was fascinated by the man. His pioneering article "The Case of Howard Phillips Lovecraft of Providence, R.I." appeared in the *Providence Sunday Journal* for 26 December 1943 (sec. III, p. 6). The very next day, Lovecraft's friend Muriel Eddy wrote to Scott:

```
Copy of Letter received Dec. 27th, 1943.

Editor:

    I enjoyed the article about Howard Phillips Lovecraft in the
Sunday Journal, by W. T. Scott, inasmuch as the late Mr. Lovecraft
was well-known to our family. It was my husband's uncle, Arthur Eddy,
who owned the bookshop on Weybosset street where H. P. Lovecraft loved
to browse. Incidentally, there was one great love of Mr. Lovecraft's
life, pehaps unknown, and therefore overlooked, by most of the public.
H. P. Lovecraft adored black cats, and would never pass a stray black
feline on the street, without stopping to pat it. Mr. Lovecraft often
brought his manuscripts to our house to read aloud to us before
submitting them to publishers. He was an excellent reader, as well as
writer, of weird and macabre tales, calculated to send cold shivers up
and down one's spine. He was a gentleman and a scholar, indeed, as
Mr. Scott has said in his most interesting article.

    H. P. Lovecraft's wife, whose name Mr. Scott did not know, was
Sonia Greene, who lived in Brooklyn, N. Y.

    We are pleased and honored to have been intimate friends of this
gifted author. I am convinced that, some day, in the not too distant
future, Providence will be proud of having produced such a prolific writer
of weird, uncanny yarns that are already known throughout the world!

                            (Signed) MRS. CLIFFORD M. EDDY.


383 Friendship Street,
Providence, 7. R. I.
Gaspeee 6680
```

Scott spoke with Mrs. Eddy after receiving her letter and typed up his notes on the verso of his transcription of her letter:

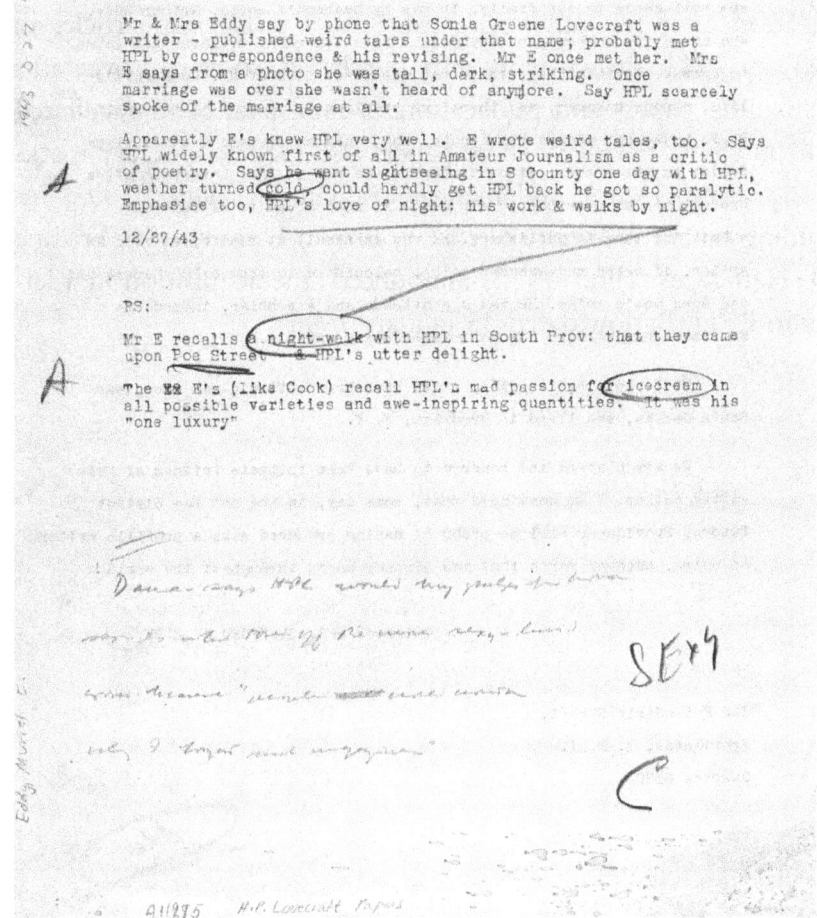

After Lovecraft's death, Robert H. Barlow came to Providence to take charge of his literary papers. He arranged with Brown librarian S. Foster Damon to deposit them at the John Hay Library. The deposit was to be uncatalogued, with access by permission from Barlow. Lovecraft's books and some residue of his papers remained in his final home at 66 College Street, which he had shared with his aunt Annie Emeline (Phillips) Gamwell. Providence bookseller H. Douglass Dana purchased the remaining books and papers after the death of Mrs. Gamwell on 29 January 1941.

Soon after the publication of Scott's pioneering article, in January 1944, Brown University purchased some of Lovecraft's remaining papers and publications from Dana. Scott facilitated the purchase. I believe these papers also included literary works by Lovecraft's uncle and mentor Franklin C. Clark, M.D., including his novel *Susan's Obituary*. Brown University's Christine D. Hathaway (1905–1972) announced the acquisition in a letter to R. H. Barlow dated 25 January 1944:

> 25 January 1944
>
> Mr. R. H. Barlow
> 2521 Benvenue
> Berkeley, California
>
> Dear Mr. Barlow:
>
> Professor S. Foster Damon, who comes in only occasionally just now as he is on sabbatical leave, has asked me to drop you a line to let you know that we have purchased a miscellaneous lot of Lovecraft material which came originally from his aunt, Mrs. Gamwell. The dealer was Dana's Old Corner Book Shop.
>
> There are a number of manuscripts by Lovecraft, odd numbers of magazines, both poetry and weird, clippings, and a few pictures, including an oil by you which we understand Lovecraft used to keep over his bed.
>
> Since Winfield T. Scott's review of the latest Lovecraft volume interest in him seems to be growing markedly. Mr. Scott himself has become quite enthusiastic and was going to get in touch with you.
>
> Sincerely yours,
>
> (Mrs. Christine D. Hathaway)
> Secretary to the Librarian

The interest stirred by Scott's 26 December 1943 article in the *Journal* doubtless originated the idea of an exhibit of Lovecraft's work and a lecture on the subject. Brown librarian Henry Bartlett Van Hoesen (1885–1965) wrote to Barlow of the acquisition of material from Dana and of Scott's interest in Lovecraft on 11 February 1944:

11 February 1944

Mr. R. H. Barlow
2521 Benvenue
Berkeley, California

Dear Mr. Barlow:

    Winfield T. Scott, a Brown man, poet and on the literary section of the Providence Journal, has become interested in Howard Lovecraft and has been in to see what material we have. He has been instrumental in helping us acquire worth while additional material which apparently had been sold by Mrs. Gamwell to a local bookseller.

    Mr. Scott wrote a very good article on Lovecraft which he may already have sent you. This is merely to say that we have every confidence in Mr. Scott's literary ability and in his friendly discretion, and I am sure that, if necessary, he would be quite willing to submit for your or our approval anything that he might write or say regarding the material we have here or regarding Lovecraft.

    Sincerely yours,

    Librarian

Van Hoesen wrote further to Scott himself on 15 February 1944:

15 February 1944

Mr. Winfield T. Scott
56 Olney Street
Providence, R.I.

Dear Mr. Scott:

    The Library Committee yesterday approved your application to examine the Lovecraft Papers, and also the Barlow Papers, providing Mr. Barlow approves also. Did you write to him and have you had a reply? I wrote the other day to tell him we had acquired the batch of stuff from Dana. The Providence Public Library has borrowed most of this last group to work up an exhibition next week.

    Sincerely yours,

    Librarian

15 February 1944 fell on a Tuesday. So presumably the Lovecraft exhibit at the Providence Public Library, based on the material acquired by Brown from Dana, was going up during the week of Sunday, 20 February, through Saturday, 26 February 1944.

Just how long the exhibit at the Providence Public Library ran I have not been able to determine. Scott wrote to Van Hoesen on 28 February 1944:

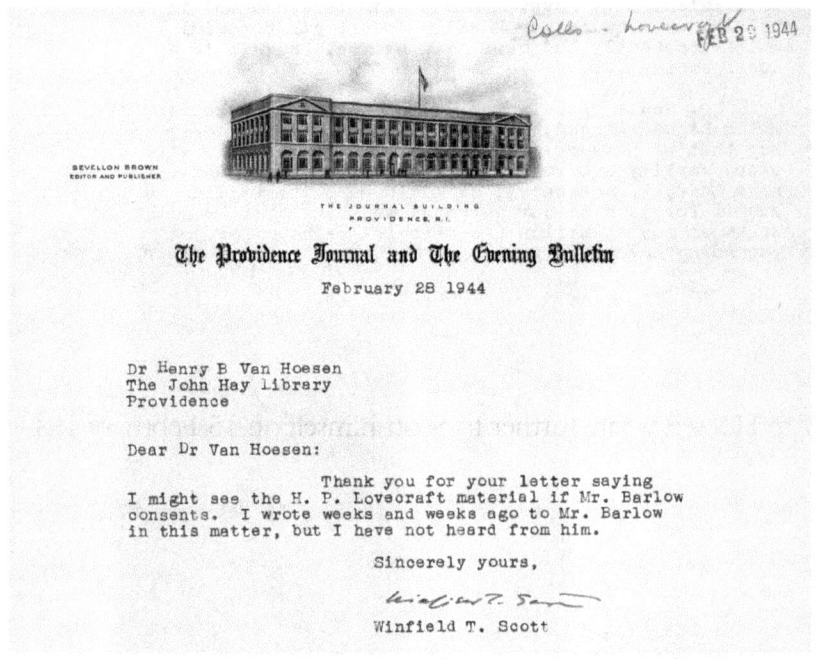

Record of the Lovecraft exhibit at the Providence Public Library in February–March 1944 is included in the *Bulletin of the Rhode Island Library Association* 16, No. 1 (May 1944):

The Providence Public Library honored the memory of the Rhode Island author Howard P. Lovecraft, teller of weird tales, with a lecture by Mr. Winfield T. Scott, literary editor of the *Providence Sunday Journal*, and an exhibition of manuscripts, books and other material owned and lent by Brown University. Two music groups met at the Library: the Rhode Island chapter of the American Federation of Organists heard a talk by Mr. Lawrence Apgar, and the Schubert Club members were told about the resources of the Music Department by Miss Marion Arnold, head of the department.

Dorothy C. Walter (1889–1967) attended Scott's lecture and took nineteen pages of notes on Scott's lecture. On the first page she dated Scott's lecture as "1944(?)":

Later in 1944 Scott published an extended version of his earlier article, titled "His Own Most Fantastic Creation," in the Arkham House collection *Marginalia*.[1]

---

1. Scott later published a revised version of this essay in his collection *Exiles and Fabrications* (Doubleday, 1961).

Scott remained interested in Lovecraft as the forties advanced. He made numerous mentions of Lovecraft in his column in the *Providence Journal* and edited a version of Sonia Davis's memoir of her husband for *Books at Brown*. He published his short article "Lovecraft as a Poet" in Donald M. Grant's and Thomas P. Hadley's *Rhode Island on Lovecraft* (Providence: Grant-Hadley, 1945).[2] Probably only the press of his duties at the *Providence Journal* and the other events of his personal life deterred him from pursuing a full biography of Lovecraft.

We can certainly speculate about who—in addition to Miss Walter—might have been in attendance for Scott's 1944 lecture on Lovecraft at the Providence Public Library. Sadly, Lovecraft's surviving aunt Mrs. Gamwell had already been dead for three years. However, a number of the residents of The Arsdale boarding house at 53–55 Waterman Street—across the backyard from 66 College Street—had known Lovecraft, including Providence Public Library periodicals librarian Marian Bonner (1883–1952). Lovecraft and Bonner were both cat-lovers, and his correspondence with her in the guise of secretary of the Kappa Alpha Tau feline fraternity is one of the most charming of the Lovecraft correspondence files preserved at the John Hay Library. Whether Bonner was off duty and available to attend when Scott's lecture transpired the record (as so far discovered) sayeth not.

Alice R. Sheppard (1870–1961) and Mary Spink (1877–1968) were downstairs neighbors of Lovecraft and his aunt at 66 College Street. Spink later compiled a listing of Lovecraft's library for the use of Mrs. Gamwell, a listing that later came to the John Hay Library. I do not know whether either of these neighbors had the opportunity to attend Scott's lecture or to see the Lovecraft exhibit.

---

2. Scott later published a revised version of this essay (under the title "A Parenthesis on Lovecraft as a Poet") in his collection *Exiles and Fabrications* (Doubleday, 1961).

Of the legal fraternity, both Albert A. Baker (1862–1959) and Ralph M. Greenlaw (1875–1951) were involved with Lovecraft's business. I do not know whether either had the opportunity to attend Scott's lecture or to see the Lovecraft exhibit.

Of course, the most important attendants were the citizens of Providence at large. Only a few had encountered Lovecraft during his lifetime. Probably a few had read his stories in *Weird Tales* and other pulp magazines. Word of the Arkham House collections of his work had only barely filtered back to Providence by this time. So the Providence Public Library, through its February–March Lovecraft exhibit and Scott's lecture, had the honor of first presenting Lovecraft and his work to the Providence reading public.

While the Providence Public Library is technically a private institution, it is supported by public funds, and any publicly supported institution must be conscious of its public. Today Lovecraft's regressive racial views have become widely known through the publication of his private correspondence.

Obviously, any public institution in Providence must today present Lovecraft with a view toward the author's known views and its own public. Nevertheless, Lovecraft's readership continues to grow. It may be that the cosmic viewpoint of his literary work has an appeal to at least a minority of readers which his social and racial views do not impede. I do not think Clarence Edgar Sherman (1887–1974) of the Providence Public Library and Henry Bartlett Van Hoesen of the Brown University Library deserve any retrospective censure for the exhibit and lecture on Lovecraft at the Providence Public Library that they and their staffs made possible in early 1944. It is fitting that Providence had the honor of hosting the first public exhibition of the work of H. P. Lovecraft and the first public lecture thereon.

Postscript

I think it is probable that a researcher on the ground in Providence may be able to discover additional particulars concerning these memorable events.

Over the years, the Providence Public Library has published an *Annual Report*. It is possible that the report for 1944 contains the dates for the Lovecraft exhibit and Scott's lecture.

Scott's journal for the period 11 January to 2 June 1944 (434 pp.)[3] is held at the John Hay Library (Ms. Harris Codex 1804). It is possible that Scott's journal contains entries pertaining to his 1944 lecture.

The *Providence Journal* may contain notices of the exhibit and Scott's lecture which an intrepid future researcher may discover. It is even possible that the *Journal* sent a photographer to cover the exhibit or Scott's lecture, in which case the newspaper's archives may offer further revelations. I do not myself have electronic access to the *Journal*.

Providence Public Library, 1900 building (225 Washington Street) (Empire Street addition was only completed in 1954.)

---

3. There is an appended note dated 4 April 1963.

Painting of Winfield Townley Scott as a young man.
Artist and date unknown.

SOURCES

All essays have been revised for publication in this collection.

Abbie Ann Hathaway (1852–1917), *Lovecraft's Teacher at Slater Avenue Primary School,* Glenview, IL: Moshassuck Press, 2020.

"Boy in Summer." As *Boy in Summer—Foster, Rhode Island: August 1896.* Evanston, IL: Moshassuck Press, 1996.

"Clergymen among Lovecraft's Paternal Ancestors." *Lovecraft Annual* No. 9 (2015): 136–82.

"Delilah Townsend (ca. 1868-1944)." Extracted from *The Site of Joseph Curwen's House in H. P. Lovecraft's* The Case of Charles Dexter Ward (with Jason C. Eckhardt), Moshassuck Press, 2013. The author is grateful to David E. Schultz, Marcos Legaria, and Graeme Phillips for their help in finding this text.

Edwin Baird: The Man Who Discovered Lovecraft. Glenview, IL: Moshassuck Press, 2023.

"The First Public Lecture on H. P. Lovecraft." *Selected Essays.* Glenview, IL: Swainwood Books, 2022. 188–200.

"Franklin C. Clark." In Franklin C. Clark, *Sketches of New England Life: I—Susan's Obituary.* Glenview, IL: Moshassuck Press, 1996. 132–67 (as "A Sketch of the Author").

"In Memoriam: Ethel Phillips Morrish (1888–1987)." As *In Memoriam: Howard Phillips Lovecraft August 20, 1890–March 15, 1937 / Ethel M. Phillips Morrish May 15, 1888–January 17, 1987.* Evanston, IL: Moshassuck Press, 15 March 1987.

"Lovecraft and the Irish." *Lovecraft Annual* No. 15 (2021): 29–45.

Lovecraft Was Our Neighbor: The People of 169 Clinton Street, Glenview, IL: Moshassuck Press, 2020.

Lovecraft Was Our Neighbor: The People of 10 Barnes Street, Glenview, IL: Moshassuck Press, 2020.

"Lovecraft's 1937 Diary." *Lovecraft Annual* No. 6 (2012): 153–78.

"Lovecraft's Travelogues of Foster, Rhode Island." *Lovecraft Annual* No. 7 (2013): 75–135.

Lovecraft's Tutor Arthur Palmer May (1880–1941). Glenview, IL: Moshassuck Press, 2020.

Mariano De Magistris (1862–1939): Lovecraft's Mortgagee on the Manton (Violet Hill) Quarry. Glenview, IL: Moshassuck Press, 2021.

"Providence's Poe Street." *Crypt of Cthulhu* No. 109 (Candlemas 2018): 20–24.

www.ingramcontent.com/pod-product-compliance
Lightning Source LLC
Chambersburg PA
CBHW060108170426
43198CB00010B/816